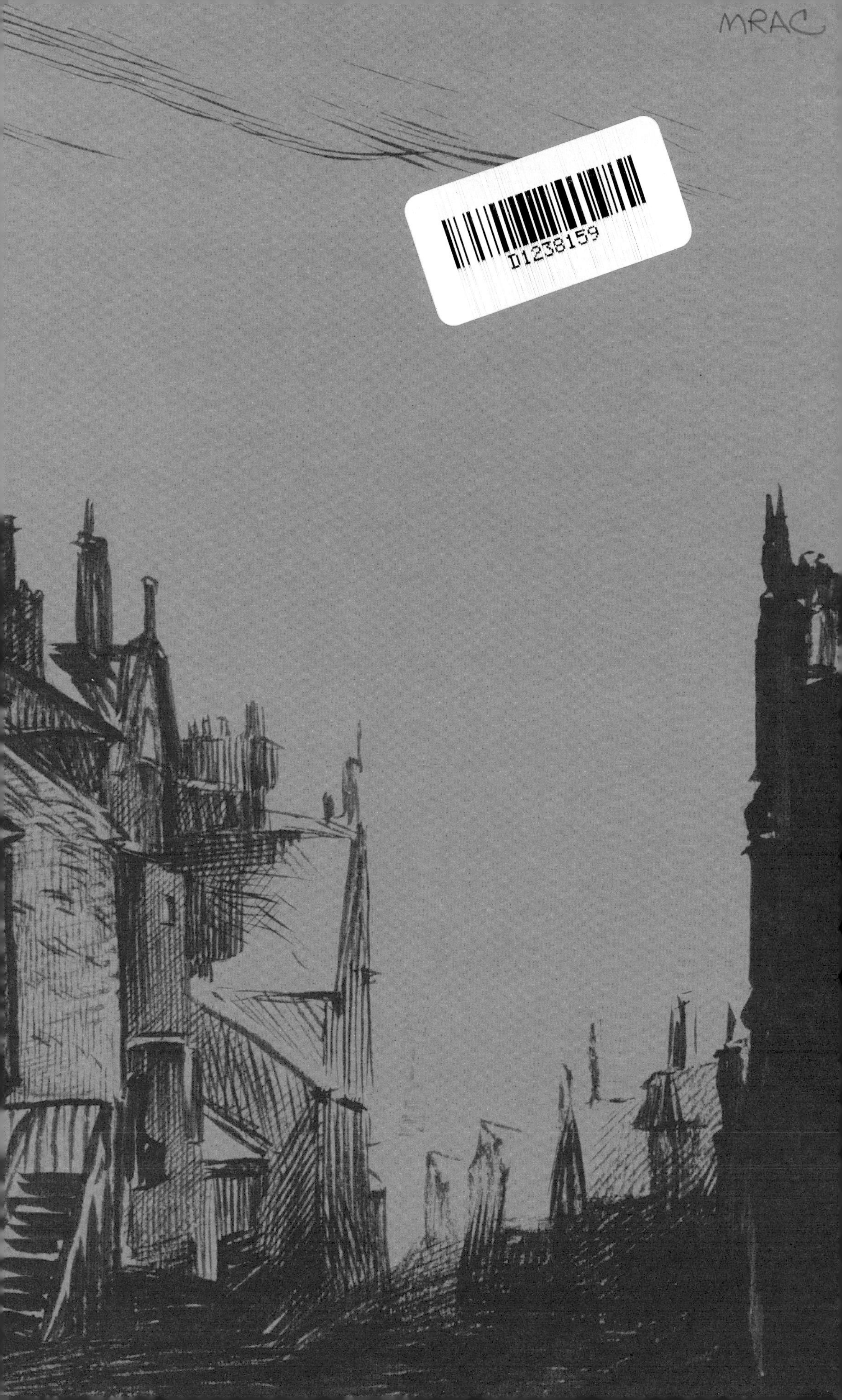

JENNY FINN ™

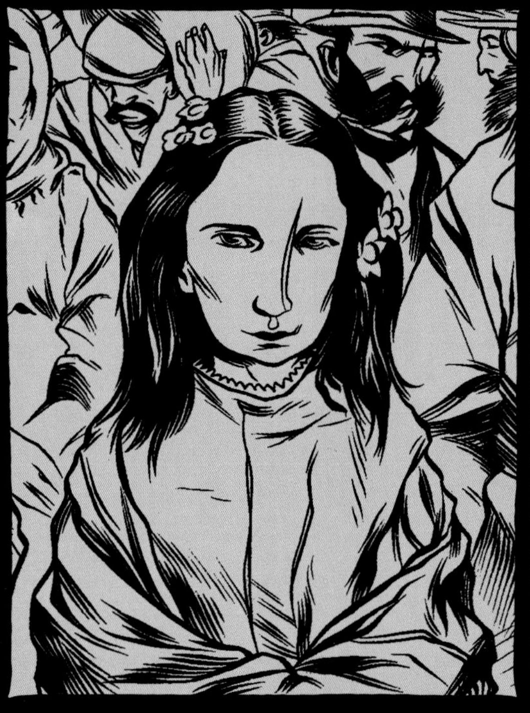

JENNY FINN

Created by
Mike Mignola and
Troy Nixey

Story by **Mike Mignola** *and* **Troy Nixey**

Art by **Troy Nixey** (chapters 1-3)
and **Farel Dalrymple** (chapter 4)

Colors by **Dave Stewart**

Letters by **Pat Brosseau** (chapters 1-2)
and **Ed Dukeshire** (chapters 3-4)

Cover art by **Mike Mignola**
with **Dave Stewart**

Chapter break art by **Troy Nixey**

Dark Horse Comics

Publisher **Mike Richardson** · *Editor* **Katii O'Brien**
Designer **Sarah Terry** · *Digital Art Technician* **Christina McKenzie**

Special thanks to Sanjay Dharawat

JENNY FINN

Published by Dark Horse Books
A division of Dark Horse Comics, Inc.
10956 SE Main Street, Milwaukie, OR 97222

Advertising Sales: (503) 905-2237
International Licensing: (503) 905-2377
Comic Shop Locator Service: Comicshoplocator.com

Neil Hankerson *Executive Vice President* • Tom Weddle *Chief Financial Officer* • Randy Stradley *Vice President of Publishing* • Nick McWhorter *Chief Business Development Officer* • Matt Parkinson *Vice President of Marketing* • Dale LaFountain *Vice President of Information Technology* • Cara Niece *Vice President of Production and Scheduling* • Mark Bernardi *Vice President of Book Trade and Digital Sales* • Ken Lizzi *General Counsel* • Dave Marshall *Editor in Chief* • Davey Estrada *Editorial Director* • Chris Warner *Senior Books Editor* • Cary Grazzini *Director of Specialty Projects* • Lia Ribacchi *Art Director* • Vanessa Todd *Director of Print Purchasing* • Matt Dryer *Director of Digital Art and Prepress* • Michael Gombos *Director of International Publishing and Licensing* • Kari Yadro *Director of Custom Programs*

DarkHorse.com
Facebook.com/DarkHorseComics · Twitter.com/DarkHorseComics

First Dark Horse edition: May 2018
ISBN: 978-1-50670-544-6

1 3 5 7 9 10 8 6 4 2
Printed in China

Library of Congress Cataloging-in-Publication Data

Names: Mignola, Michael, author, artist.   Nixey, Troy, author, artist.
  Dalrymple, Farel, artist.   Stewart, Dave, colourist, artist.   Brosseau,
  Pat, letterer.   Dukeshire, Ed, letterer.
Title: Jenny Finn / story by Mike Mignola and Troy Nixey ; art by Troy Nixey
  (chapters 1-3), Farel Dalrymple (chapter 4) ; colors by Dave Stewart ;
  letters by Pat Brosseau (chapters 1-2), Ed Dukeshire (chapters 3-4) ;
  cover art by Mike Mignola with Dave Stewart ; chapter break art by Troy
  Nixey.
Description: First Dark Horse edition.   Milwaukie, OR : Dark Horse Books,
  2018.   "Created by Mike Mignola and Troy Nixey"   "Originally printed as
  Jenny Finn: Doom and Jenny Finn: Messiah, and later reprinted as Jenny
  Finn: Doom Messiah"
Identifiers: LCCN 2017060946   ISBN 9781506705446 (hardback)
Subjects: LCSH: Graphic novels.   BISAC: COMICS & GRAPHIC NOVELS / Horror.
  COMICS & GRAPHIC NOVELS / Fantasy.   COMICS & GRAPHIC NOVELS / General.
Classification: LCC PN6727.M53 J46 2018   DDC 741.5/973--dc23
LC record available at https://lccn.loc.gov/2017060946

CHAPTER
ONE

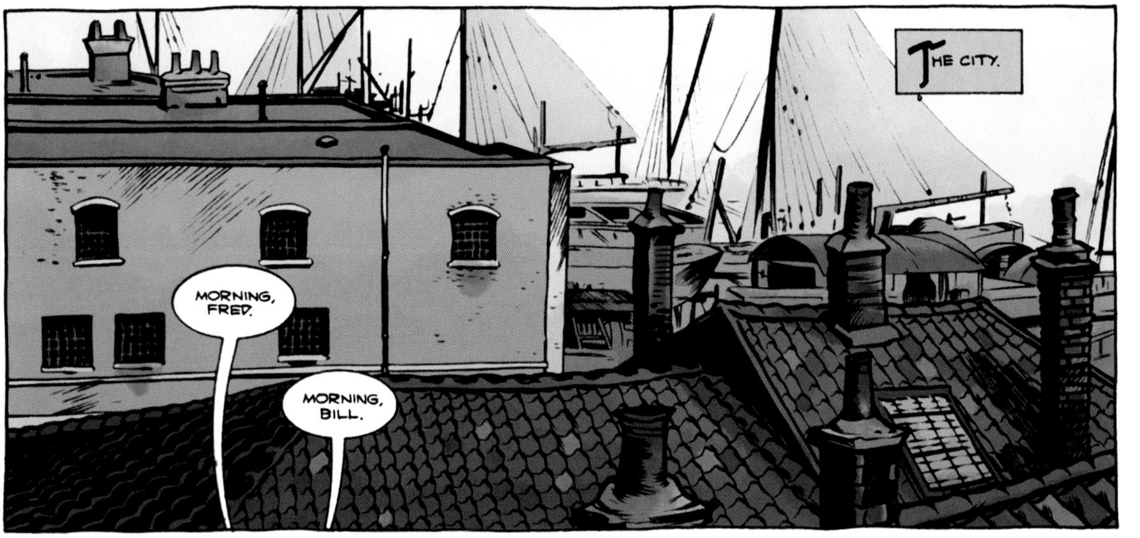
THE CITY.
MORNING, FRED.
MORNING, BILL.

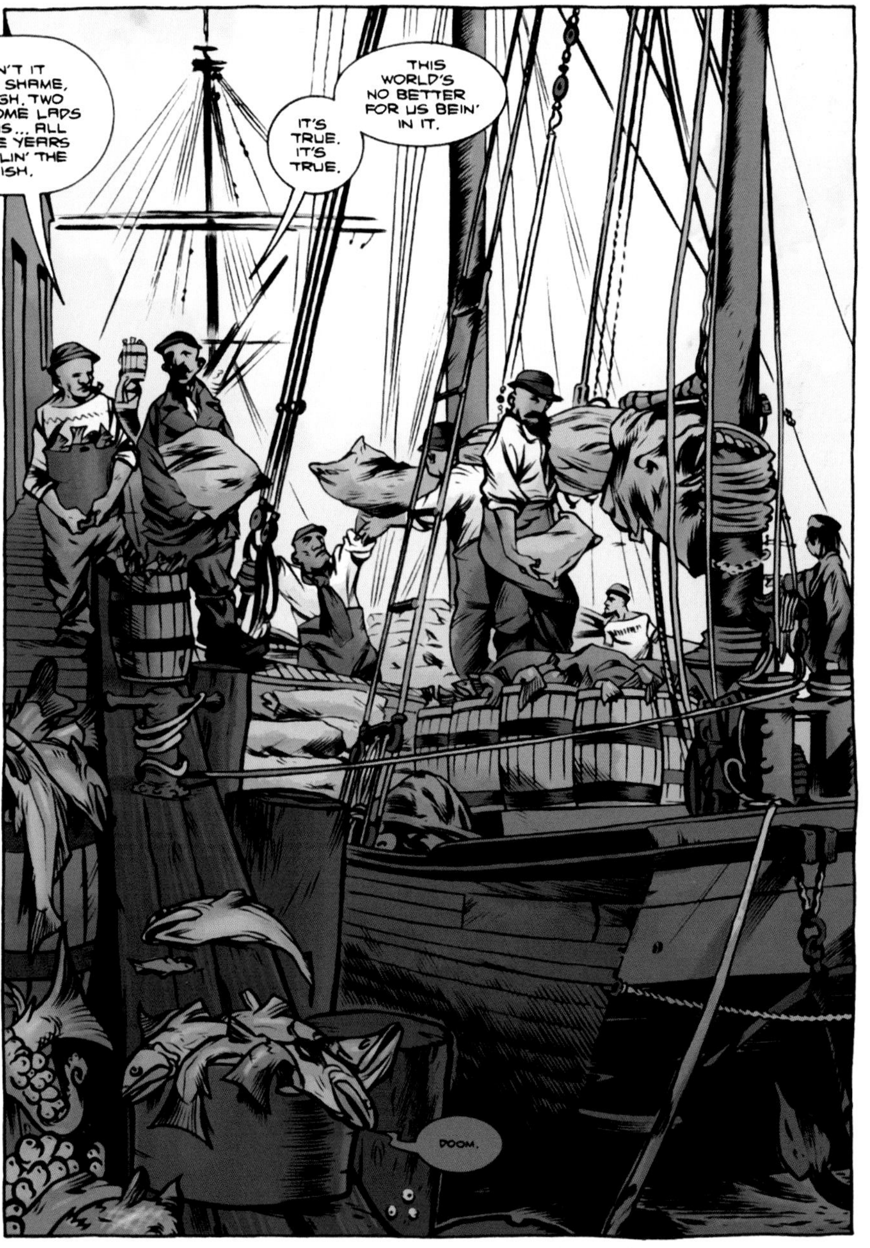
AIN'T IT THE SHAME, THOUGH. TWO HANDSOME LADS LIKE US... ALL THESE YEARS HAULIN' THE FISH.
IT'S TRUE. IT'S TRUE.
THIS WORLD'S NO BETTER FOR US BEIN' IN IT.
DOOM.

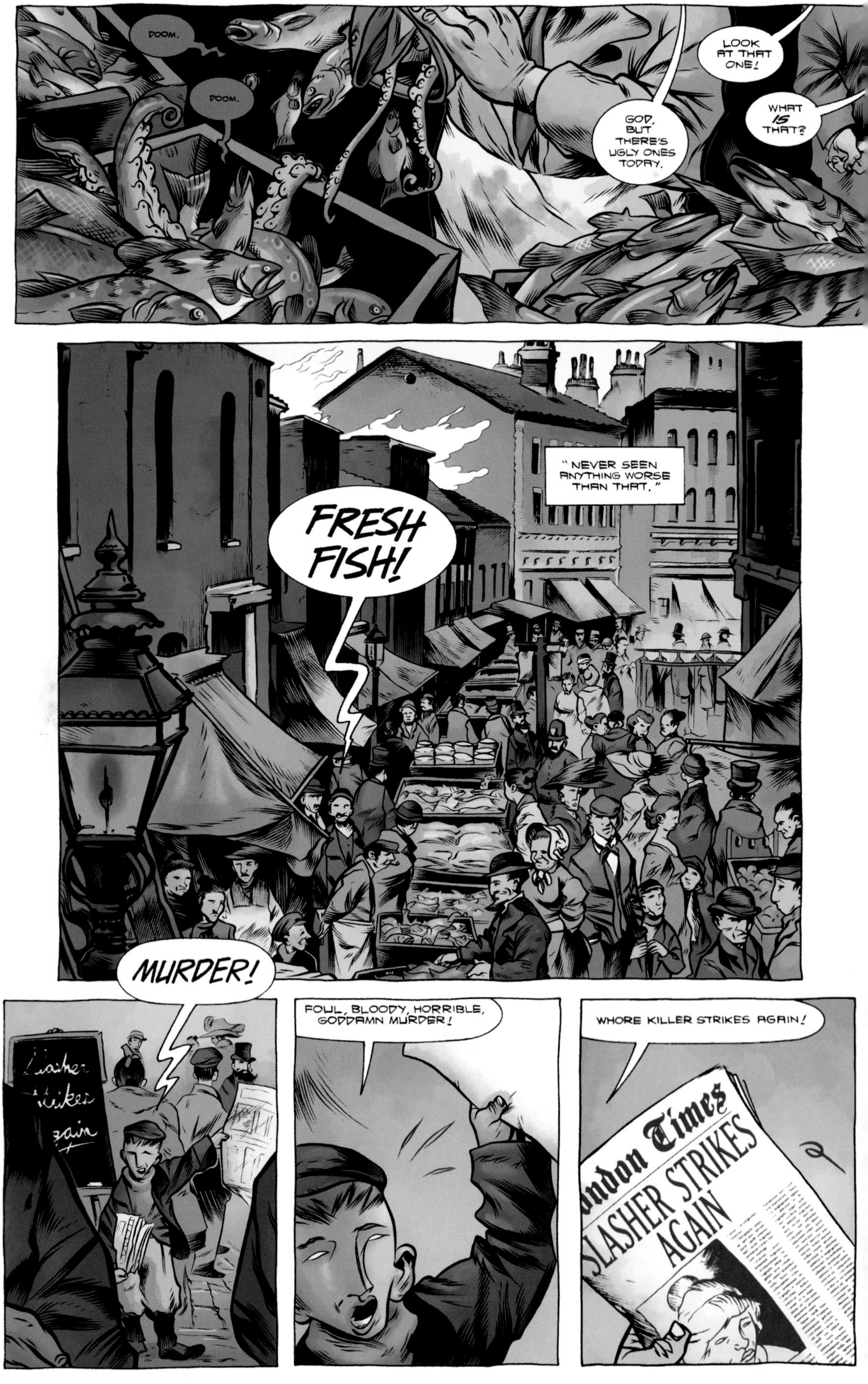
DOOM.
DOOM.
GOD, BUT THERE'S UGLY ONES TODAY.
LOOK AT THAT ONE!
WHAT IS THAT?
"NEVER SEEN ANYTHING WORSE THAN THAT."
FRESH FISH!
MURDER!
FOUL, BLOODY, HORRIBLE, GODDAMN MURDER!
WHORE KILLER STRIKES AGAIN!
ondon Times
SLASHER STRIKES AGAIN

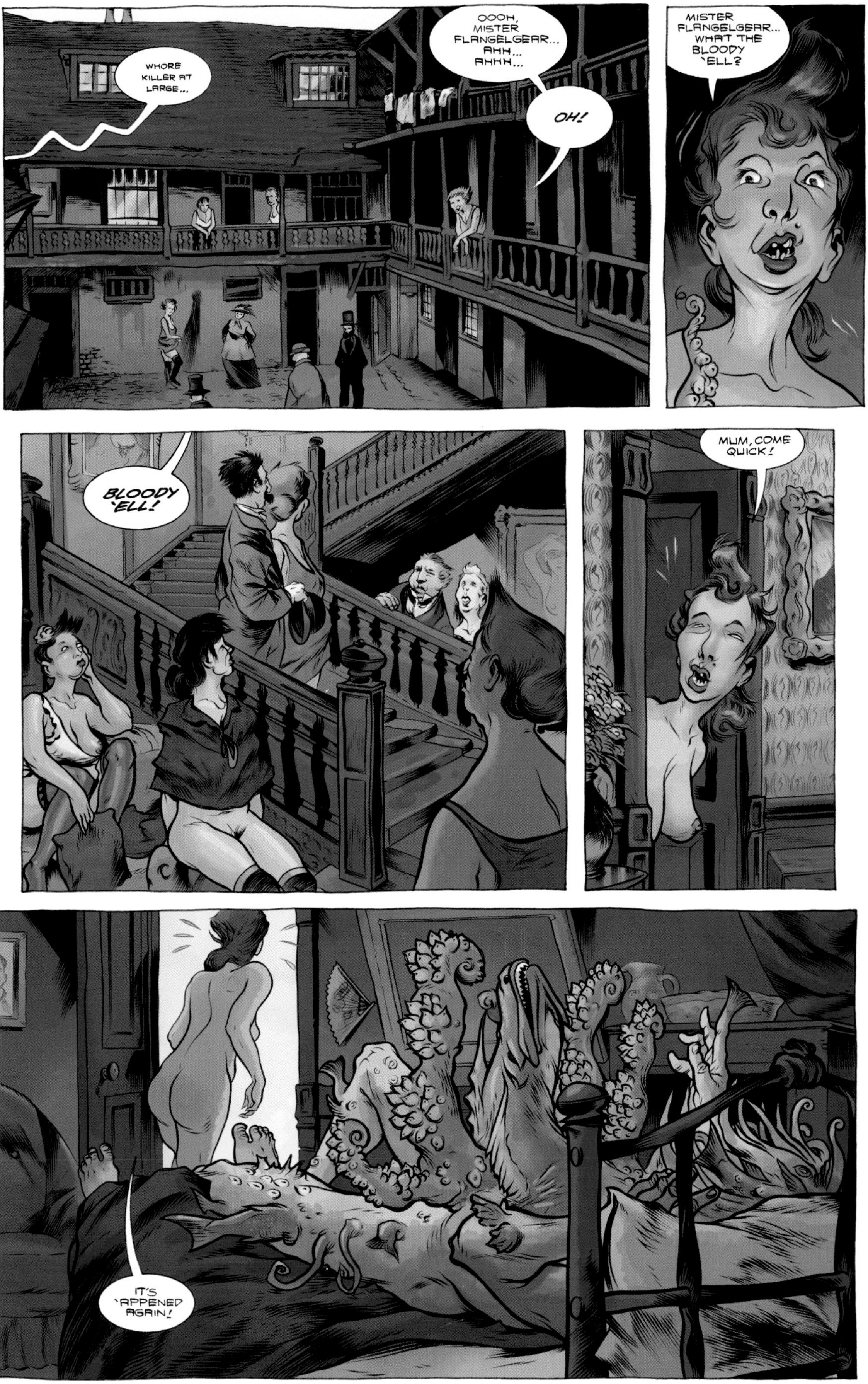
WHORE KILLER AT LARGE...
OOOH, MISTER FLANGELGEAR... AHH... AHHH...
OH!
MISTER FLANGELGEAR... WHAT THE BLOODY 'ELL?
BLOODY 'ELL!
MUM, COME QUICK!
IT'S 'APPENED AGAIN!

THIS IS THE WORST ONE YET.

'E DIDN'T LOOK SO BAD AT THE START...

...OH, A LITTLE SCALY, BUT THIS ... *THIS* COME ON 'IM ALLA THE SUDDEN.

HMM...

WELL, I HOPE HE PAID UP FRONT.

HE DID...

...BUT THAT ONE ATE THE MONEY.

SNAP

GOD, IT'S A BLOODY AWFUL MESS...

WE'LL DRAG 'IM OUT BACK--

I WILL TAKE CHARGE OF HIM.

PRIME MINISTER...!

TELL ME, WAS HE A "REGULAR"?

I SEEN 'IM IN 'ERE LAST WEEK... WITH THE NEW GIRL.

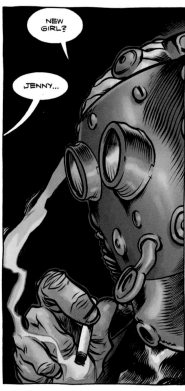

NEW GIRL?

JENNY...

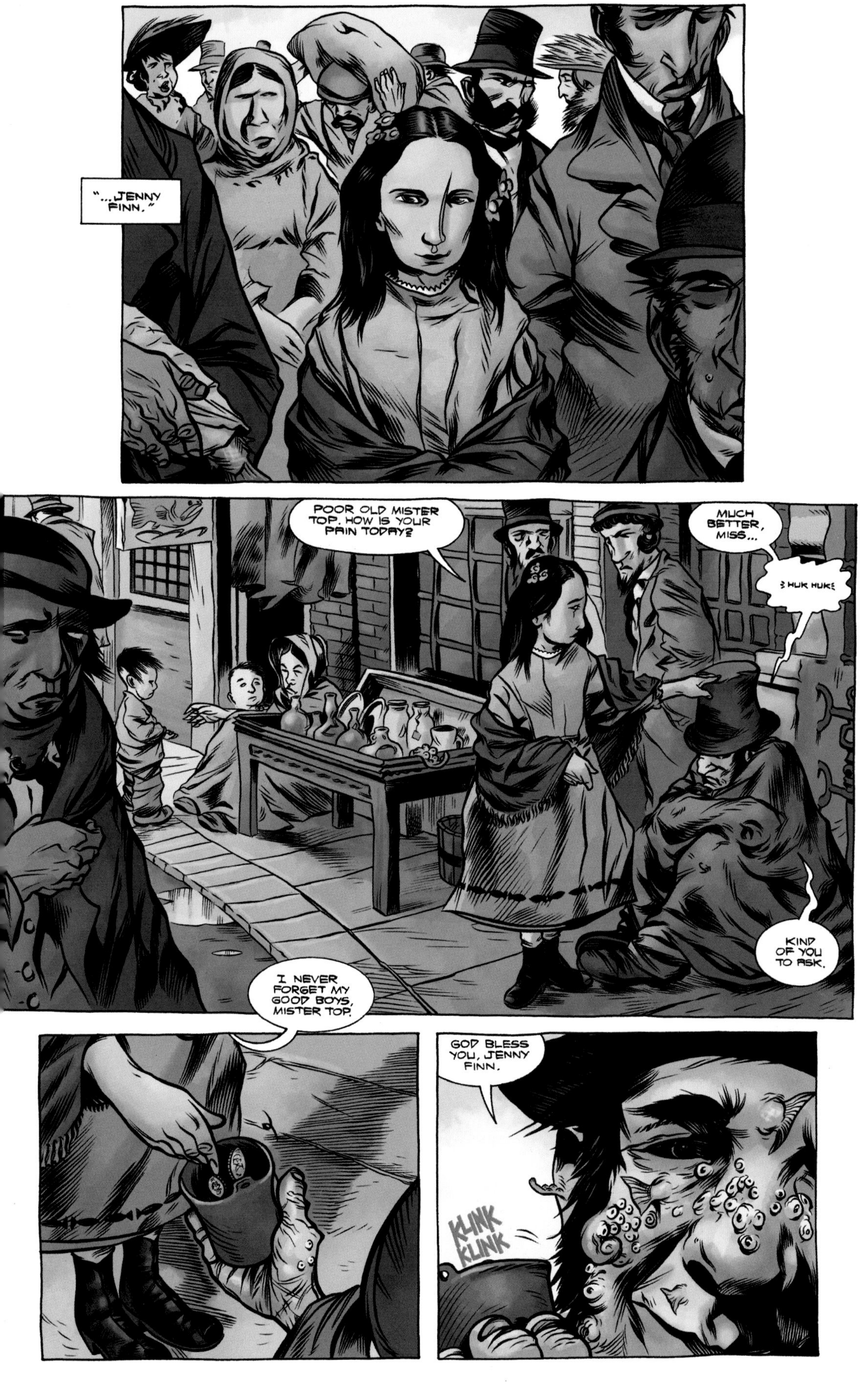
"...JENNY FINN."
POOR OLD MISTER TOP. HOW IS YOUR PAIN TODAY?
MUCH BETTER, MISS...
HUK HUK
KIND OF YOU TO ASK.
I NEVER FORGET MY GOOD BOYS, MISTER TOP.
GOD BLESS YOU, JENNY FINN.
KLINK KLINK

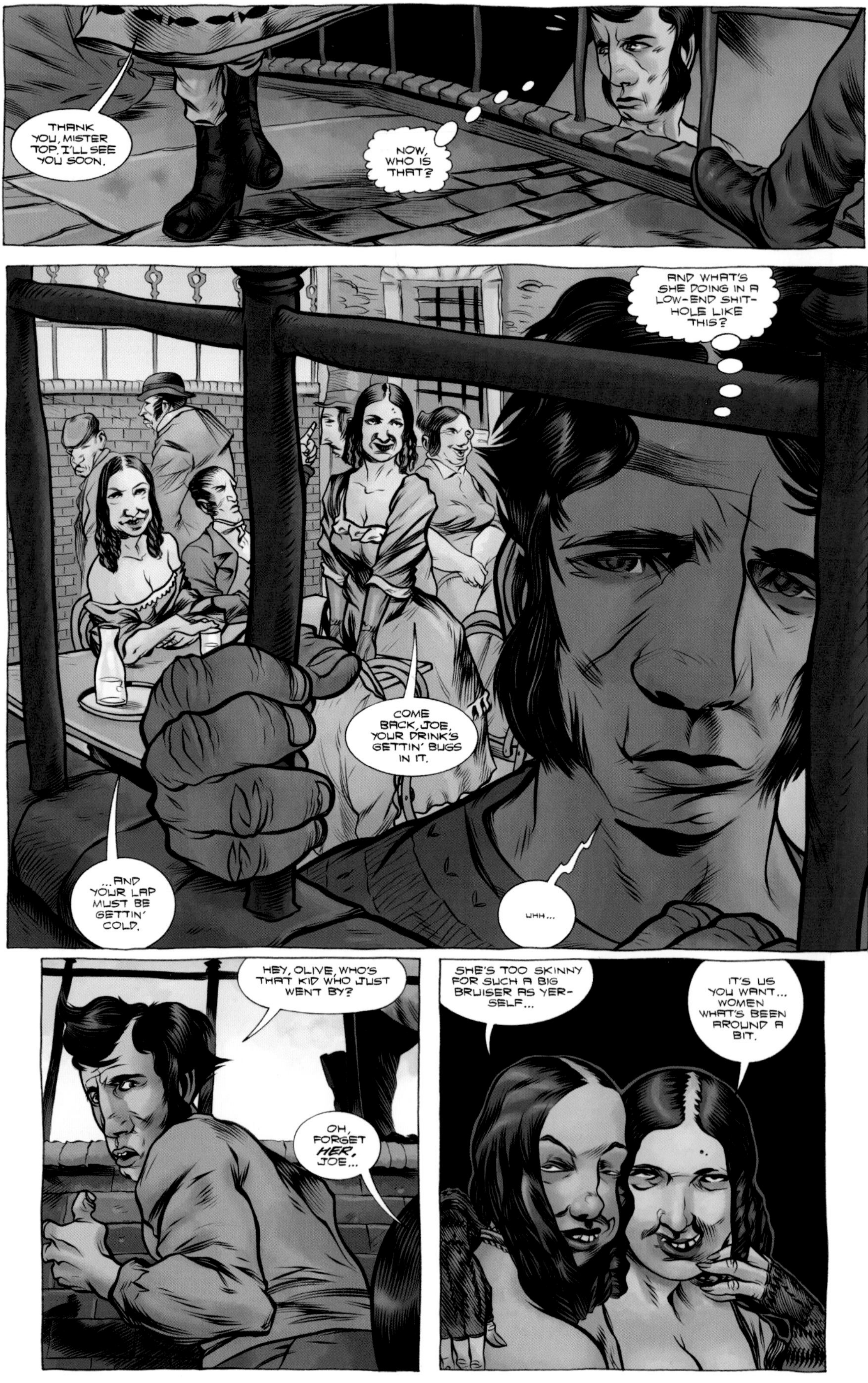
THANK YOU, MISTER TOP. I'LL SEE YOU SOON.
NOW, WHO IS THAT?
AND WHAT'S SHE DOING IN A LOW-END SHIT-HOLE LIKE THIS?
COME BACK, JOE, YOUR DRINK'S GETTIN' BUGS IN IT.
...AND YOUR LAP MUST BE GETTIN' COLD.
UHH...
HEY, OLIVE, WHO'S THAT KID WHO JUST WENT BY?
OH, FORGET HER, JOE...
SHE'S TOO SKINNY FOR SUCH A BIG BRUISER AS YER-SELF...
IT'S US YOU WANT... WOMEN WHAT'S BEEN AROUND A BIT.

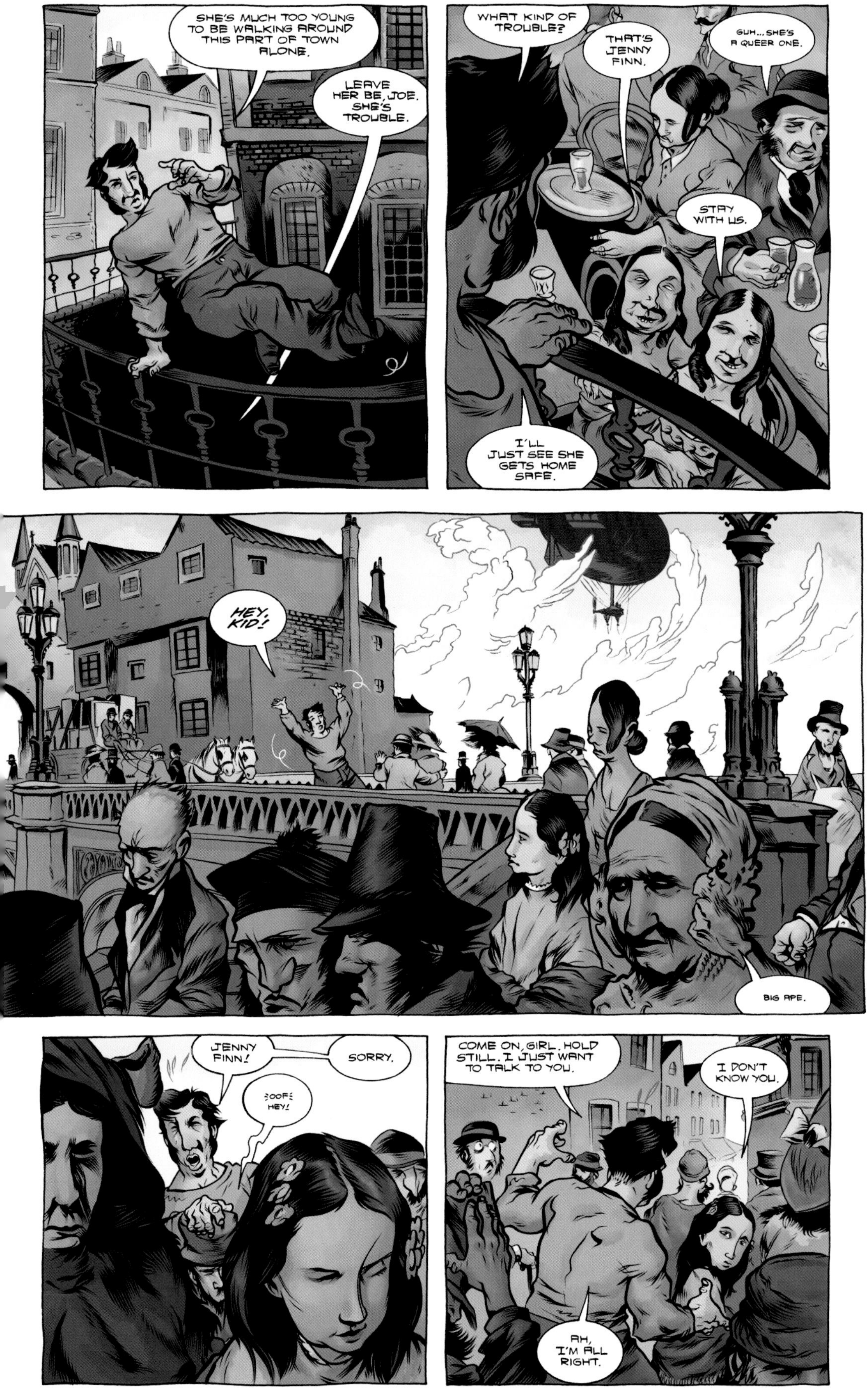
SHE'S MUCH TOO YOUNG TO BE WALKING AROUND THIS PART OF TOWN ALONE.
LEAVE HER BE, JOE. SHE'S TROUBLE.
WHAT KIND OF TROUBLE?
THAT'S JENNY FINN.
GUH... SHE'S A QUEER ONE.
STAY WITH US.
I'LL JUST SEE SHE GETS HOME SAFE.
HEY, KID!
BIG APE.
JENNY FINN!
SORRY.
OOF! HEY!
COME ON, GIRL. HOLD STILL. I JUST WANT TO TALK TO YOU.
I DON'T KNOW YOU.
AH, I'M ALL RIGHT.

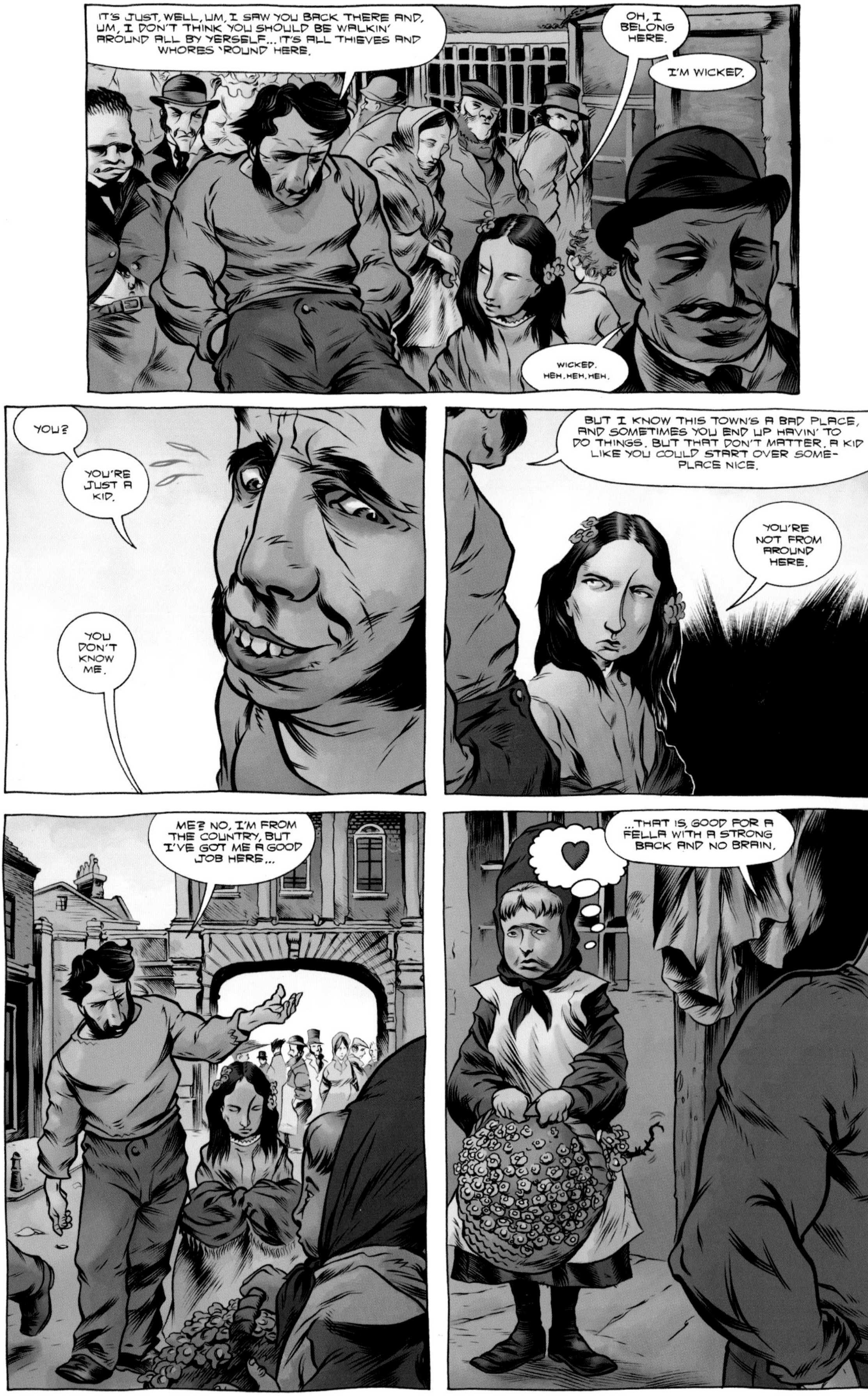
IT'S JUST, WELL, UM, I SAW YOU BACK THERE AND, UM, I DON'T THINK YOU SHOULD BE WALKIN' AROUND ALL BY YERSELF... IT'S ALL THIEVES AND WHORES 'ROUND HERE.
OH, I BELONG HERE.
I'M WICKED.
WICKED. HEH. HEH. HEH.
YOU?
YOU'RE JUST A KID.
YOU DON'T KNOW ME.
BUT I KNOW THIS TOWN'S A BAD PLACE, AND SOMETIMES YOU END UP HAVIN' TO DO THINGS. BUT THAT DON'T MATTER. A KID LIKE YOU COULD START OVER SOME-PLACE NICE.
YOU'RE NOT FROM AROUND HERE.
ME? NO, I'M FROM THE COUNTRY, BUT I'VE GOT ME A GOOD JOB HERE...
...THAT IS, GOOD FOR A FELLA WITH A STRONG BACK AND NO BRAIN.

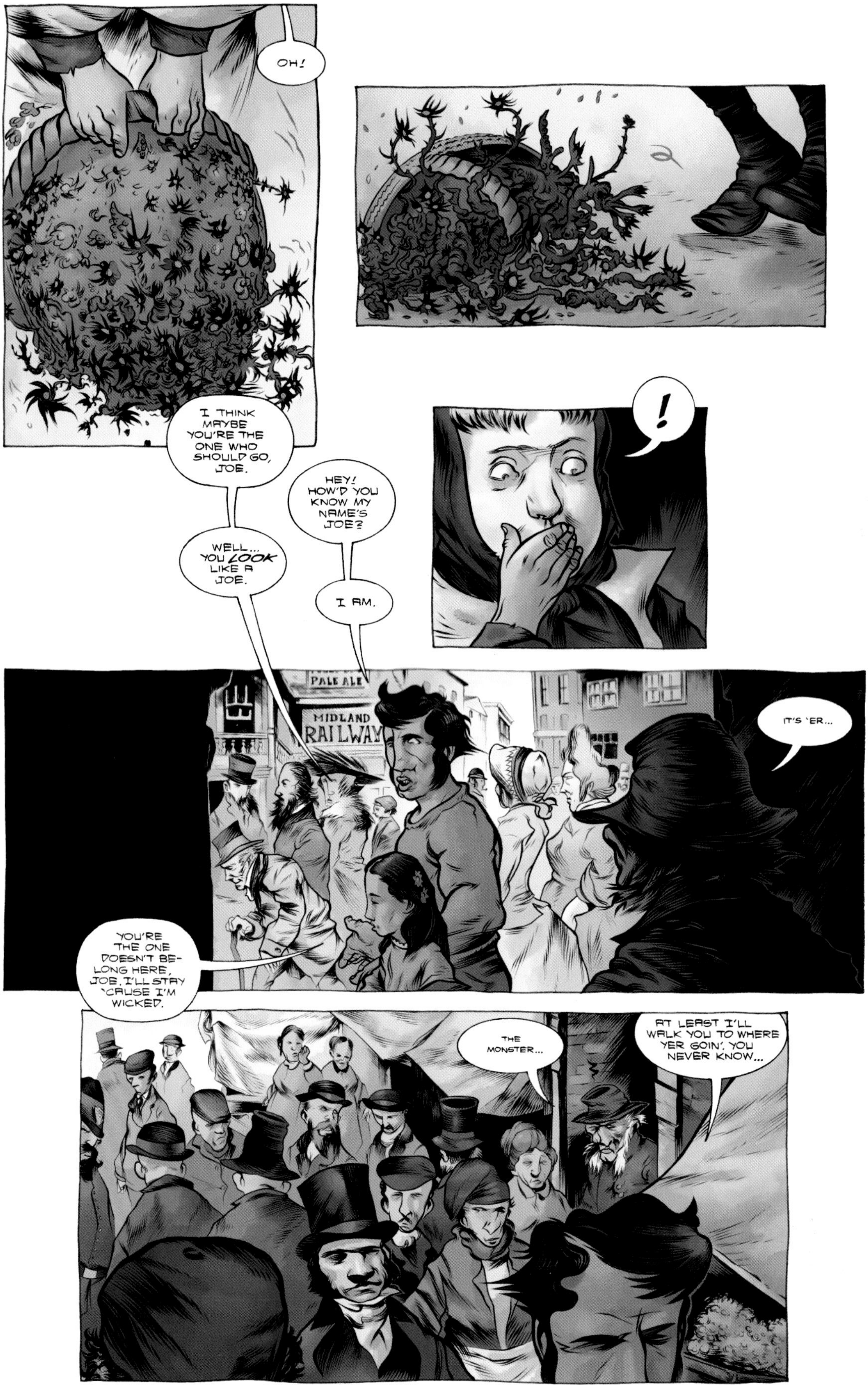
OH!
I THINK MAYBE YOU'RE THE ONE WHO SHOULD GO, JOE.
HEY! HOW'D YOU KNOW MY NAME'S JOE?
WELL... YOU LOOK LIKE A JOE.
I AM.
!
PALE ALE
MIDLAND RAILWAY
IT'S 'ER...
YOU'RE THE ONE DOESN'T BE-LONG HERE, JOE. I'LL STAY 'CAUSE I'M WICKED.
THE MONSTER...
AT LEAST I'LL WALK YOU TO WHERE YER GOIN'. YOU NEVER KNOW...

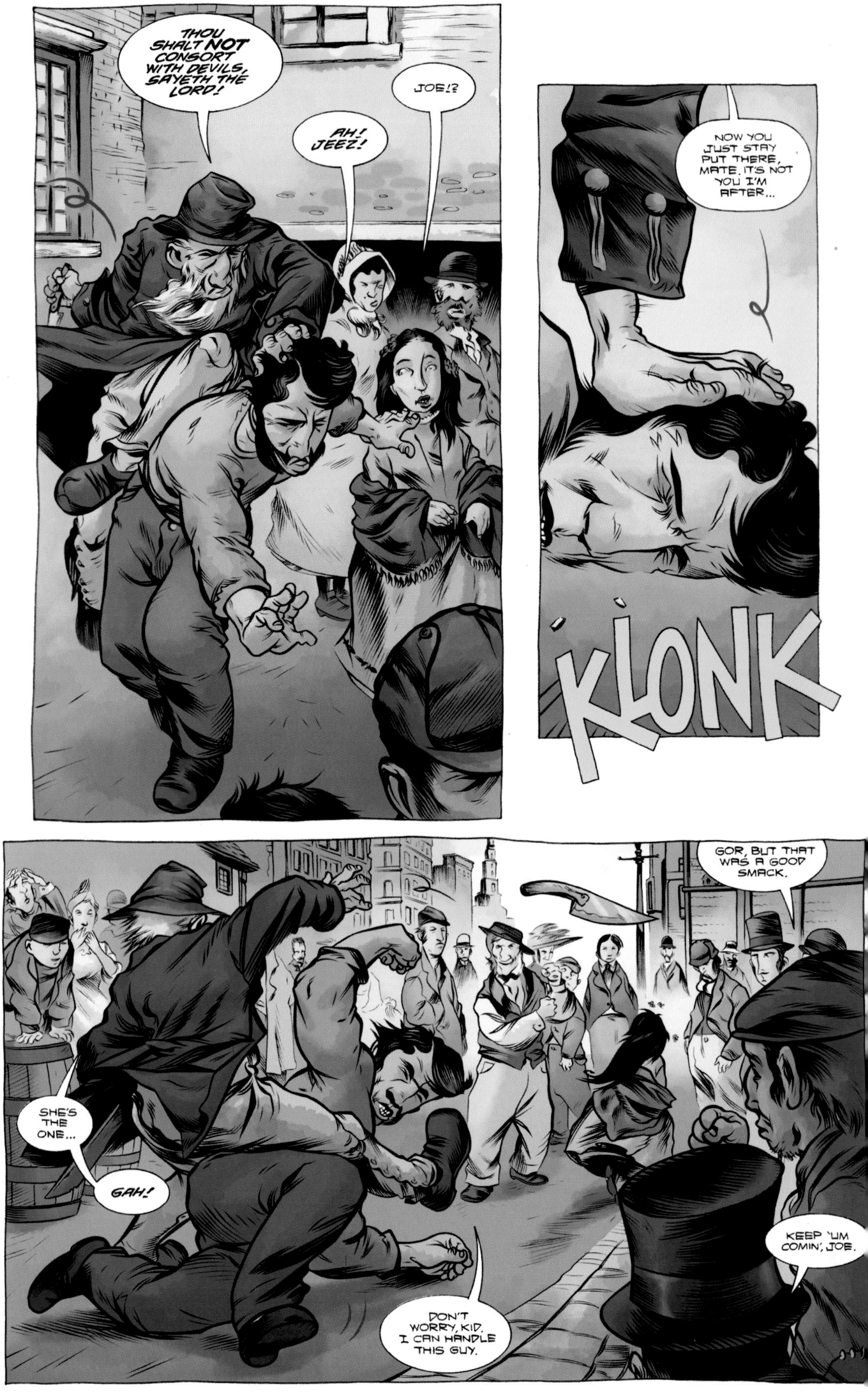
THOU SHALT NOT CONSORT WITH DEVILS, SAYETH THE LORD!
JOE!?
AH! JEEZ!
NOW YOU JUST STAY PUT THERE, MATE, IT'S NOT YOU I'M AFTER...
KLONK
SHE'S THE ONE...
GAH!
GOR, BUT THAT WAS A GOOD SMACK.
DON'T WORRY, KID, I CAN HANDLE THIS GUY.
KEEP 'UM COMIN', JOE.

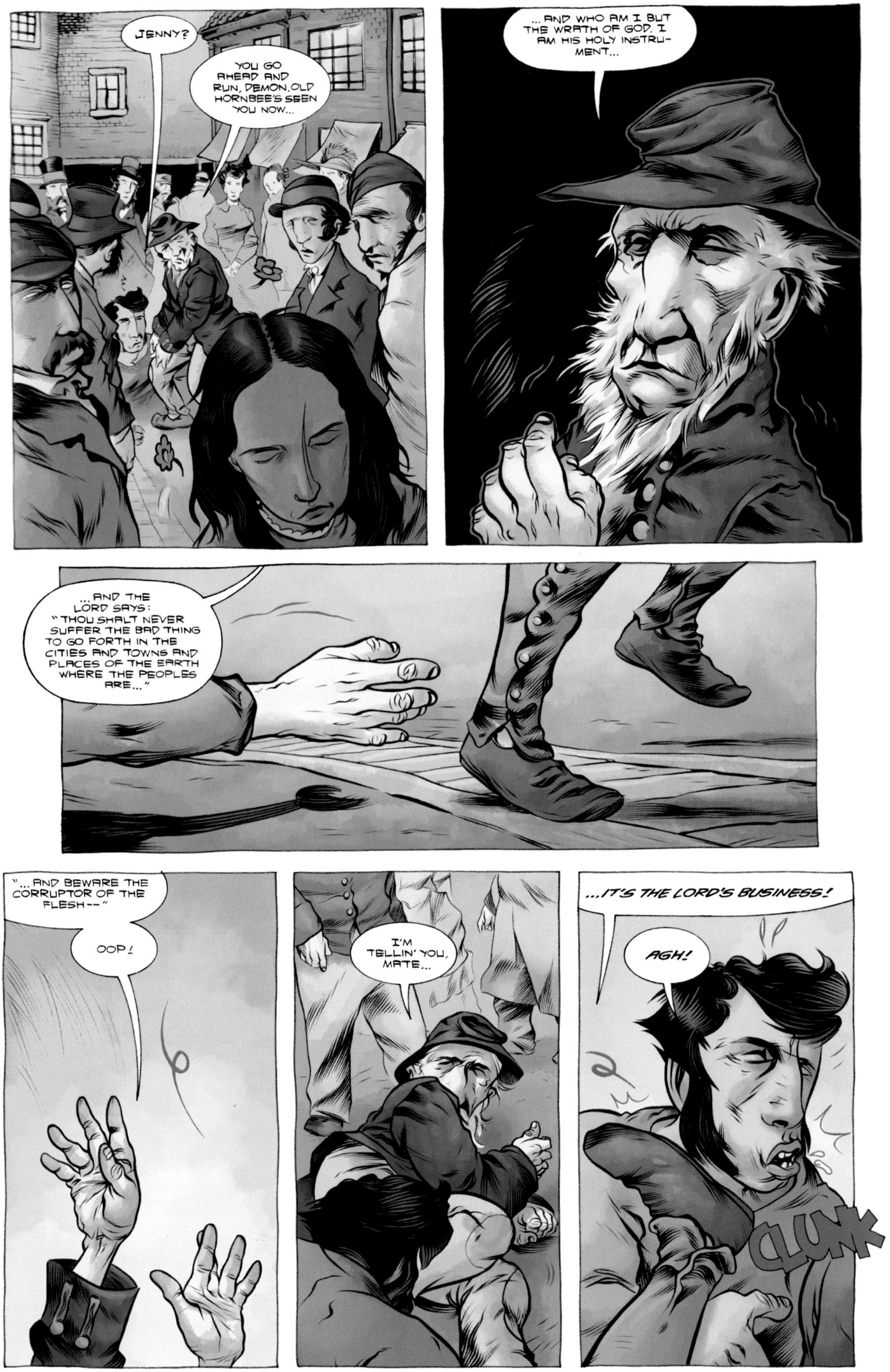
JENNY?
YOU GO AHEAD AND RUN, DEMON, OLD HORNBEE'S SEEN YOU NOW...
... AND WHO AM I BUT THE WRATH OF GOD. I AM HIS HOLY INSTRU-MENT...
...AND THE LORD SAYS: "THOU SHALT NEVER SUFFER THE BAD THING TO GO FORTH IN THE CITIES AND TOWNS AND PLACES OF THE EARTH WHERE THE PEOPLES ARE..."
"... AND BEWARE THE CORRUPTOR OF THE FLESH--"
OOP!
I'M TELLIN' YOU, MATE...
...IT'S THE LORD'S BUSINESS!
AGH!
CLUNK

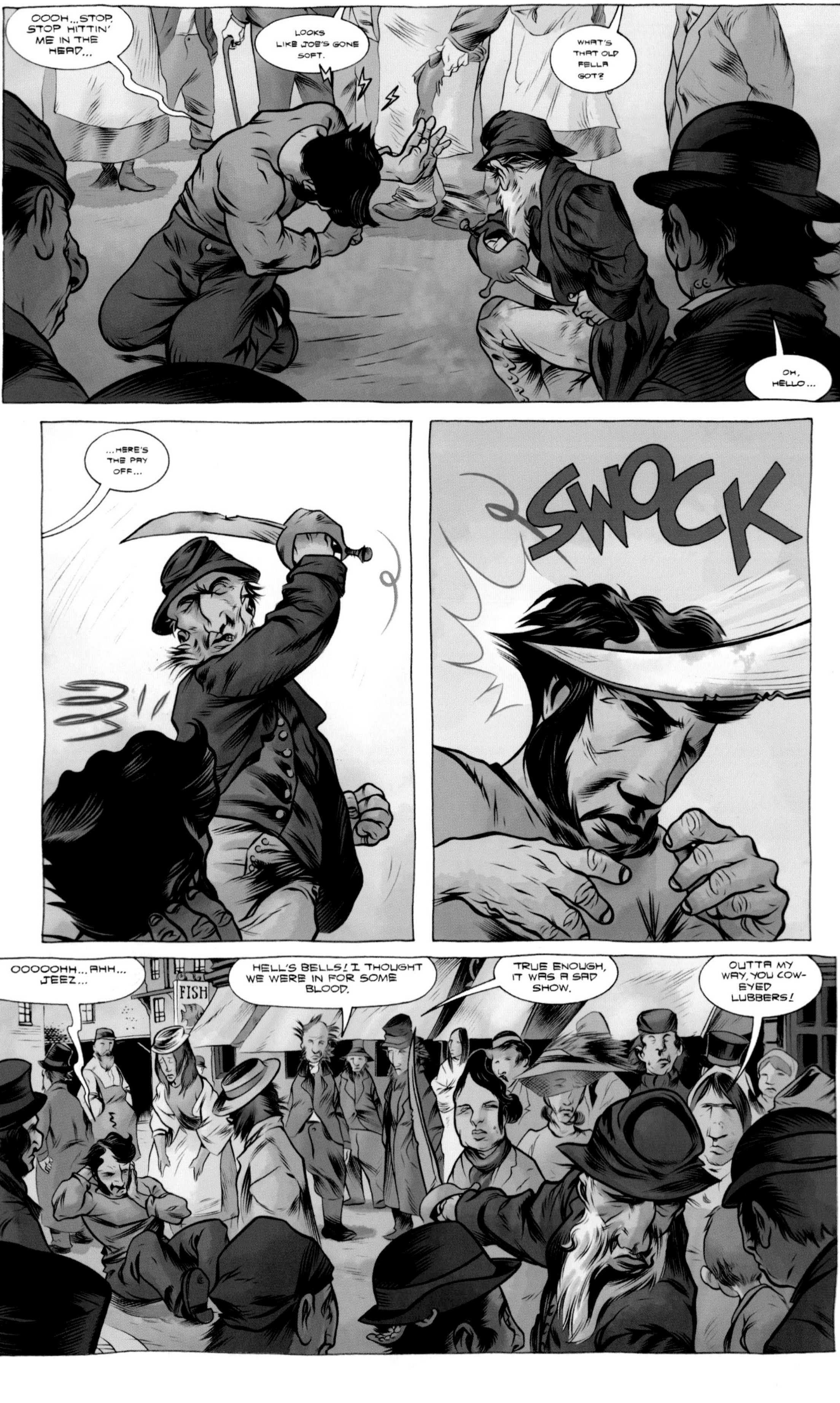
OOOH... STOP, STOP HITTIN' ME IN THE HEAD...
LOOKS LIKE JOE'S GONE SOFT.
WHAT'S THAT OLD FELLA GOT?
OH, HELLO...
...HERE'S THE PAY OFF...
SWOCK
OOOOOHH... AHH... JEEZ...
HELL'S BELLS! I THOUGHT WE WERE IN FOR SOME BLOOD.
TRUE ENOUGH, IT WAS A SAD SHOW.
OUTTA MY WAY, YOU COW-EYED LUBBERS!
FISH

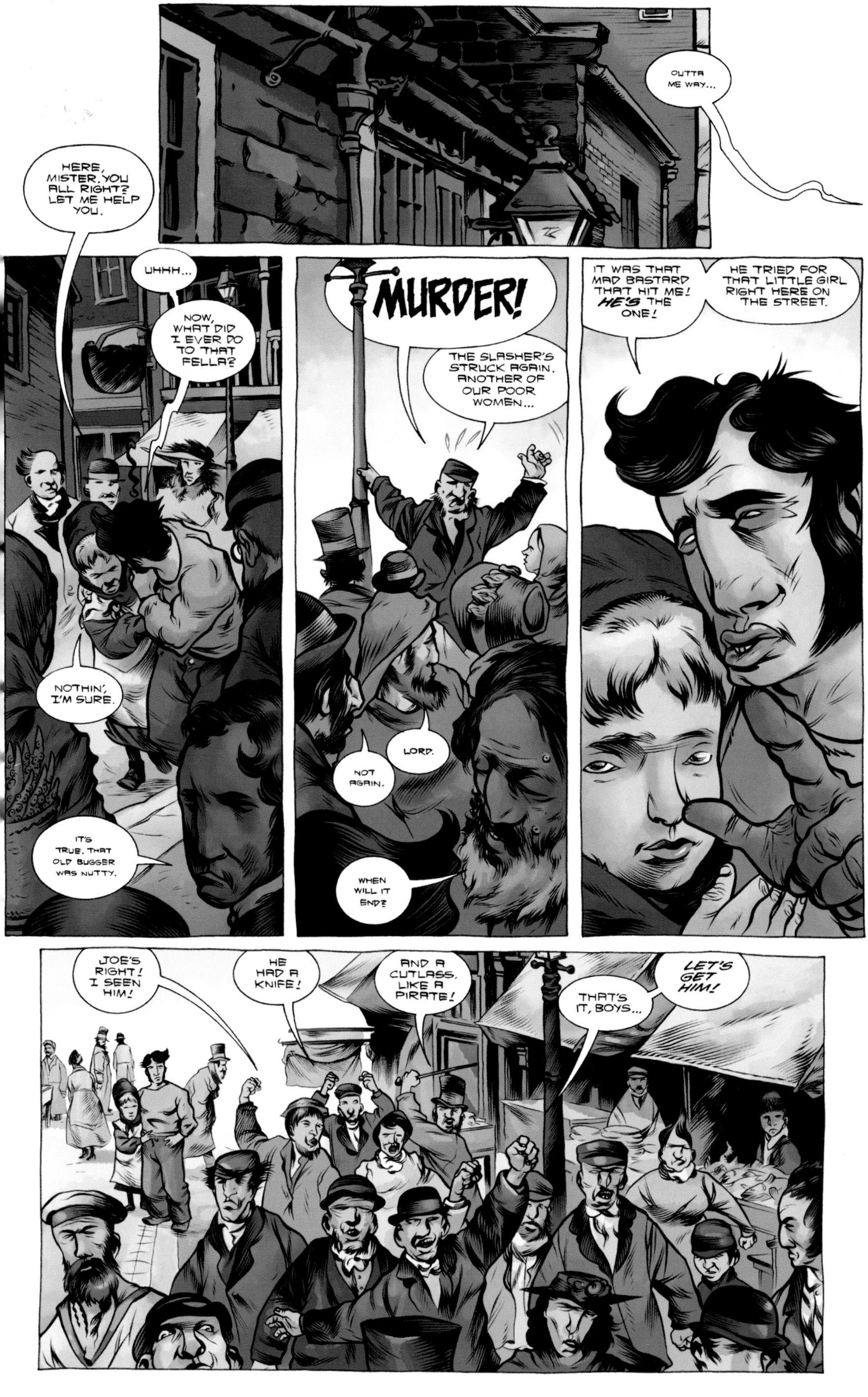
OUTTA ME WAY...
HERE, MISTER. YOU ALL RIGHT? LET ME HELP YOU.
UHHH...
NOW, WHAT DID I EVER DO TO THAT FELLA?
NOTHIN', I'M SURE.
IT'S TRUE. THAT OLD BUGGER WAS NUTTY.
MURDER!
THE SLASHER'S STRUCK AGAIN. ANOTHER OF OUR POOR WOMEN...
LORD.
NOT AGAIN.
WHEN WILL IT END?
IT WAS THAT MAD BASTARD THAT HIT ME! HE'S THE ONE!
HE TRIED FOR THAT LITTLE GIRL RIGHT HERE ON THE STREET.
JOE'S RIGHT! I SEEN HIM!
HE HAD A KNIFE!
AND A CUTLASS, LIKE A PIRATE!
THAT'S IT, BOYS...
LET'S GET HIM!

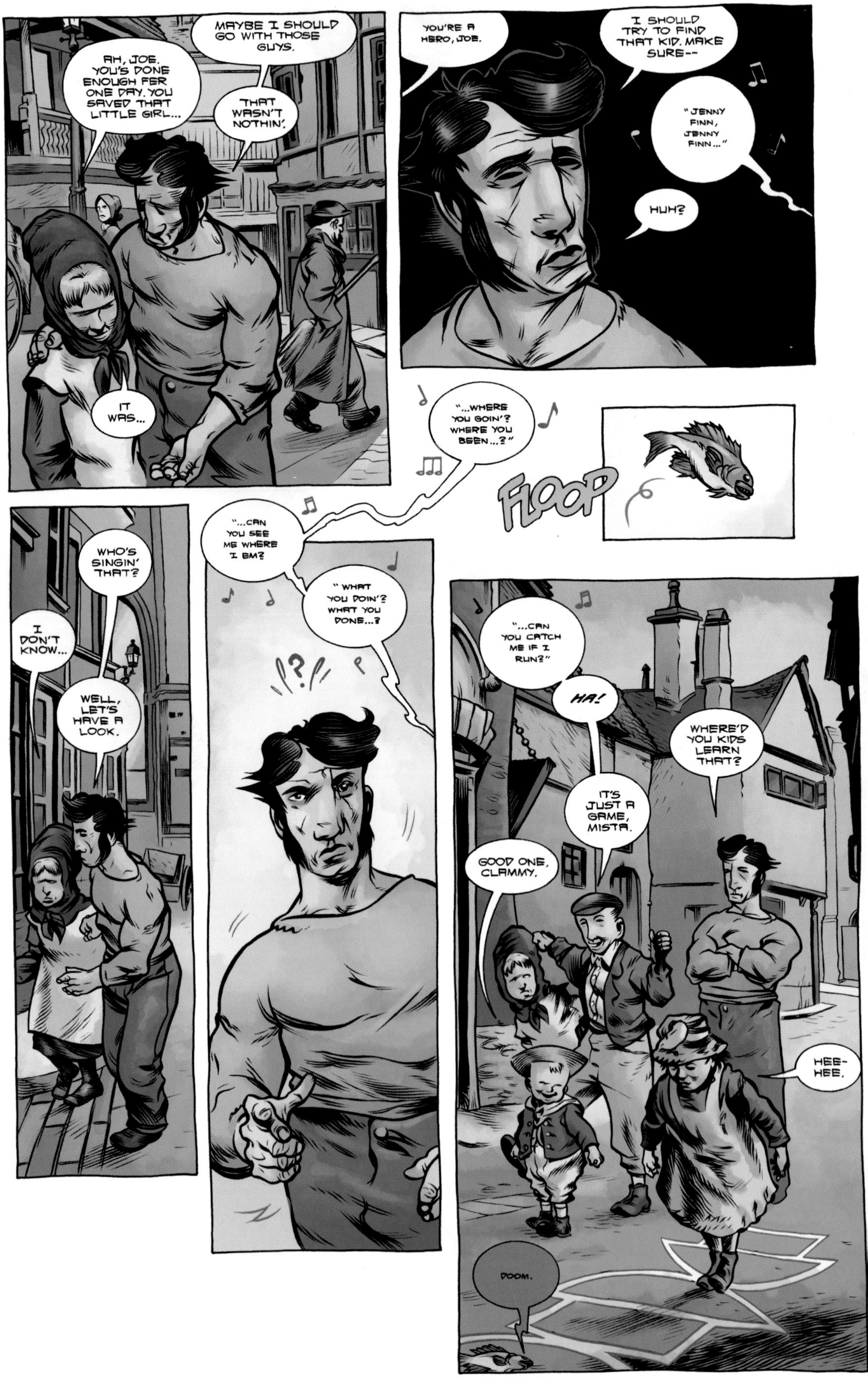
MAYBE I SHOULD GO WITH THOSE GUYS.
AH, JOE. YOU'S DONE ENOUGH FER ONE DAY. YOU SAVED THAT LITTLE GIRL...
THAT WASN'T NOTHIN'.
IT WAS...
YOU'RE A HERO, JOE.
I SHOULD TRY TO FIND THAT KID. MAKE SURE--
"JENNY FINN, JENNY FINN..."
HUH?
"...WHERE YOU GOIN'? WHERE YOU BEEN...?"
FLOOP
WHO'S SINGIN' THAT?
I DON'T KNOW...
WELL, LET'S HAVE A LOOK.
"...CAN YOU SEE ME WHERE I AM?
" WHAT YOU DOIN'? WHAT YOU DONE...?
?
"...CAN YOU CATCH ME IF I RUN?"
HA!
WHERE'D YOU KIDS LEARN THAT?
IT'S JUST A GAME, MISTA.
GOOD ONE, CLAMMY.
HEE-HEE.
DOOM.

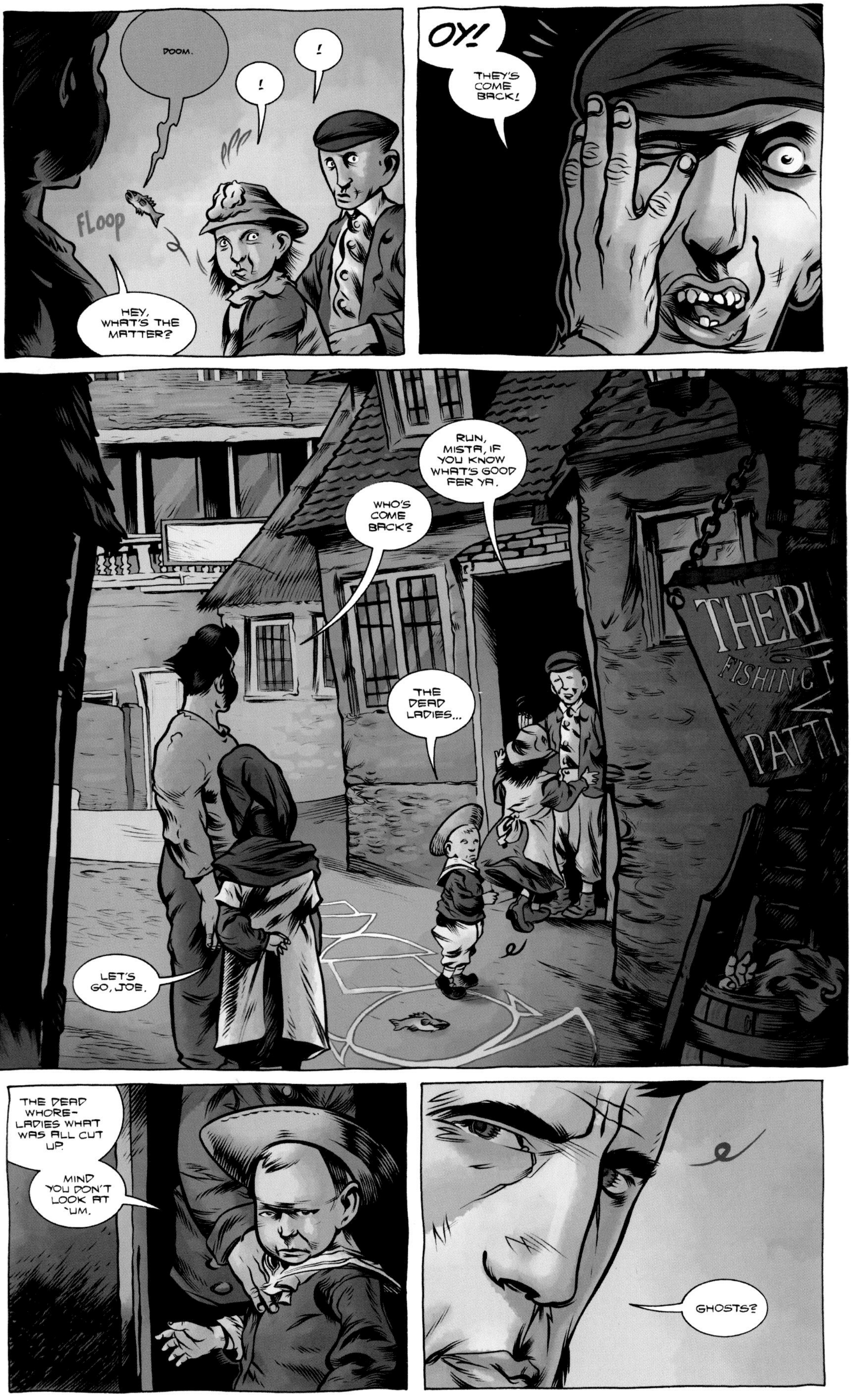
DOOM.
!
!
PPP
FLoop
HEY, WHAT'S THE MATTER?
OY!
THEY'S COME BACK!
RUN, MISTA, IF YOU KNOW WHAT'S GOOD FER YA.
WHO'S COME BACK?
THE DEAD LADIES...
LET'S GO, JOE.
THER
FISHING
PATT
THE DEAD WHORE-LADIES WHAT WAS ALL CUT UP.
MIND YOU DON'T LOOK AT 'UM.
GHOSTS?

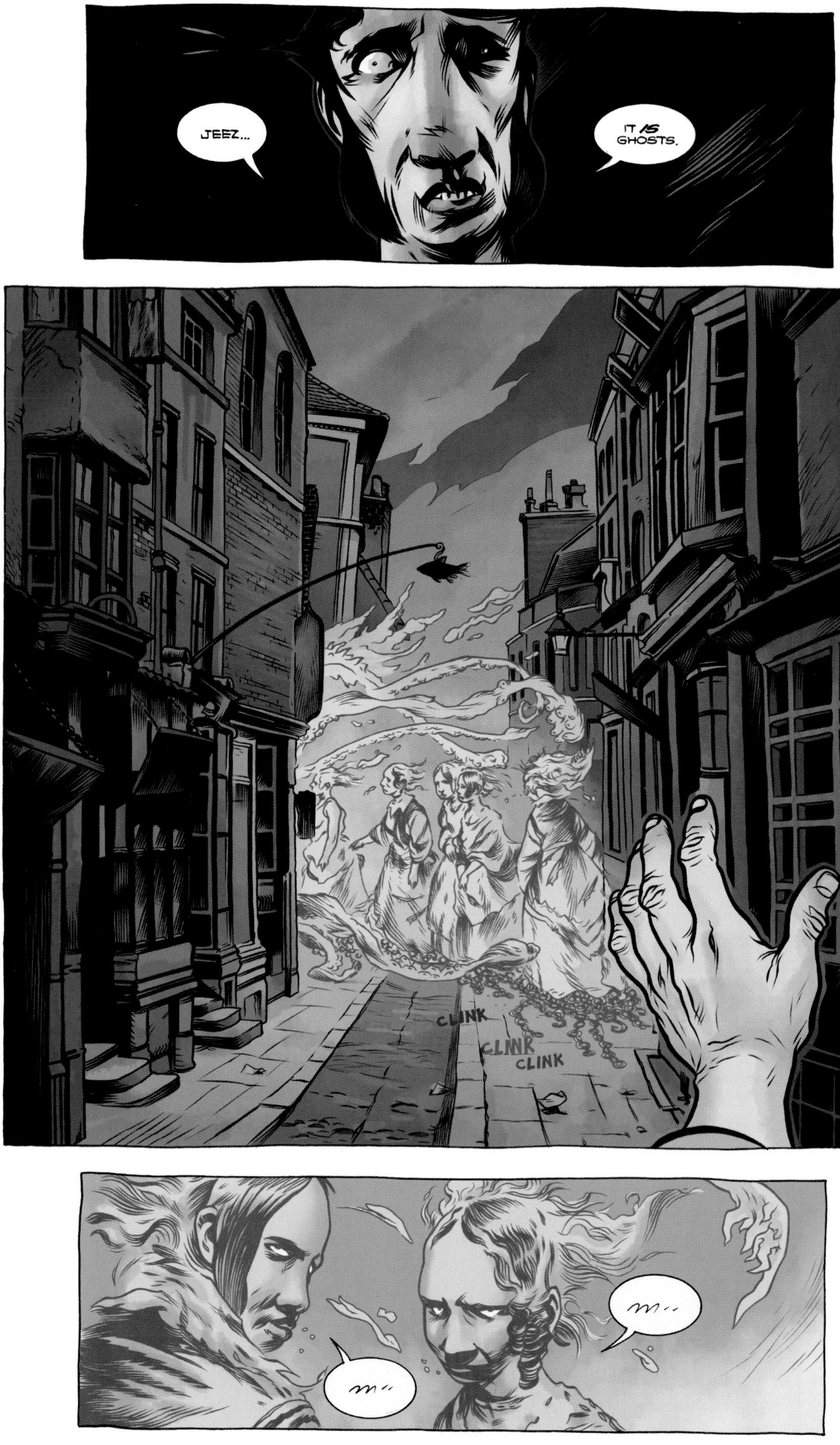
JEEZ...
IT IS GHOSTS.
CLINK
CLINK
CLINK
m..
m..

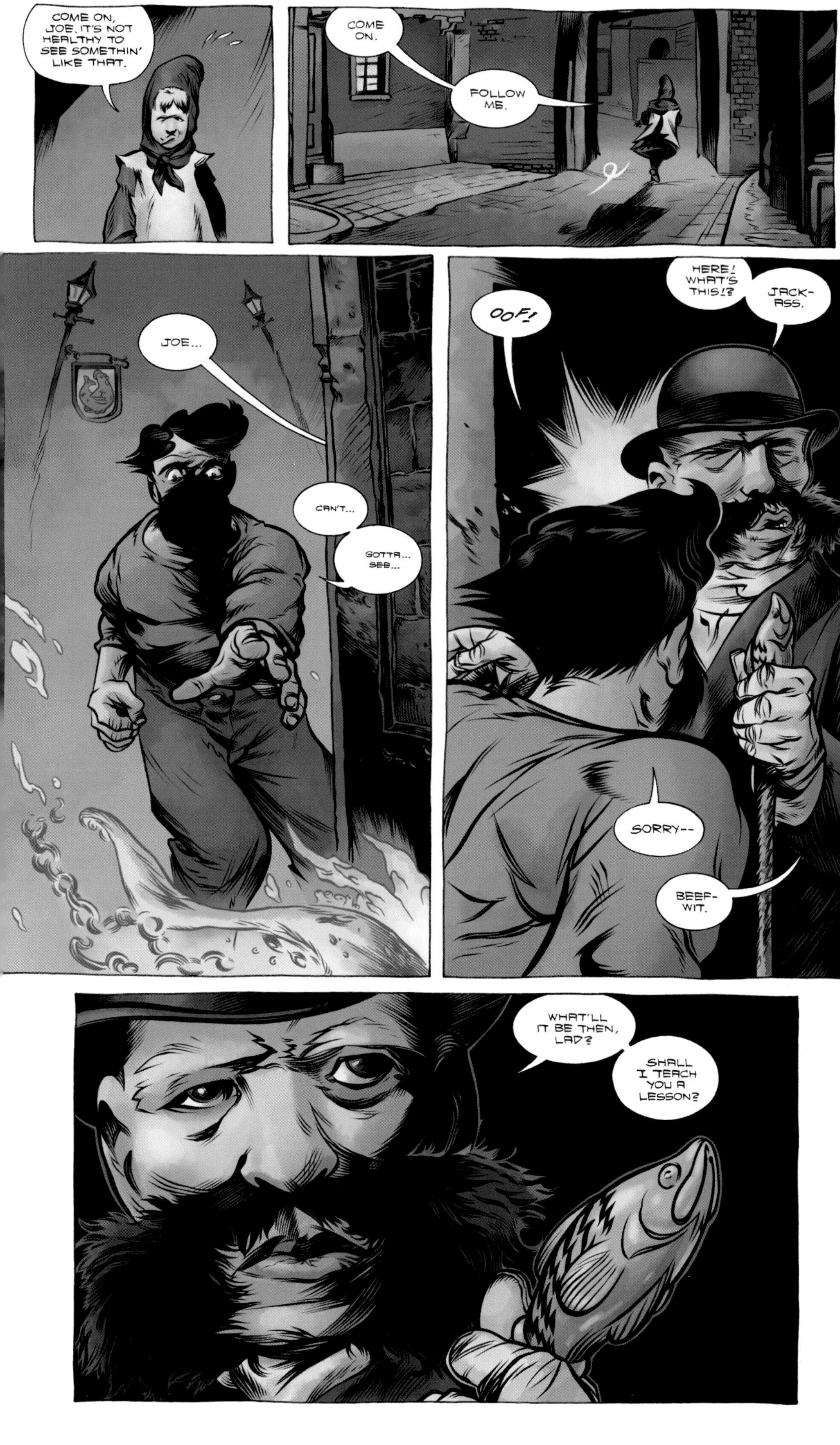
COME ON, JOE. IT'S NOT HEALTHY TO SEE SOMETHIN' LIKE THAT.
COME ON.
FOLLOW ME.
JOE...
CAN'T...
GOTTA... SEE...
OOF!
HERE! WHAT'S THIS!?
JACK-ASS.
SORRY--
BEEF-WIT.
WHAT'LL IT BE THEN, LAD?
SHALL I TEACH YOU A LESSON?

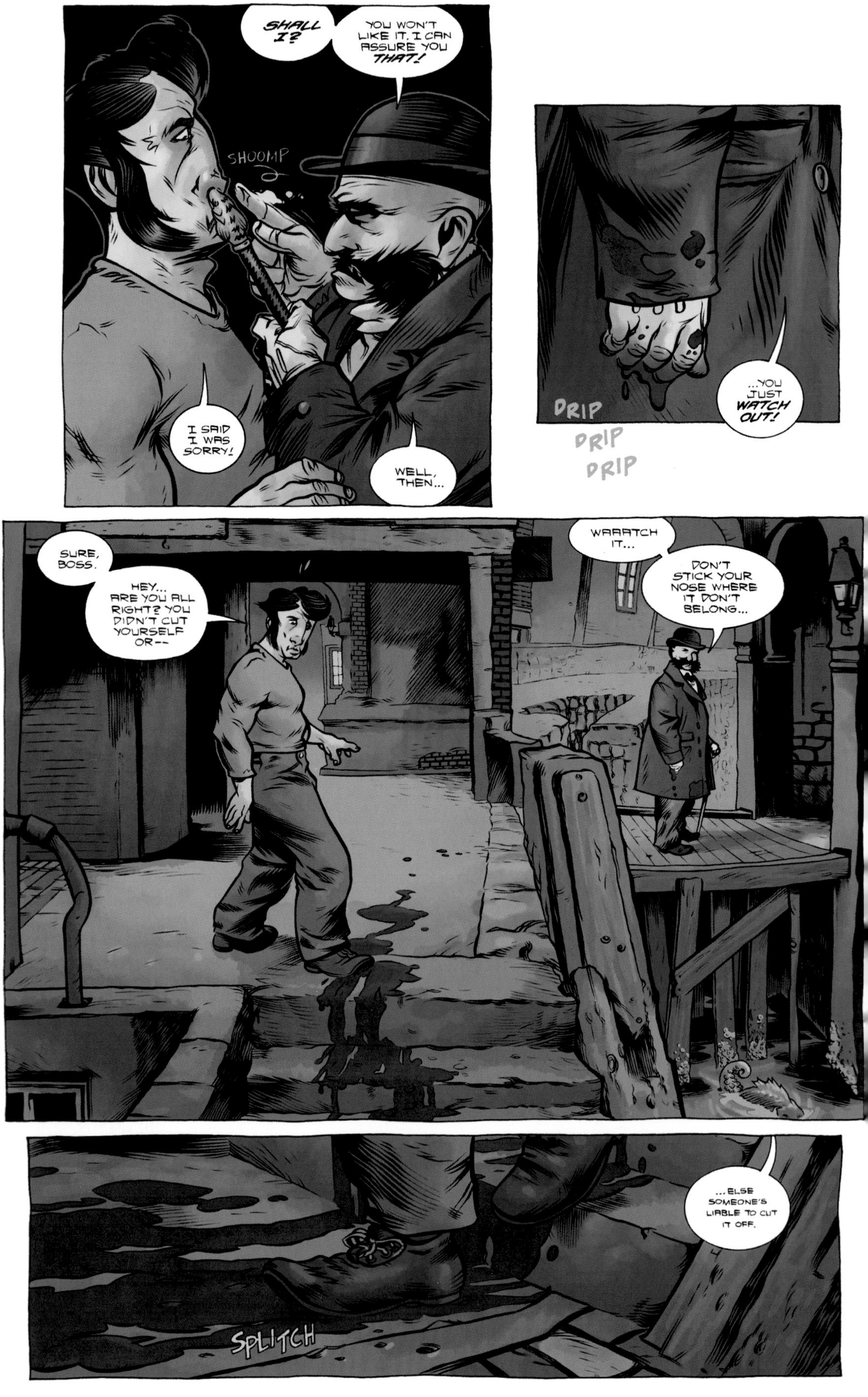
SHALL I?
YOU WON'T LIKE IT. I CAN ASSURE YOU THAT!
SHOOMP
I SAID I WAS SORRY!
WELL, THEN...
...YOU JUST WATCH OUT!
DRIP
DRIP
DRIP
SURE, BOSS.
HEY... ARE YOU ALL RIGHT? YOU DIDN'T CUT YOURSELF OR--
WAAATCH IT...
DON'T STICK YOUR NOSE WHERE IT DON'T BELONG...
...ELSE SOMEONE'S LIABLE TO CUT IT OFF.
SPLITCH

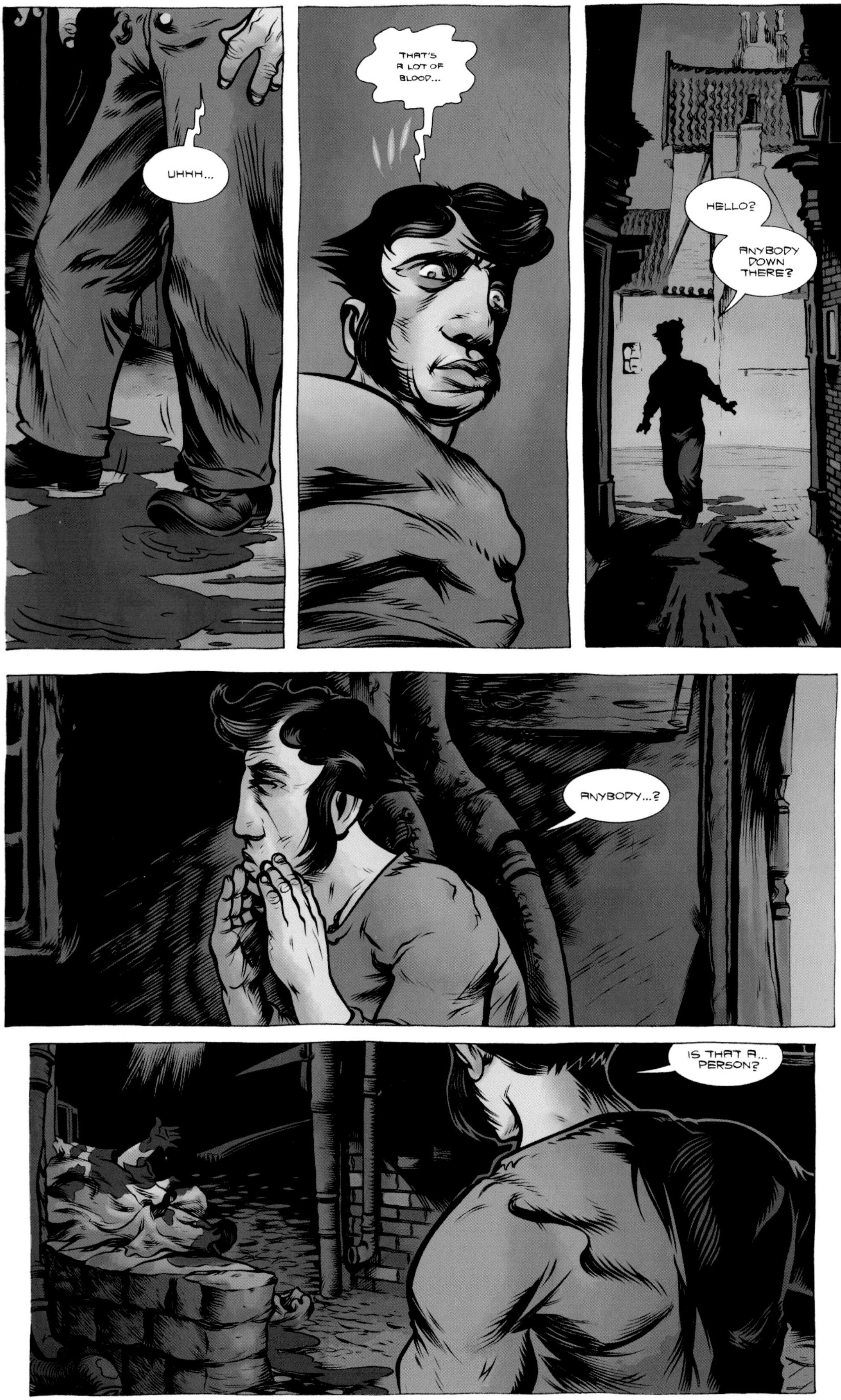
UHHH...
THAT'S A LOT OF BLOOD...
HELLO?
ANYBODY DOWN THERE?
ANYBODY...?
IS THAT A... PERSON?

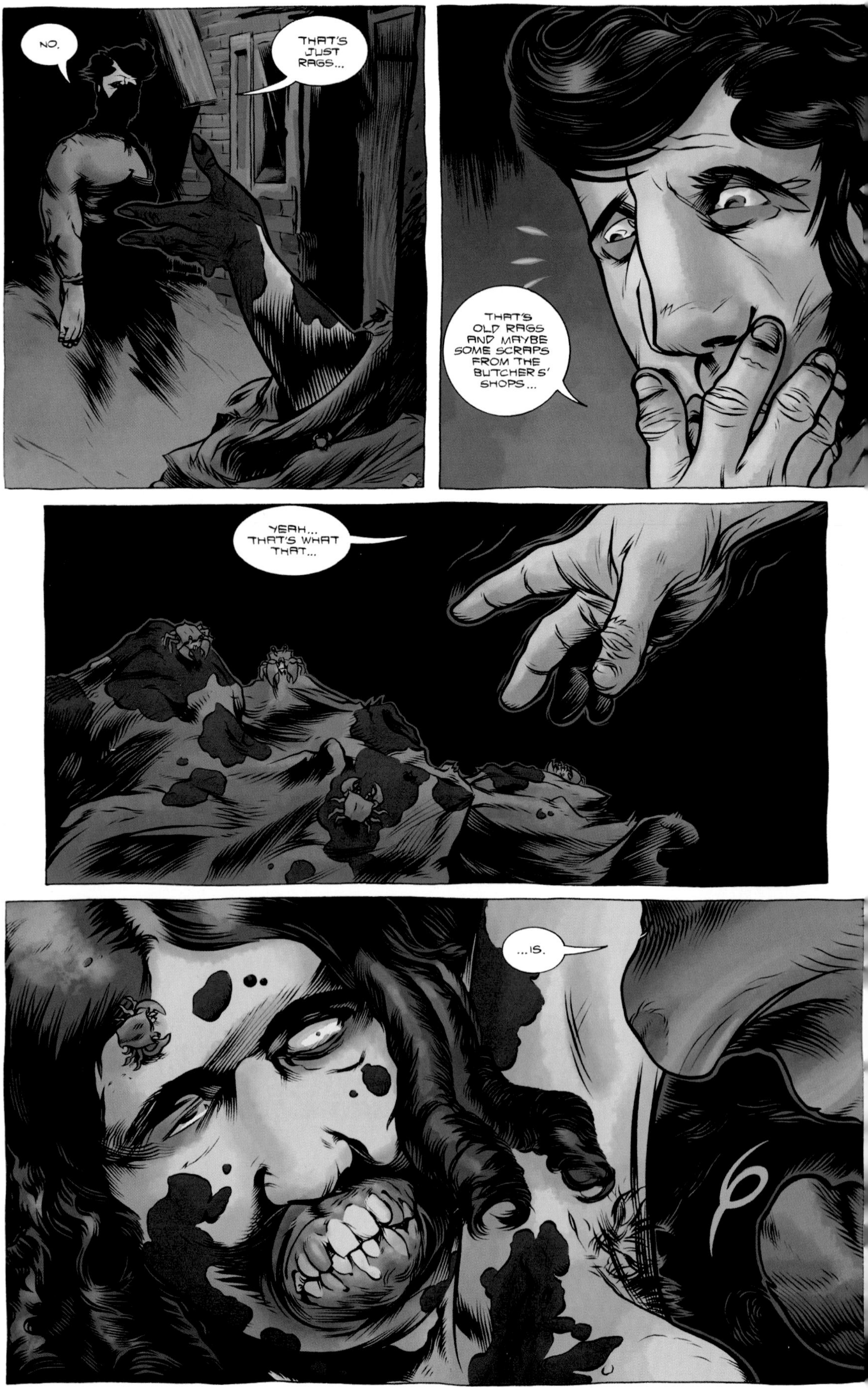
NO.
THAT'S JUST RAGS...
THAT'S OLD RAGS AND MAYBE SOME SCRAPS FROM THE BUTCHER'S' SHOPS...
YEAH... THAT'S WHAT THAT...
...IS.

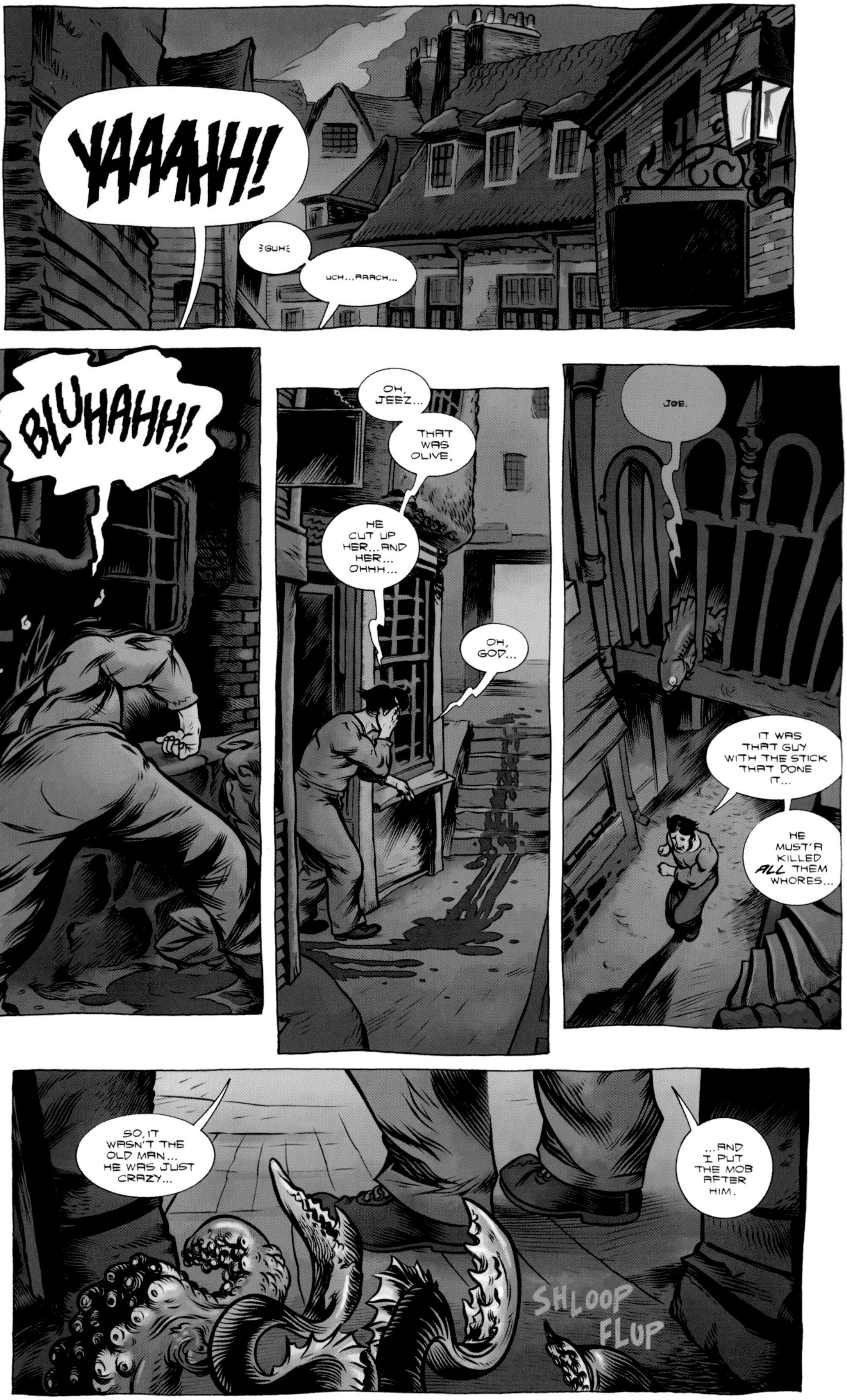
YAAAHH!
GUH
UCH... RAACH...
BLUHAHH!
OH, JEEZ...
THAT WAS OLIVE.
HE CUT UP HER... AND HER... OHHH...
OH, GOD...
JOE.
IT WAS THAT GUY WITH THE STICK THAT DONE IT...
HE MUST'A KILLED ALL THEM WHORES...
SO, IT WASN'T THE OLD MAN... HE WAS JUST CRAZY...
...AND I PUT THE MOB AFTER HIM.
SHLOOP
FLUP

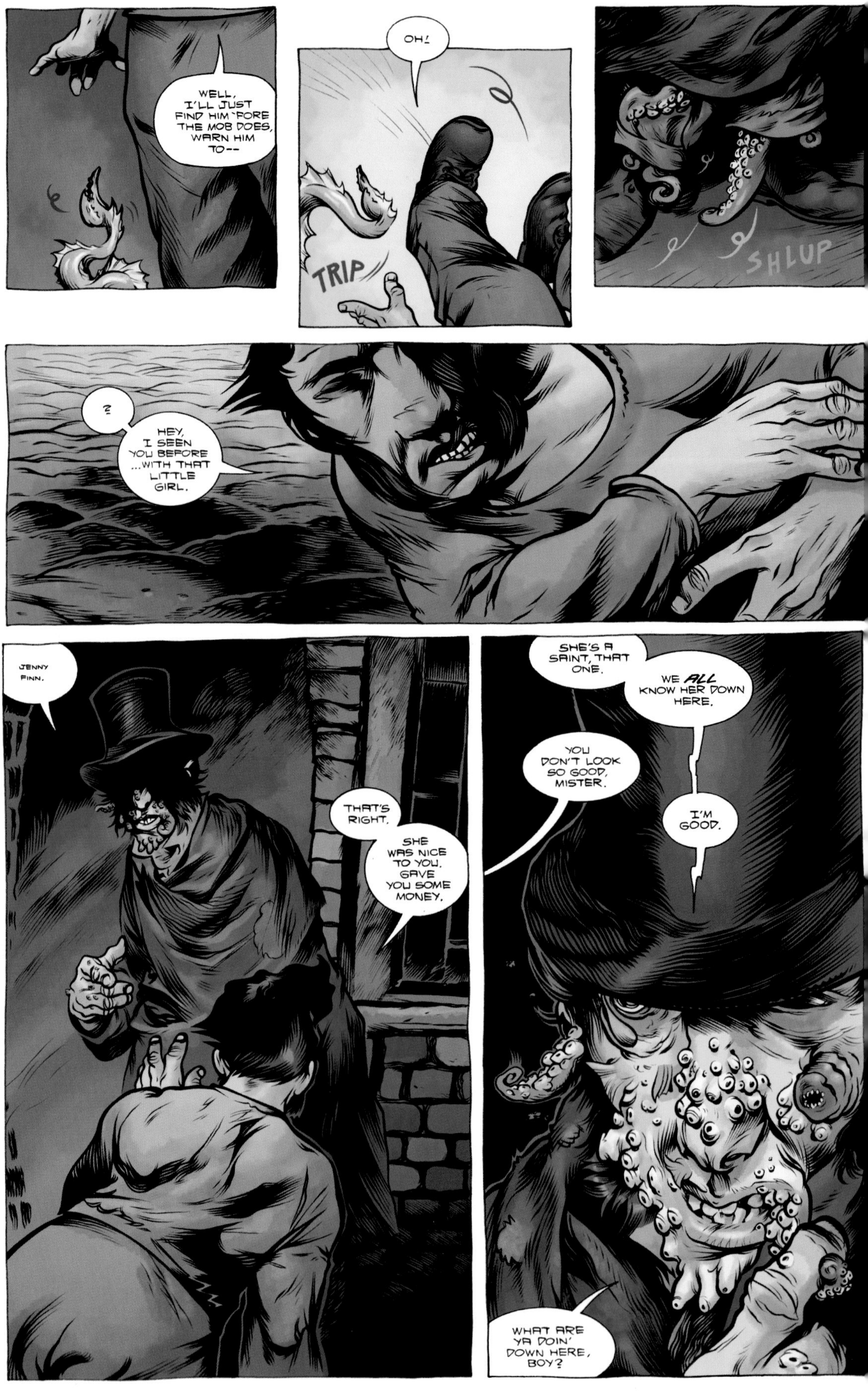
WELL, I'LL JUST FIND HIM 'FORE THE MOB DOES, WARN HIM TO--
OH!
TRIP
SHLUP
?
HEY, I SEEN YOU BEFORE ...WITH THAT LITTLE GIRL.
JENNY FINN.
THAT'S RIGHT.
SHE WAS NICE TO YOU. GAVE YOU SOME MONEY.
SHE'S A SAINT, THAT ONE.
WE ALL KNOW HER DOWN HERE.
YOU DON'T LOOK SO GOOD, MISTER.
I'M GOOD.
WHAT ARE YA DOIN' DOWN HERE, BOY?

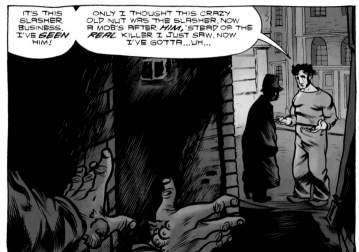

IT'S THIS SLASHER BUSINESS. I'VE *SEEN* HIM!

ONLY I THOUGHT THIS CRAZY OLD NUT WAS THE SLASHER. NOW A MOB'S AFTER *HIM,* 'STEAD OF THE *REAL* KILLER I JUST SAW. NOW I'VE GOTTA...UH...

BLUP
GLUTCH

WELL, NEVER MIND, MISTER. IT'S MY PROBLEM.

I'LL JUST BE GOIN' NOW--

DON'T GO.

YES, STAY...

STAY...

SHE'LL BE COMIN' THIS WAY SOON.

ALWAYS DOES.

WHO'S COMIN'?

SHE'S FOND OF YOU.

YES. STAY.

YES.

WHO?

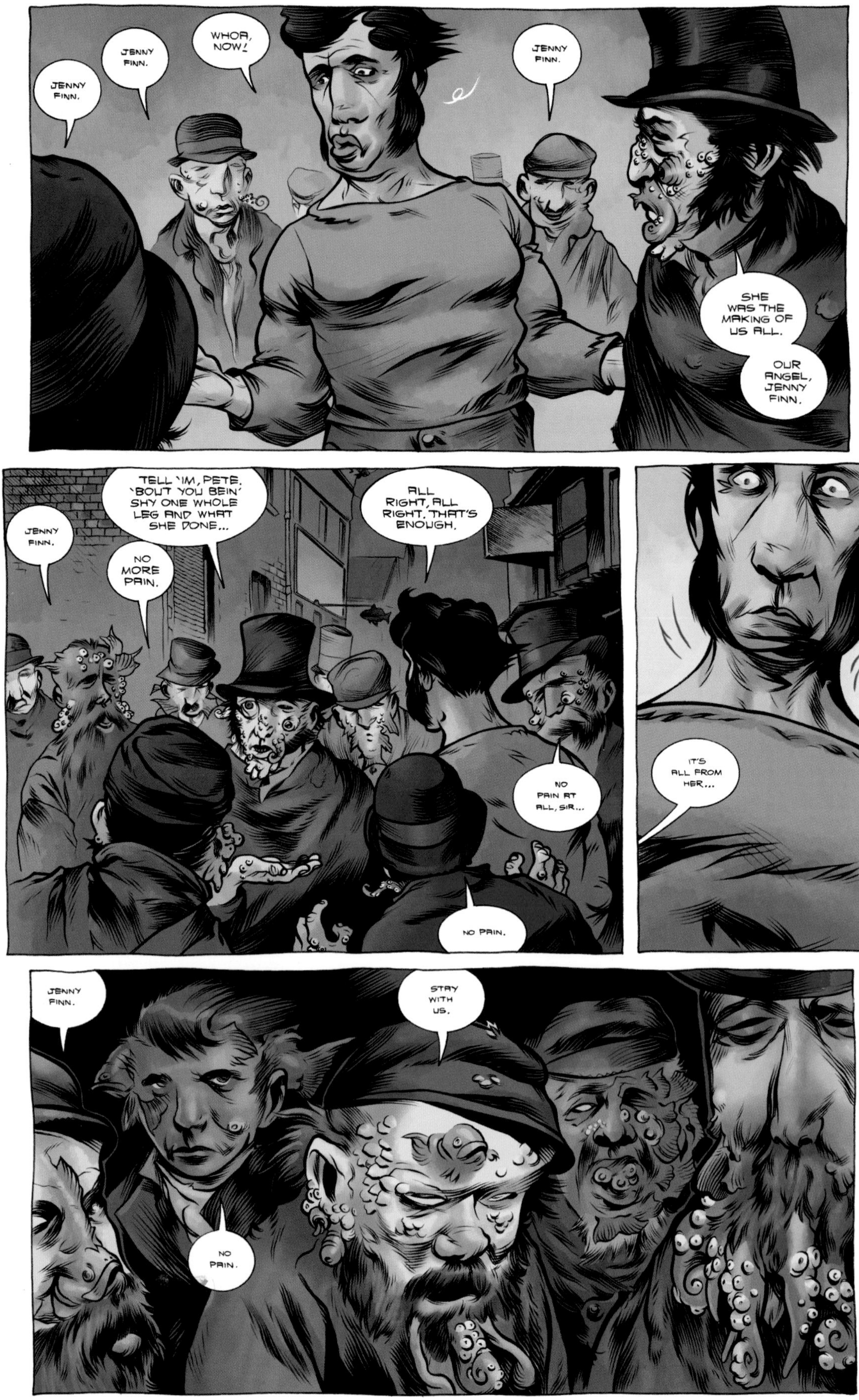

JENNY FINN.
JENNY FINN.
WHOA, NOW!
JENNY FINN.
SHE WAS THE MAKING OF US ALL.
OUR ANGEL, JENNY FINN.
JENNY FINN.
TELL 'IM, PETE. 'BOUT YOU BEIN' SHY ONE WHOLE LEG AND WHAT SHE DONE...
NO MORE PAIN.
ALL RIGHT, ALL RIGHT. THAT'S ENOUGH.
NO PAIN AT ALL, SIR...
NO PAIN.
IT'S ALL FROM HER...
JENNY FINN.
STAY WITH US.
NO PAIN.

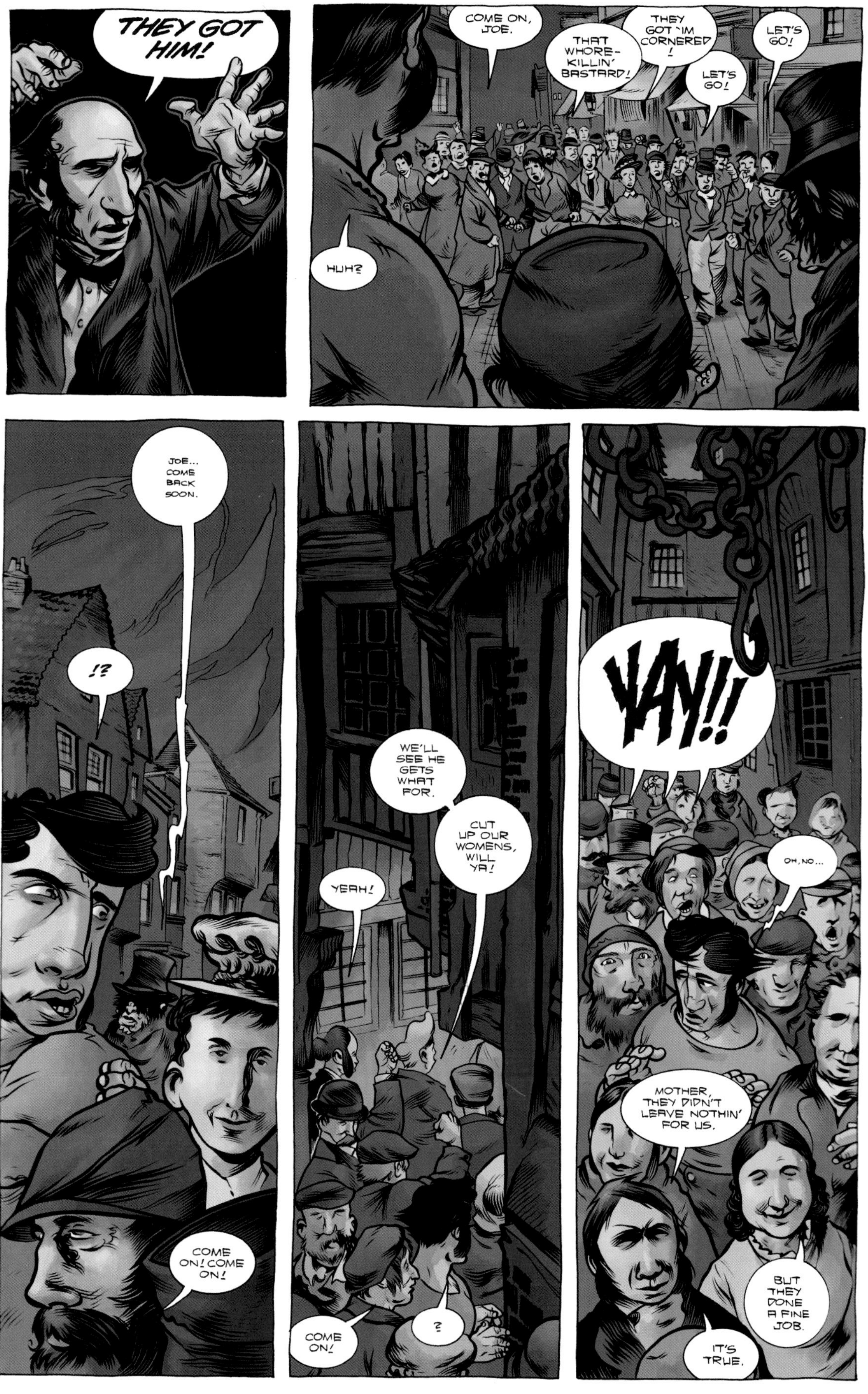
THEY GOT HIM!
COME ON, JOE.
THAT WHORE-KILLIN' BASTARD!
THEY GOT 'IM CORNERED!
LET'S GO!
LET'S GO!
HUH?
JOE... COME BACK SOON.
!?
COME ON! COME ON!
WE'LL SEE HE GETS WHAT FOR.
CUT UP OUR WOMENS, WILL YA!
YEAH!
COME ON!
?
YAY!!
OH, NO...
MOTHER, THEY DIDN'T LEAVE NOTHIN' FOR US.
BUT THEY DONE A FINE JOB.
IT'S TRUE.

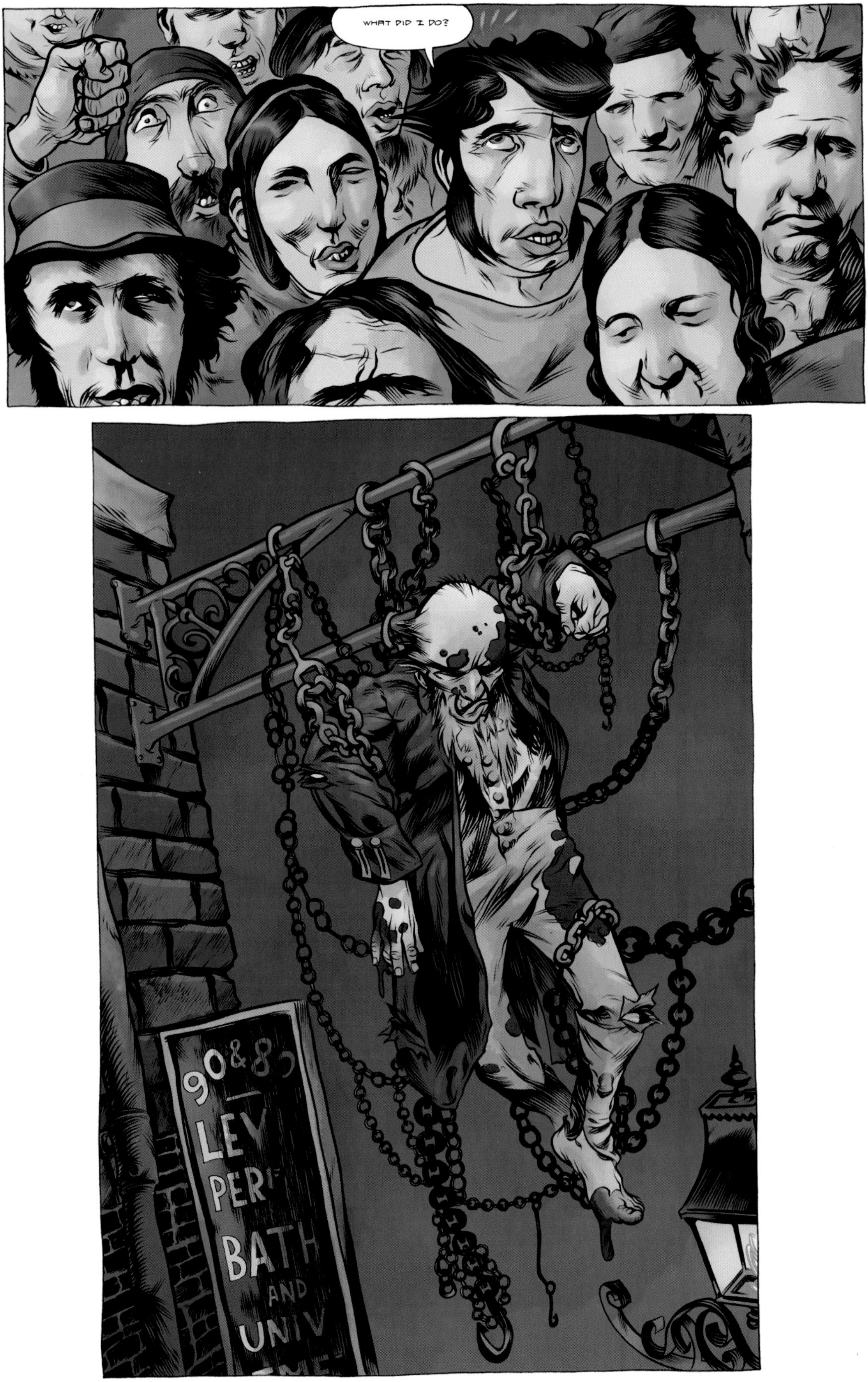
WHAT DID I DO?
BATH
AND

CHAPTER TWO

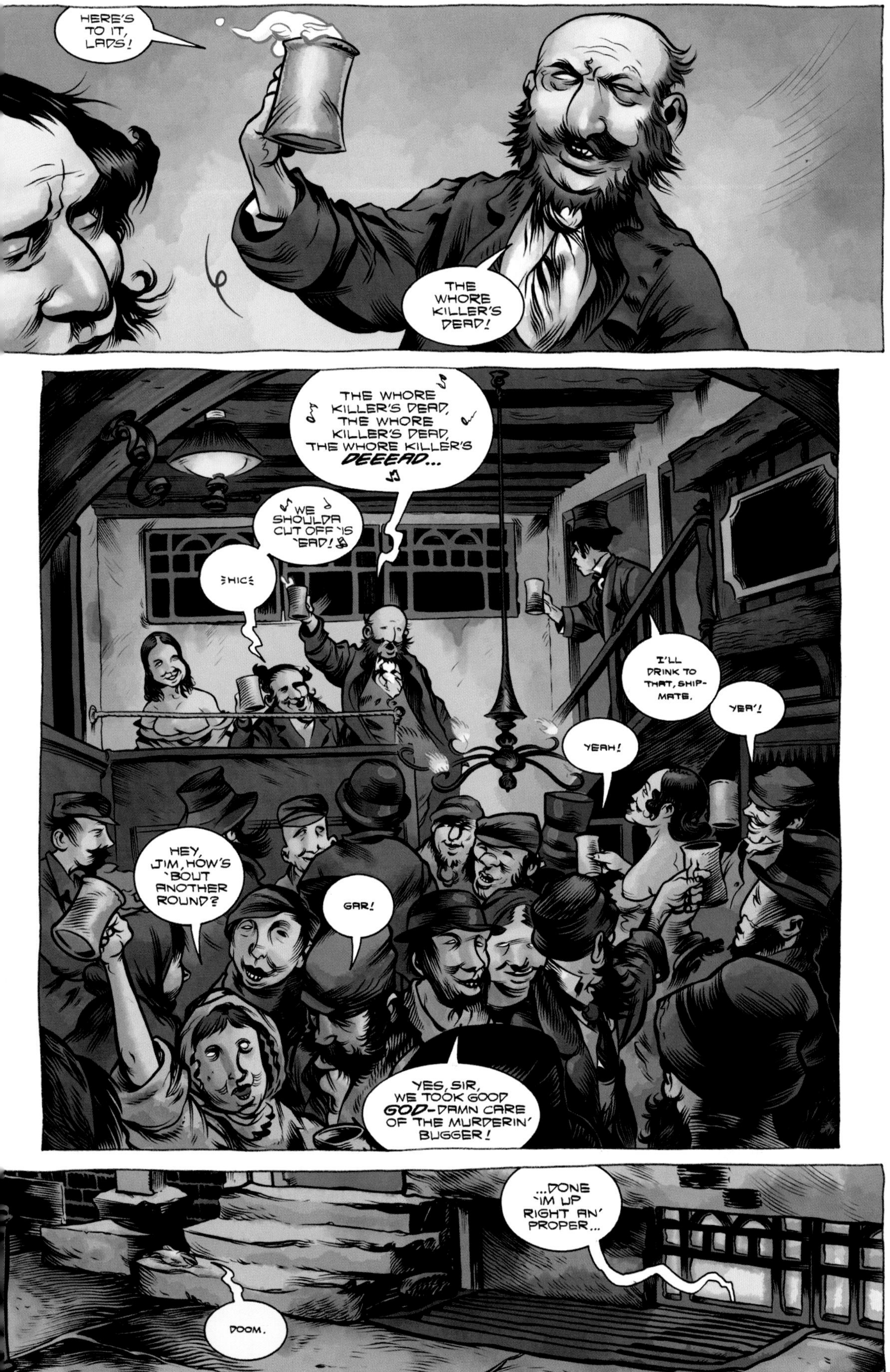
HERE'S TO IT, LADS!
THE WHORE KILLER'S DEAD!
THE WHORE KILLER'S DEAD, THE WHORE KILLER'S DEAD, THE WHORE KILLER'S DEEEAD...
WE SHOULDA CUT OFF 'IS 'EAD!
HIC
I'LL DRINK TO THAT, SHIP-MATE.
YEA'!
YEAH!
HEY, JIM, HOW'S 'BOUT ANOTHER ROUND?
GAR!
YES, SIR, WE TOOK GOOD GOD-DAMN CARE OF THE MURDERIN' BUGGER!
...DONE 'IM UP RIGHT AN' PROPER...
DOOM.

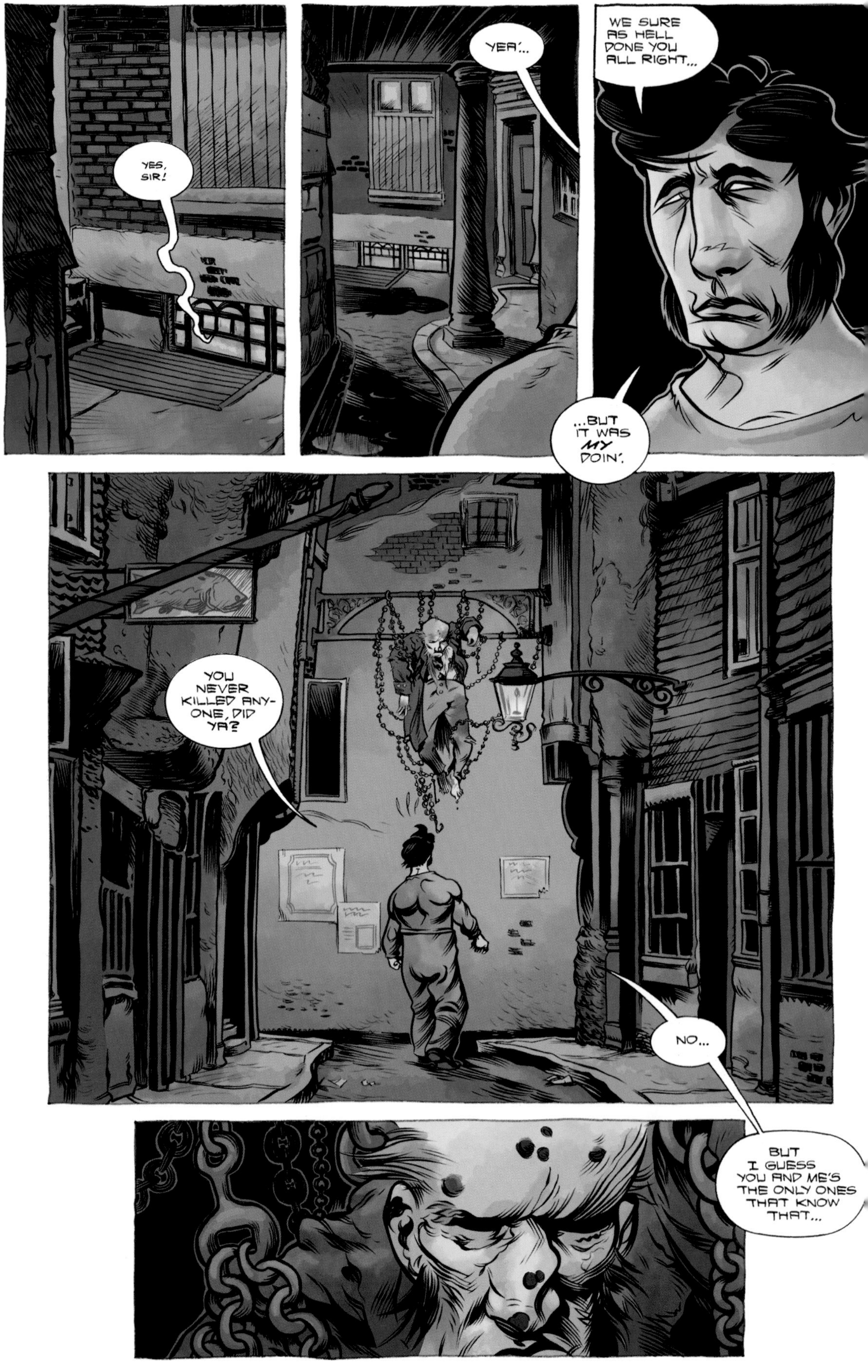
YES, SIR!
YEA'...
WE SURE AS HELL DONE YOU ALL RIGHT...
...BUT IT WAS MY DOIN'.
YOU NEVER KILLED ANY-ONE, DID YA?
NO...
BUT I GUESS YOU AND ME'S THE ONLY ONES THAT KNOW THAT...

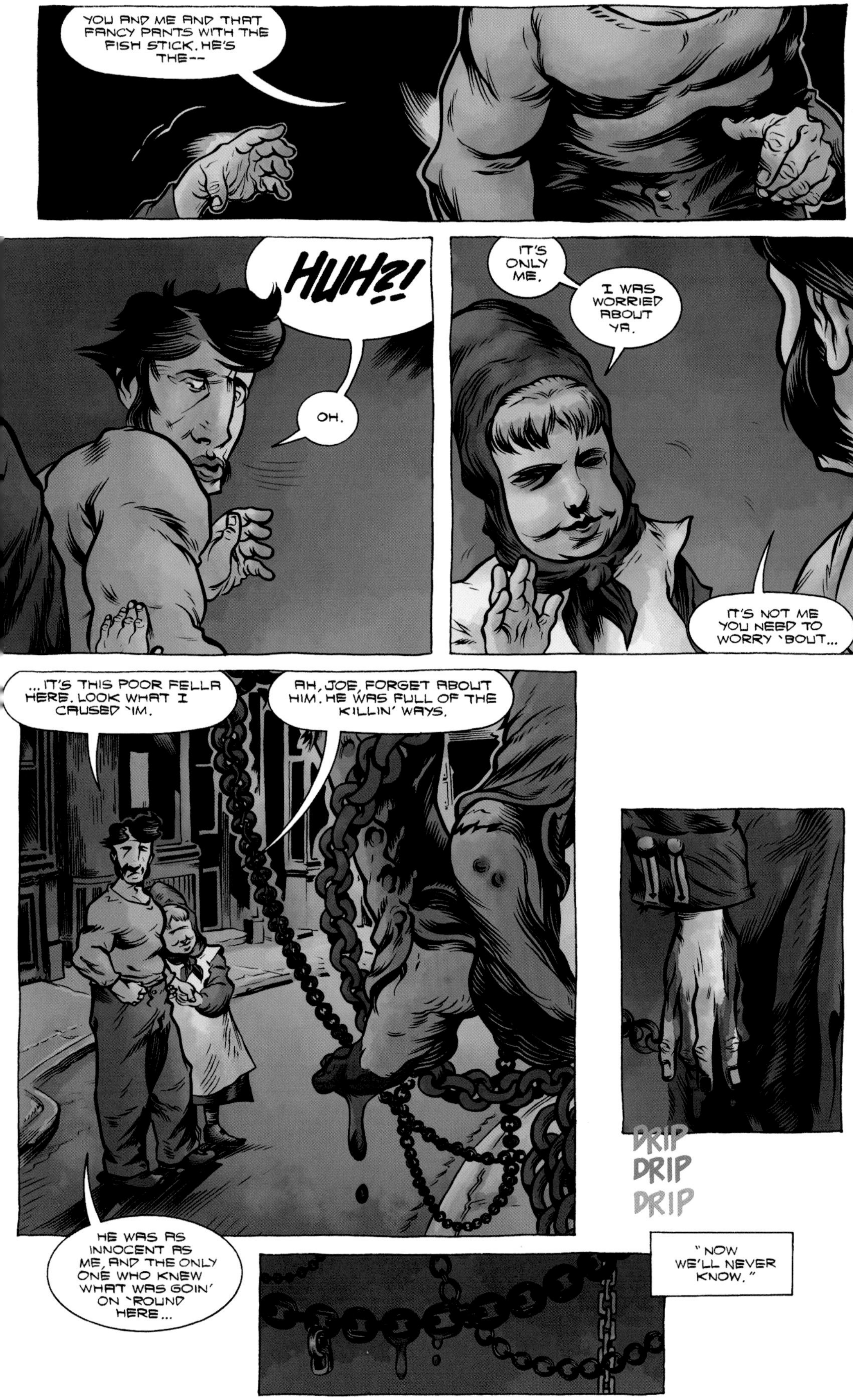
YOU AND ME AND THAT FANCY PANTS WITH THE FISH STICK. HE'S THE--
HUH?!
OH.
IT'S ONLY ME.
I WAS WORRIED ABOUT YA.
IT'S NOT ME YOU NEED TO WORRY 'BOUT...
...IT'S THIS POOR FELLA HERE. LOOK WHAT I CAUSED 'IM.
AH, JOE, FORGET ABOUT HIM. HE WAS FULL OF THE KILLIN' WAYS.
HE WAS AS INNOCENT AS ME, AND THE ONLY ONE WHO KNEW WHAT WAS GOIN' ON 'ROUND HERE...
DRIP
DRIP
DRIP
"NOW WE'LL NEVER KNOW."

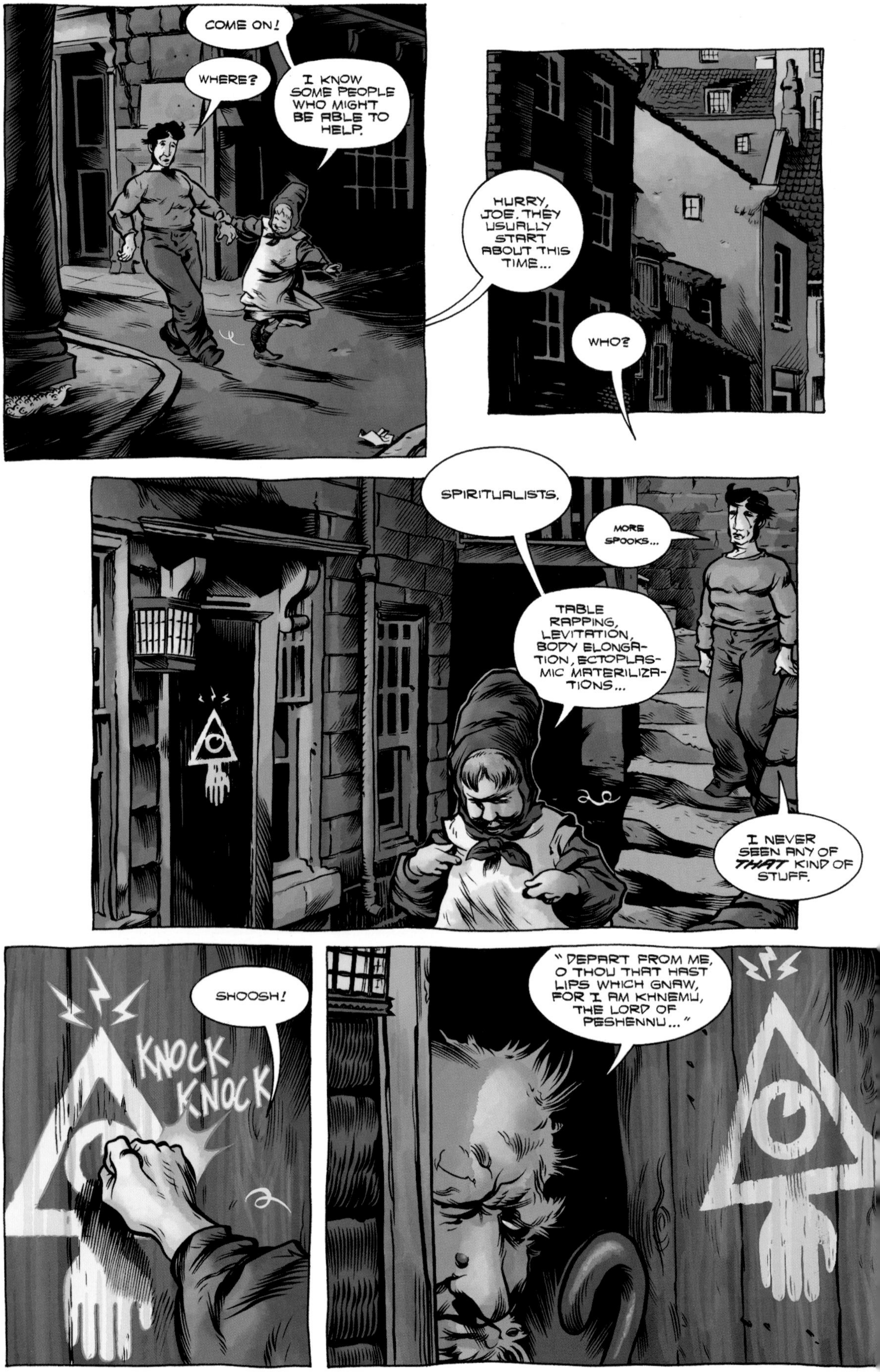
COME ON!
WHERE?
I KNOW SOME PEOPLE WHO MIGHT BE ABLE TO HELP.
HURRY, JOE. THEY USUALLY START ABOUT THIS TIME...
WHO?
SPIRITUALISTS.
MORE SPOOKS...
TABLE RAPPING, LEVITATION, BODY ELONGATION, ECTOPLASMIC MATERILIZATIONS...
I NEVER SEEN ANY OF THAT KIND OF STUFF.
SHOOSH!
KNOCK KNOCK
"DEPART FROM ME, O THOU THAT HAST LIPS WHICH GNAW, FOR I AM KHNEMU, THE LORD OF PESHENNU..."

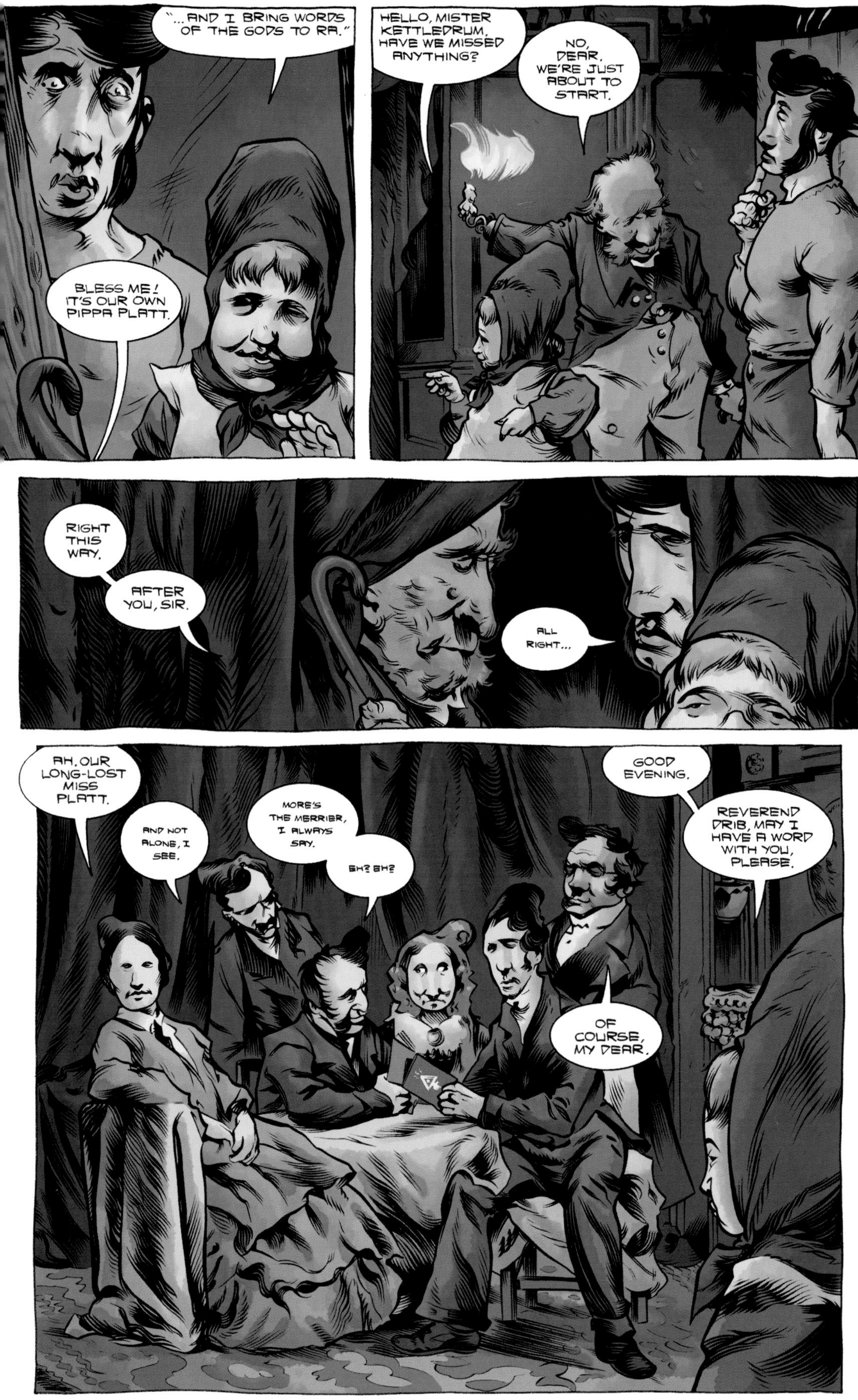
"...AND I BRING WORDS OF THE GODS TO RA."
BLESS ME! IT'S OUR OWN PIPPA PLATT.
HELLO, MISTER KETTLEDRUM, HAVE WE MISSED ANYTHING?
NO, DEAR, WE'RE JUST ABOUT TO START.
RIGHT THIS WAY.
AFTER YOU, SIR.
ALL RIGHT...
AH, OUR LONG-LOST MISS PLATT.
AND NOT ALONE, I SEE.
MORE'S THE MERRIER, I ALWAYS SAY.
EH? EH?
GOOD EVENING.
REVEREND DRIB, MAY I HAVE A WORD WITH YOU, PLEASE.
OF COURSE, MY DEAR.

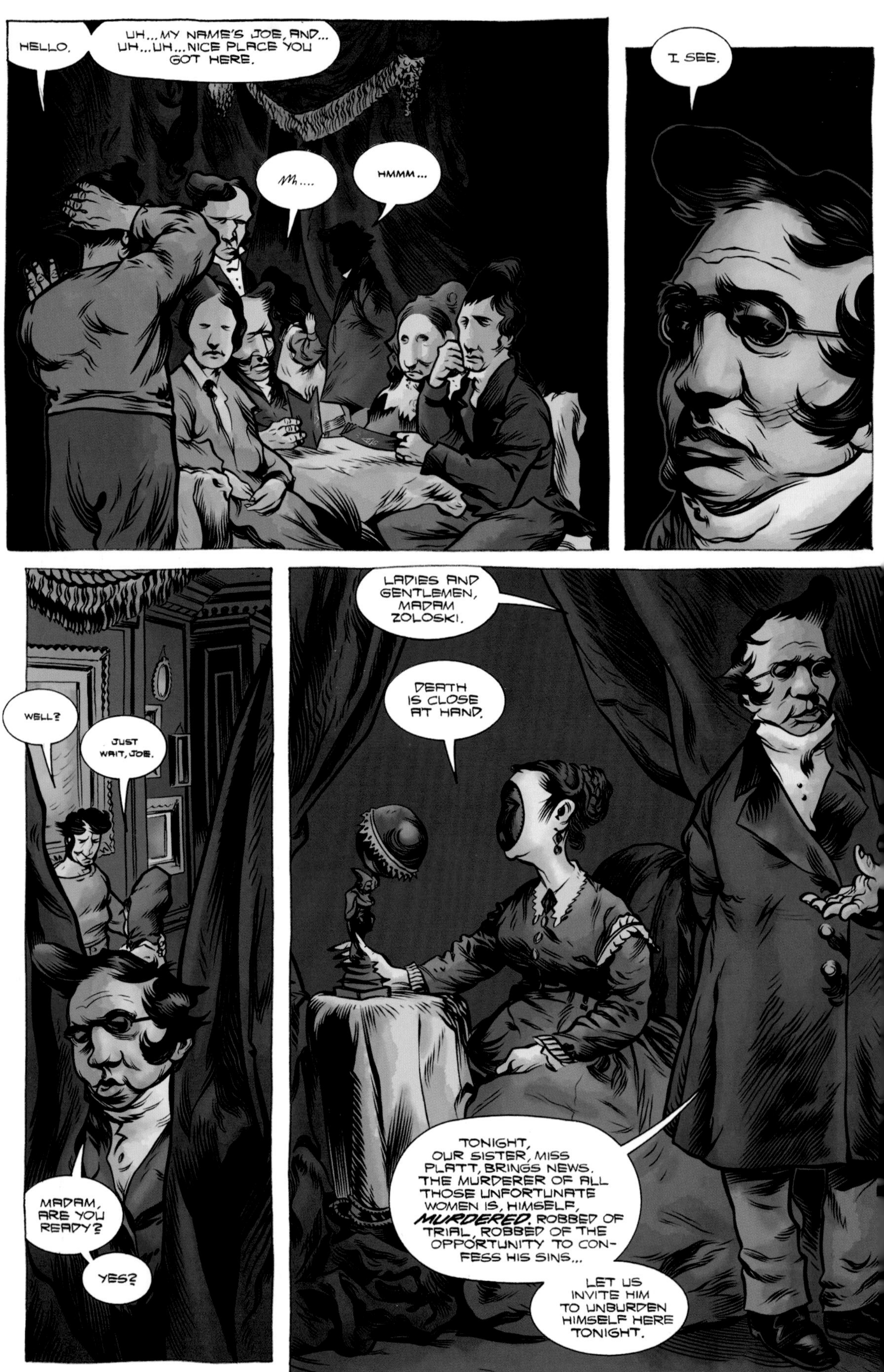
HELLO.
UH... MY NAME'S JOE, AND... UH... UH... NICE PLACE YOU GOT HERE.
I SEE.
HMMM...
WELL?
JUST WAIT, JOE.
MADAM, ARE YOU READY?
YES?
LADIES AND GENTLEMEN, MADAM ZOLOSKI.
DEATH IS CLOSE AT HAND.
TONIGHT, OUR SISTER, MISS PLATT, BRINGS NEWS. THE MURDERER OF ALL THOSE UNFORTUNATE WOMEN IS, HIMSELF, MURDERED. ROBBED OF TRIAL, ROBBED OF THE OPPORTUNITY TO CONFESS HIS SINS...
LET US INVITE HIM TO UNBURDEN HIMSELF HERE TONIGHT.

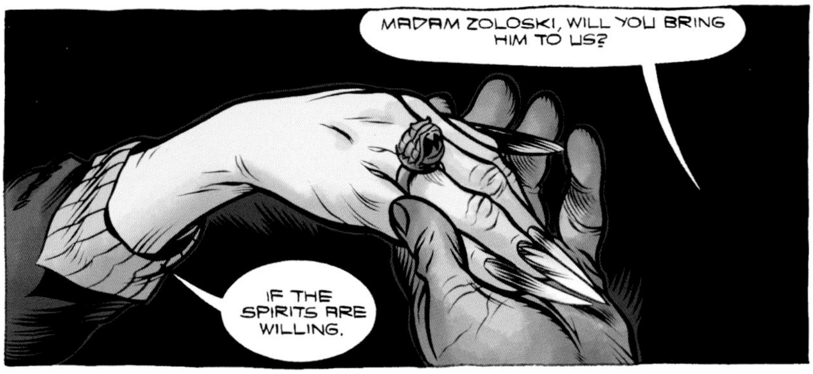
MADAM ZOLOSKI, WILL YOU BRING HIM TO US?
IF THE SPIRITS ARE WILLING.

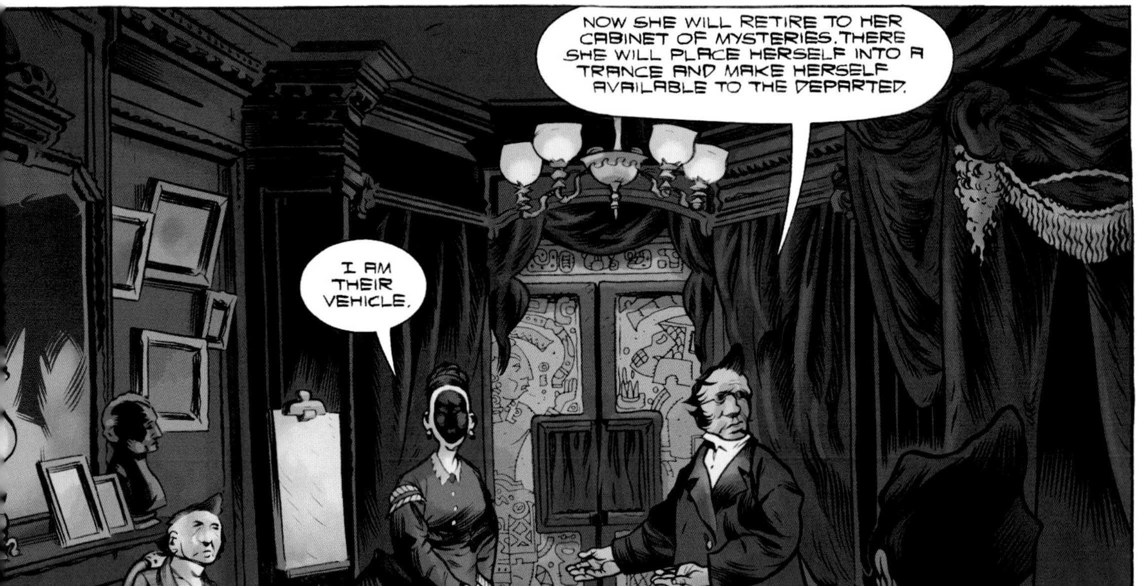
NOW SHE WILL RETIRE TO HER CABINET OF MYSTERIES. THERE SHE WILL PLACE HERSELF INTO A TRANCE AND MAKE HERSELF AVAILABLE TO THE DEPARTED.
I AM THEIR VEHICLE.

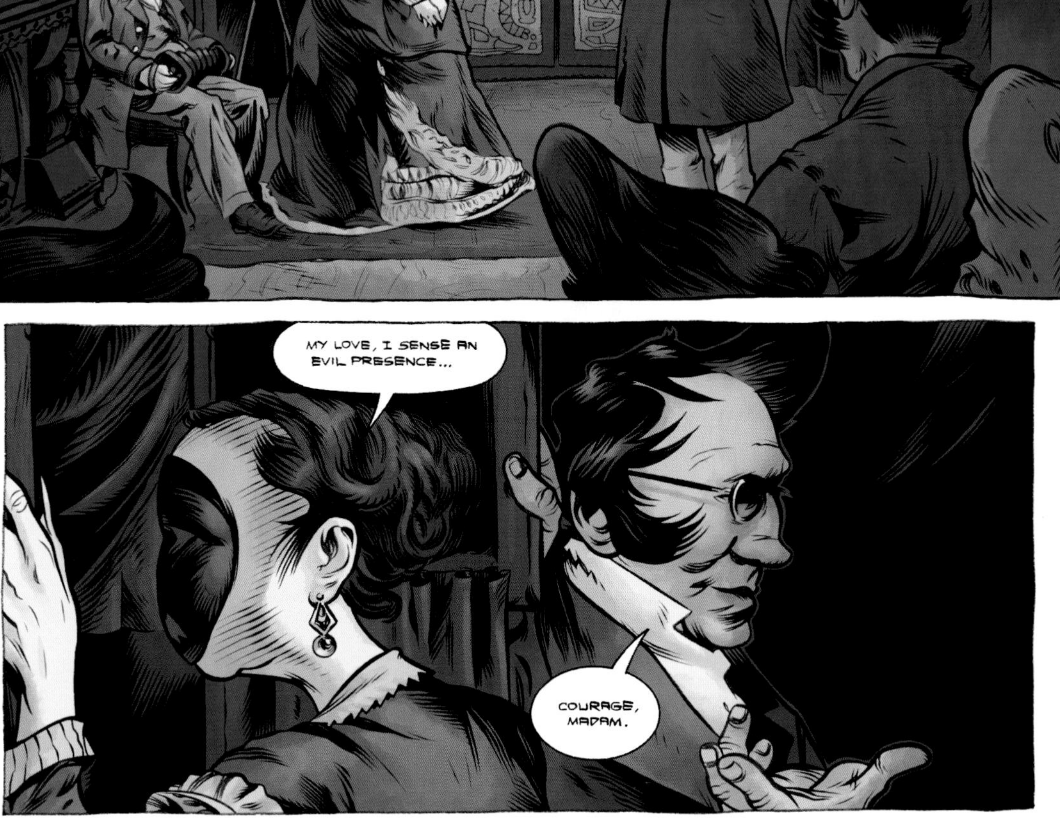
MY LOVE, I SENSE AN EVIL PRESENCE...
COURAGE, MADAM.

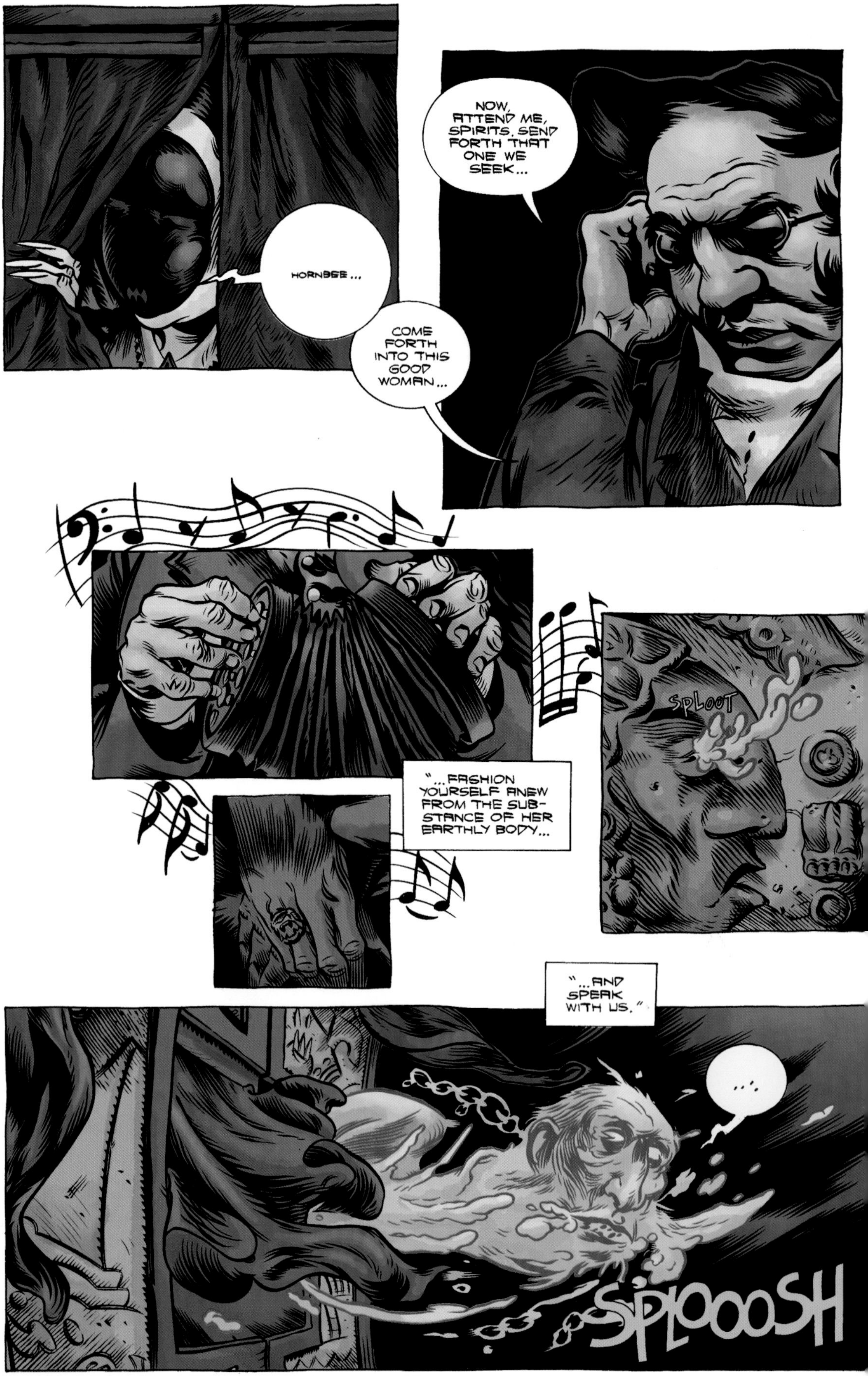
NOW, ATTEND ME, SPIRITS. SEND FORTH THAT ONE WE SEEK...
HORNBEE...
COME FORTH INTO THIS GOOD WOMAN...
SPLOOT
"...FASHION YOURSELF ANEW FROM THE SUB-STANCE OF HER EARTHLY BODY...
"...AND SPEAK WITH US."
...
SPLOOOSH

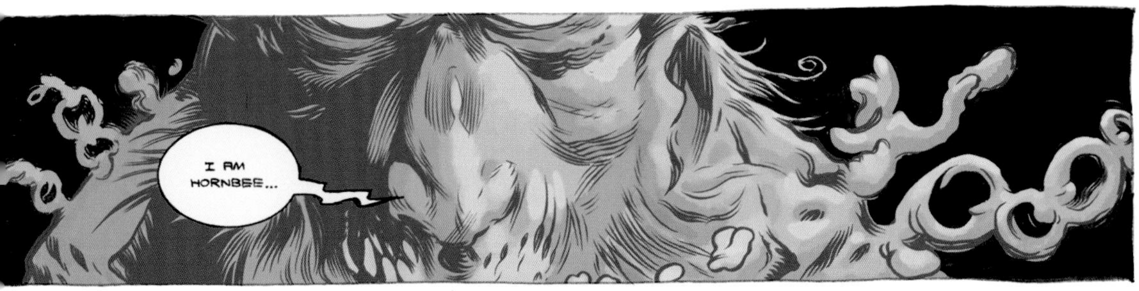
I AM HORNBEE...

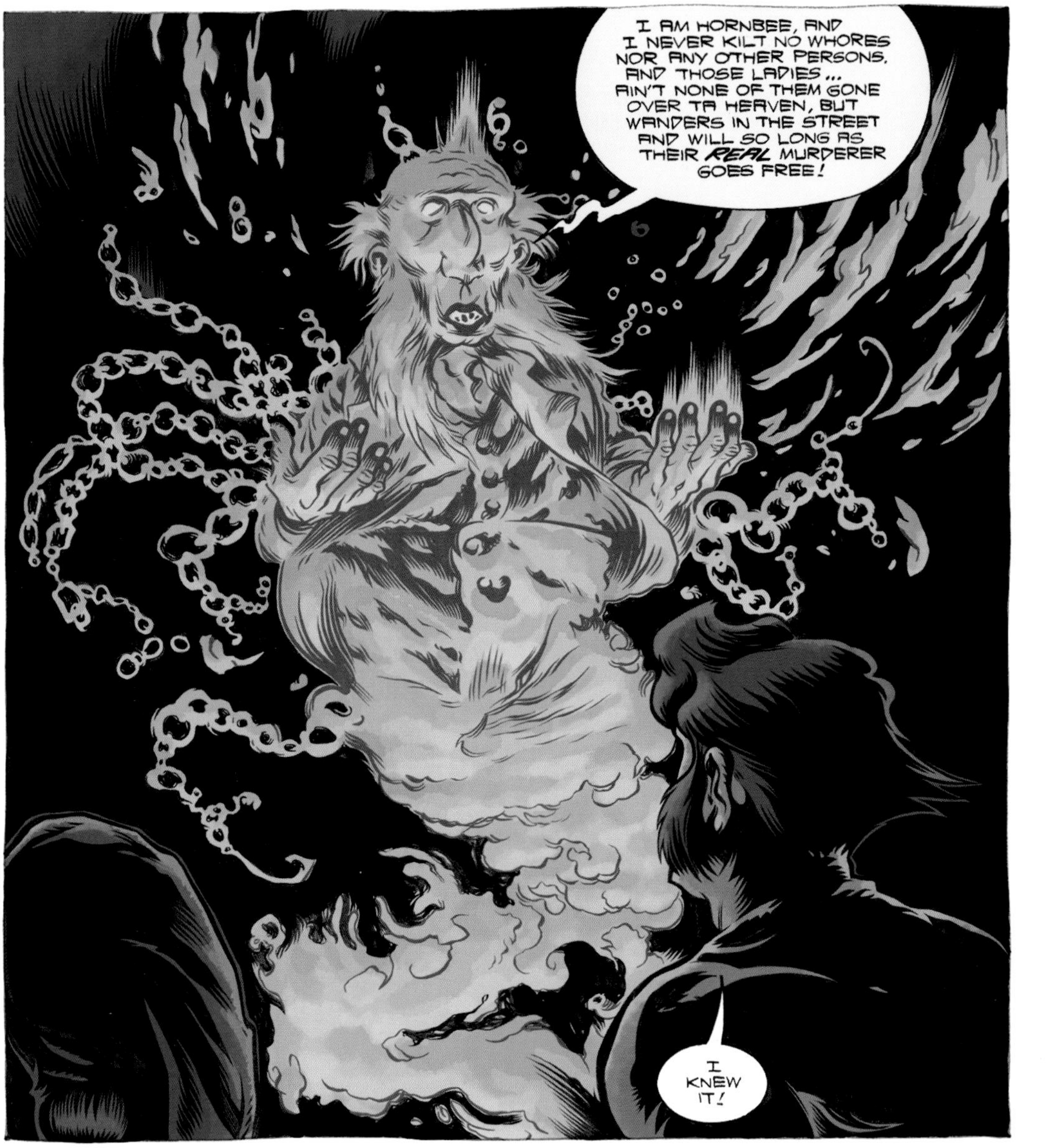
I AM HORNBEE, AND I NEVER KILT NO WHORES NOR ANY OTHER PERSONS, AND THOSE LADIES... AIN'T NONE OF THEM GONE OVER TA HEAVEN, BUT WANDERS IN THE STREET AND WILL SO LONG AS THEIR REAL MURDERER GOES FREE!
I KNEW IT!

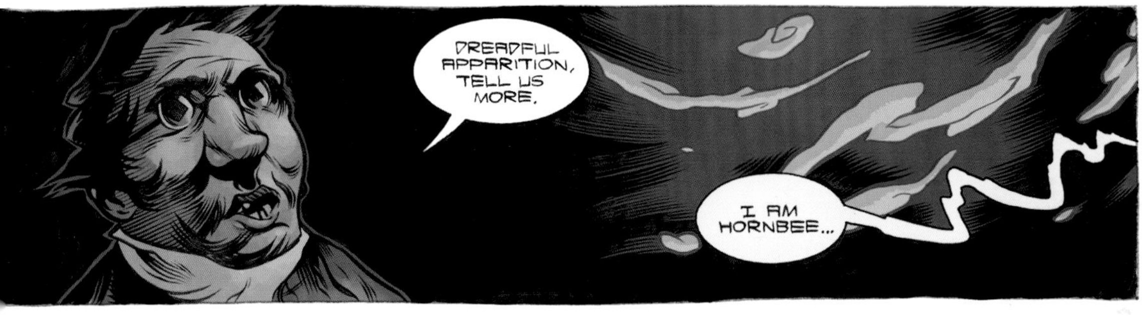
DREADFUL APPARITION, TELL US MORE.
I AM HORNBEE...

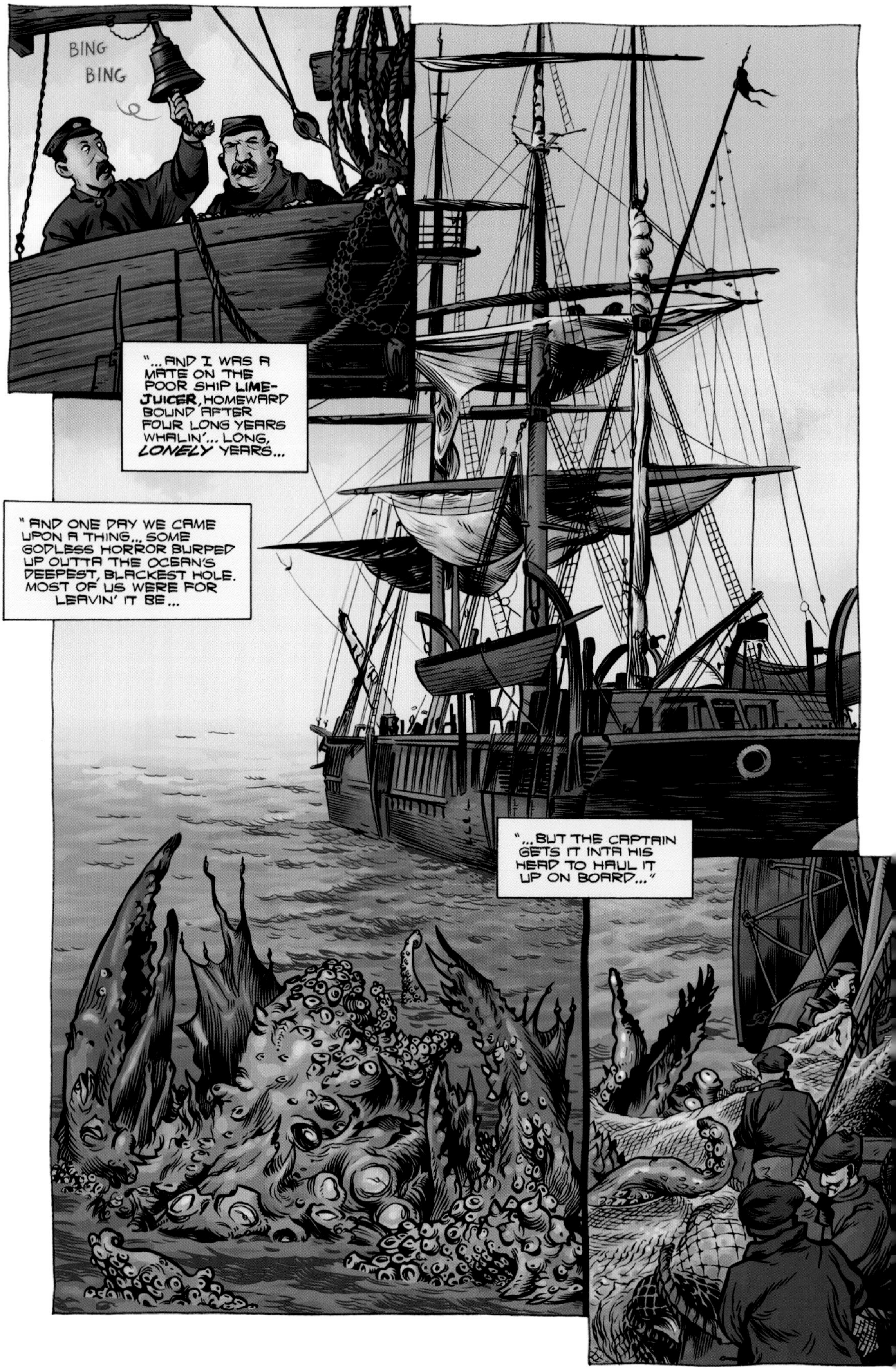
BING BING
"...AND I WAS A MATE ON THE POOR SHIP LIME-JUICER, HOMEWARD BOUND AFTER FOUR LONG YEARS WHALIN'... LONG, LONELY YEARS...
"AND ONE DAY WE CAME UPON A THING... SOME GODLESS HORROR BURPED UP OUTTA THE OCEAN'S DEEPEST, BLACKEST HOLE. MOST OF US WERE FOR LEAVIN' IT BE...
"...BUT THE CAPTAIN GETS IT INTA HIS HEAD TO HAUL IT UP ON BOARD..."

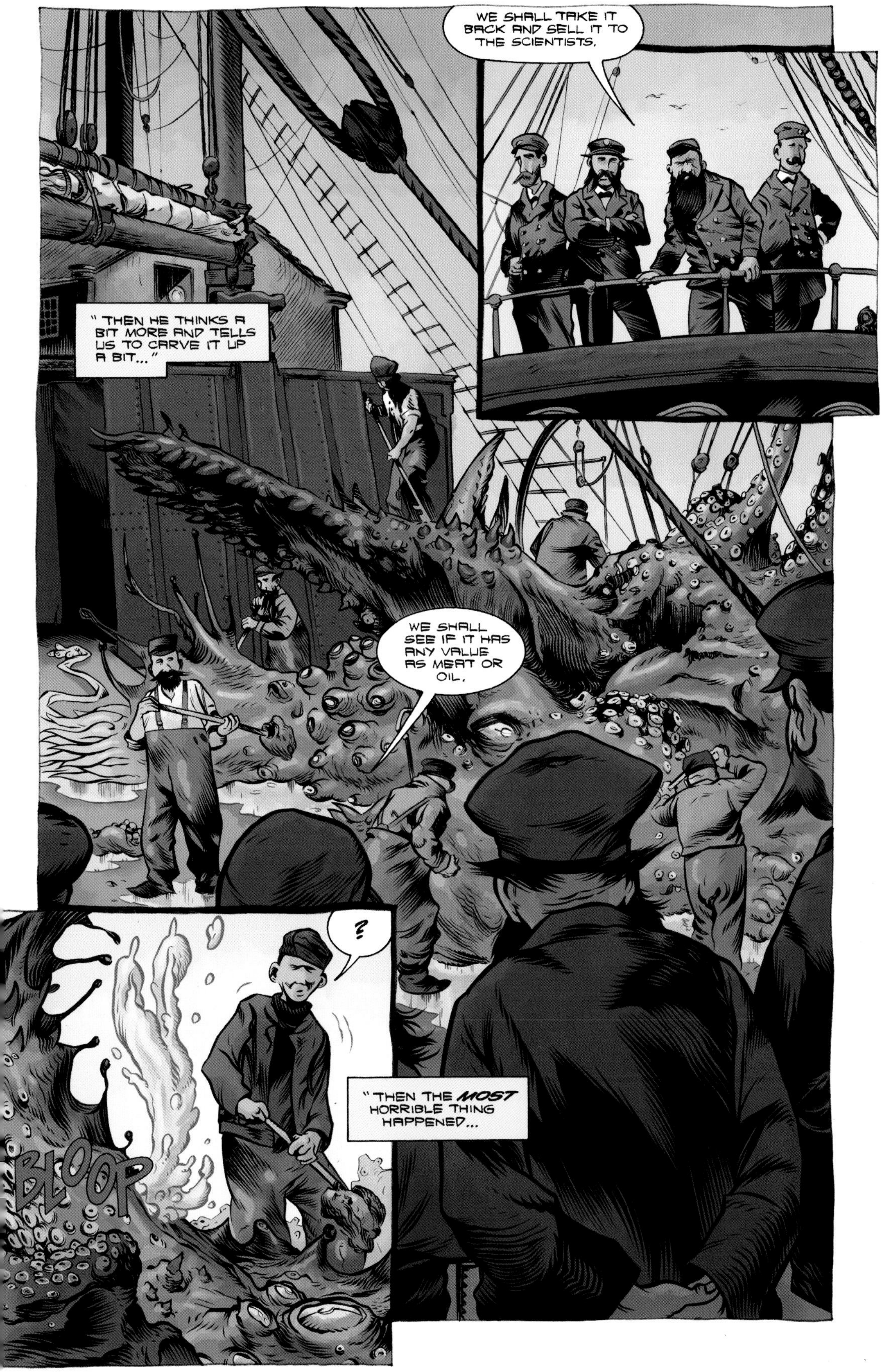
WE SHALL TAKE IT BACK AND SELL IT TO THE SCIENTISTS.
"THEN HE THINKS A BIT MORE AND TELLS US TO CARVE IT UP A BIT..."
WE SHALL SEE IF IT HAS ANY VALUE AS MEAT OR OIL.
?
"THEN THE *MOST* HORRIBLE THING HAPPENED...
BLOOP

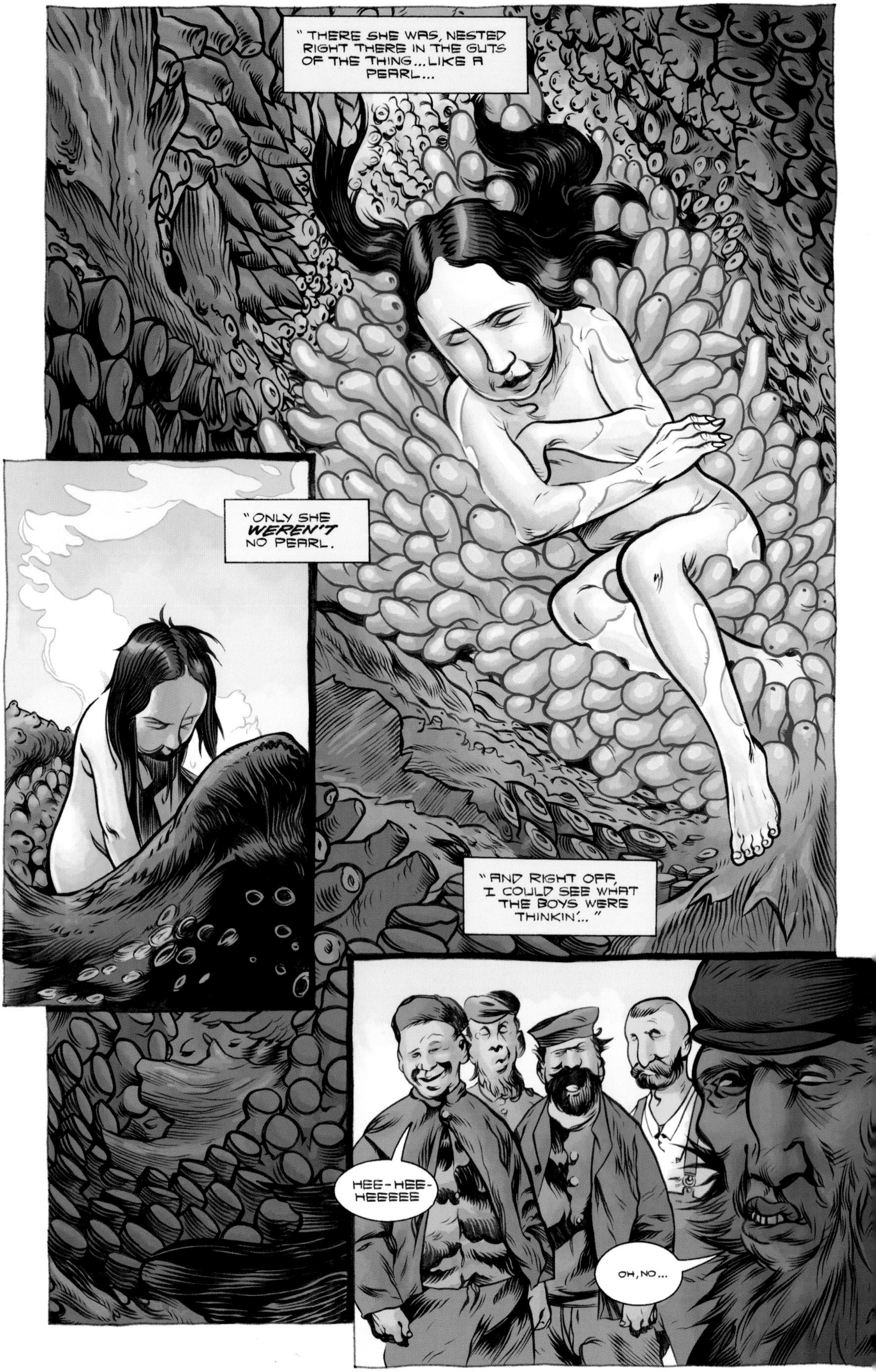
"THERE SHE WAS, NESTED RIGHT THERE IN THE GUTS OF THE THING...LIKE A PEARL...
"ONLY SHE *WEREN'T* NO PEARL.
"AND RIGHT OFF, I COULD SEE WHAT THE BOYS WERE THINKIN'..."
HEE-HEE-HEEEEE
OH, NO...

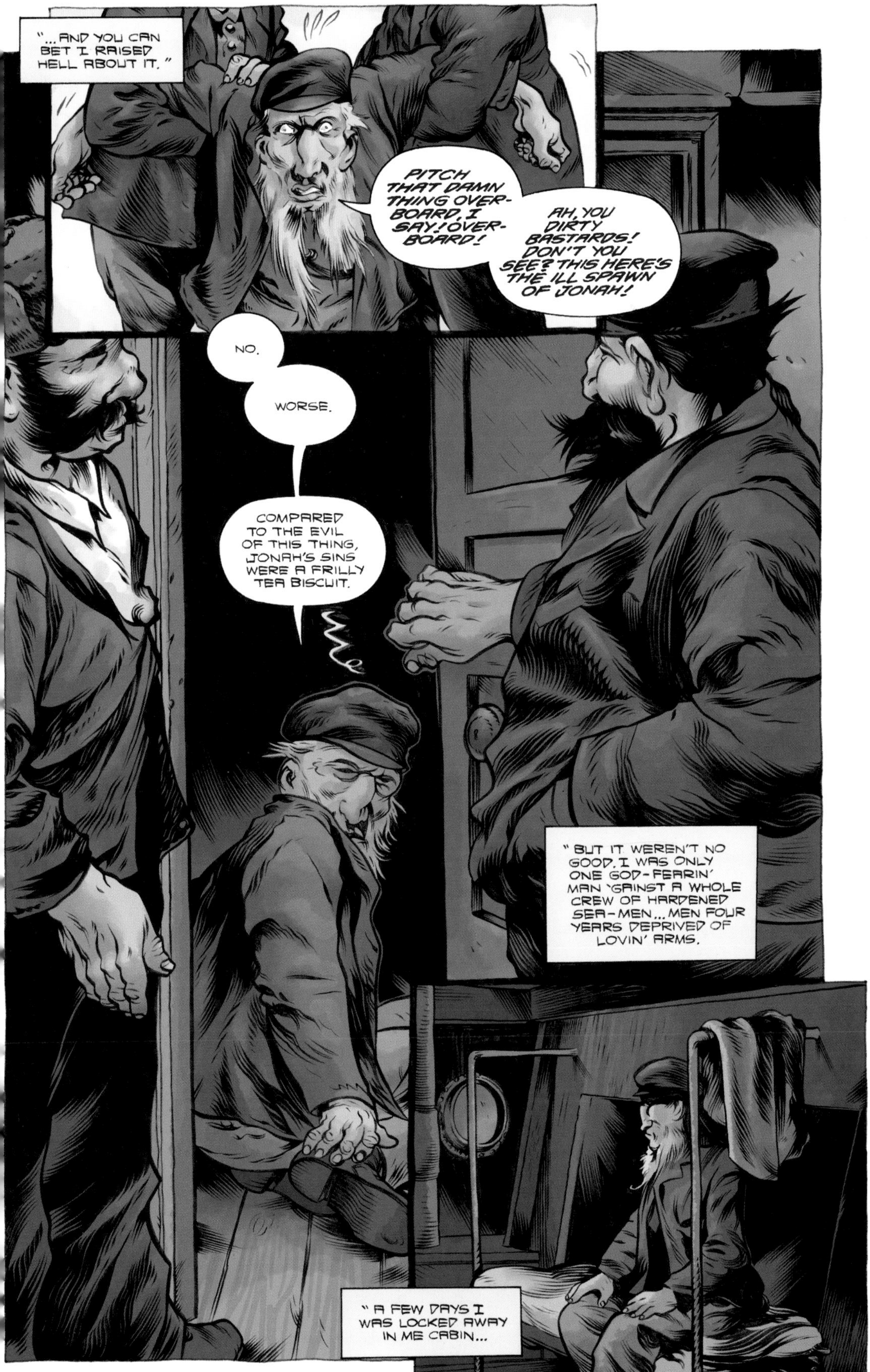
"...AND YOU CAN BET I RAISED HELL ABOUT IT."
PITCH THAT DAMN THING OVER-BOARD, I SAY! OVER-BOARD!
AH, YOU DIRTY BASTARDS! DON'T YOU SEE? THIS HERE'S THE ILL SPAWN OF JONAH!
NO.
WORSE.
COMPARED TO THE EVIL OF THIS THING, JONAH'S SINS WERE A FRILLY TEA BISCUIT.
"BUT IT WEREN'T NO GOOD. I WAS ONLY ONE GOD-FEARIN' MAN 'GAINST A WHOLE CREW OF HARDENED SEA-MEN... MEN FOUR YEARS DEPRIVED OF LOVIN' ARMS.
"A FEW DAYS I WAS LOCKED AWAY IN ME CABIN...

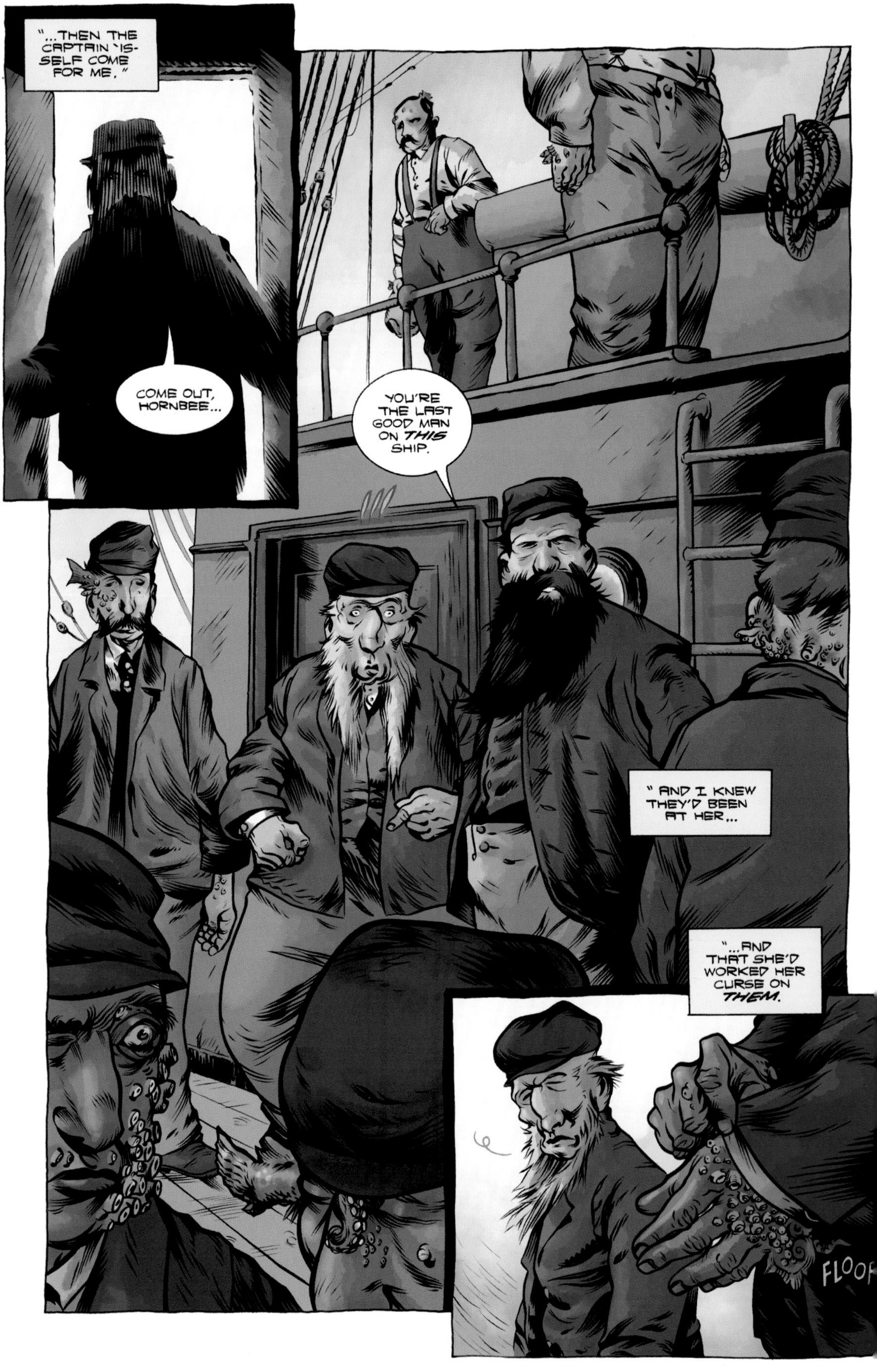

"...THEN THE CAPTAIN 'IS-SELF COME FOR ME."
COME OUT, HORNBEE...
YOU'RE THE LAST GOOD MAN ON THIS SHIP.
"AND I KNEW THEY'D BEEN AT HER...
"...AND THAT SHE'D WORKED HER CURSE ON THEM.
FLOOP

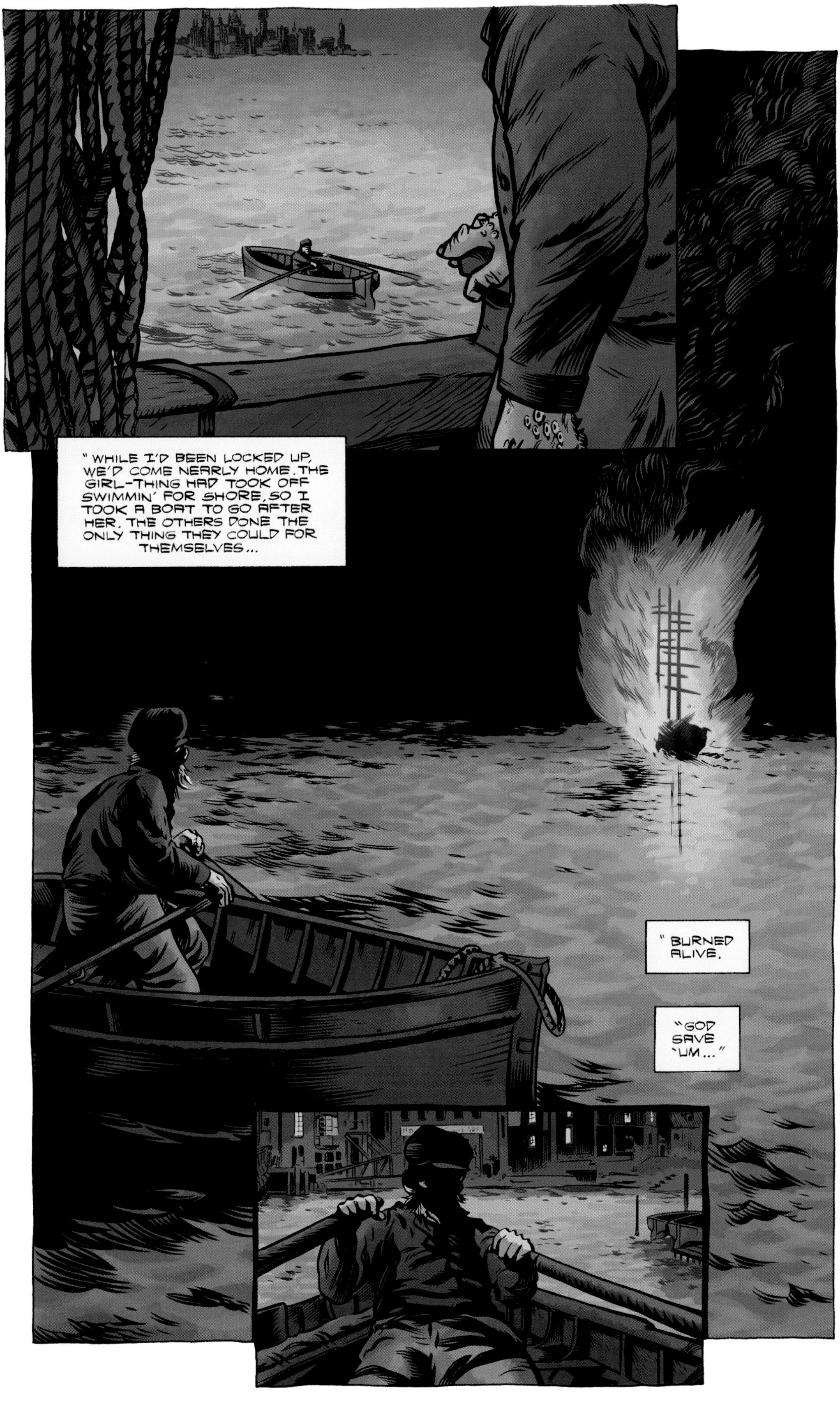
"WHILE I'D BEEN LOCKED UP, WE'D COME NEARLY HOME. THE GIRL-THING HAD TOOK OFF SWIMMIN' FOR SHORE, SO I TOOK A BOAT TO GO AFTER HER. THE OTHERS DONE THE ONLY THING THEY COULD FOR THEMSELVES...
"BURNED ALIVE.
"GOD SAVE 'UM..."

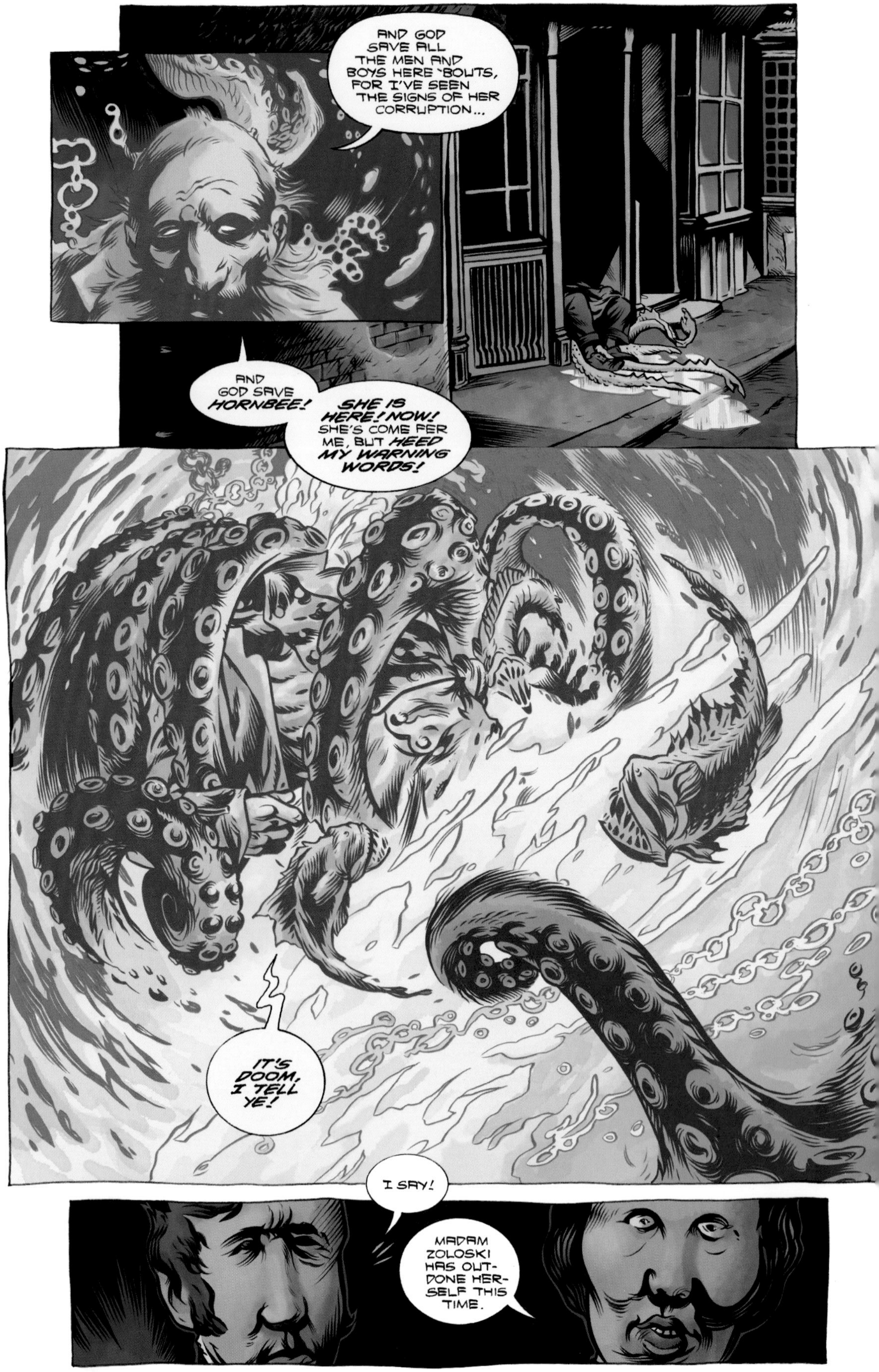
AND GOD SAVE ALL THE MEN AND BOYS HERE 'BOUTS, FOR I'VE SEEN THE SIGNS OF HER CORRUPTION...
AND GOD SAVE HORNBEE!
SHE IS HERE! NOW! SHE'S COME FER ME, BUT HEED MY WARNING WORDS!
IT'S DOOM, I TELL YE!
I SAY!
MADAM ZOLOSKI HAS OUT-DONE HER-SELF THIS TIME.

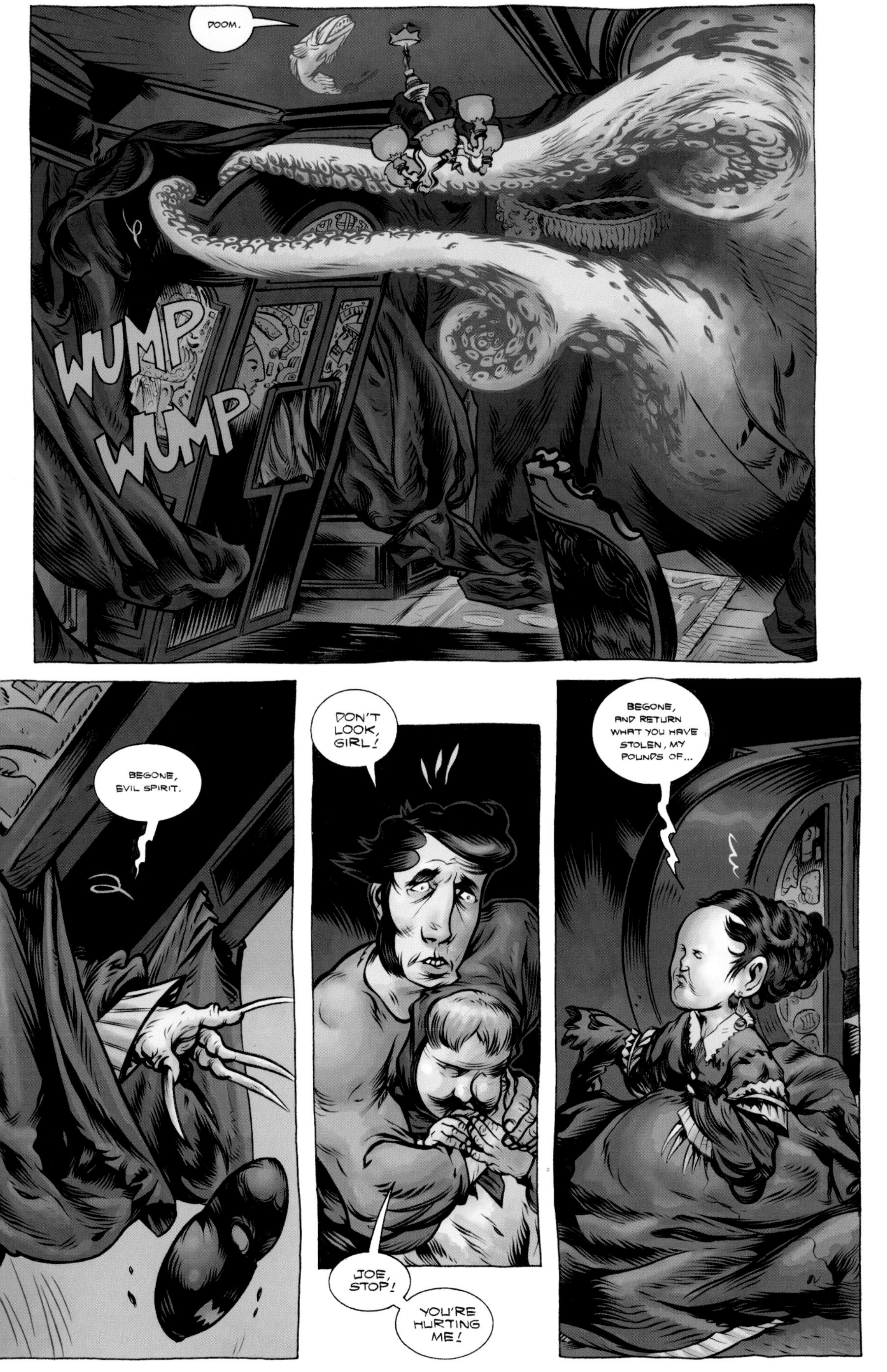
DOOM.
WUMP
WUMP
BEGONE, EVIL SPIRIT.
DON'T LOOK, GIRL!
JOE, STOP!
YOU'RE HURTING ME!
BEGONE, AND RETURN WHAT YOU HAVE STOLEN, MY POUNDS OF...

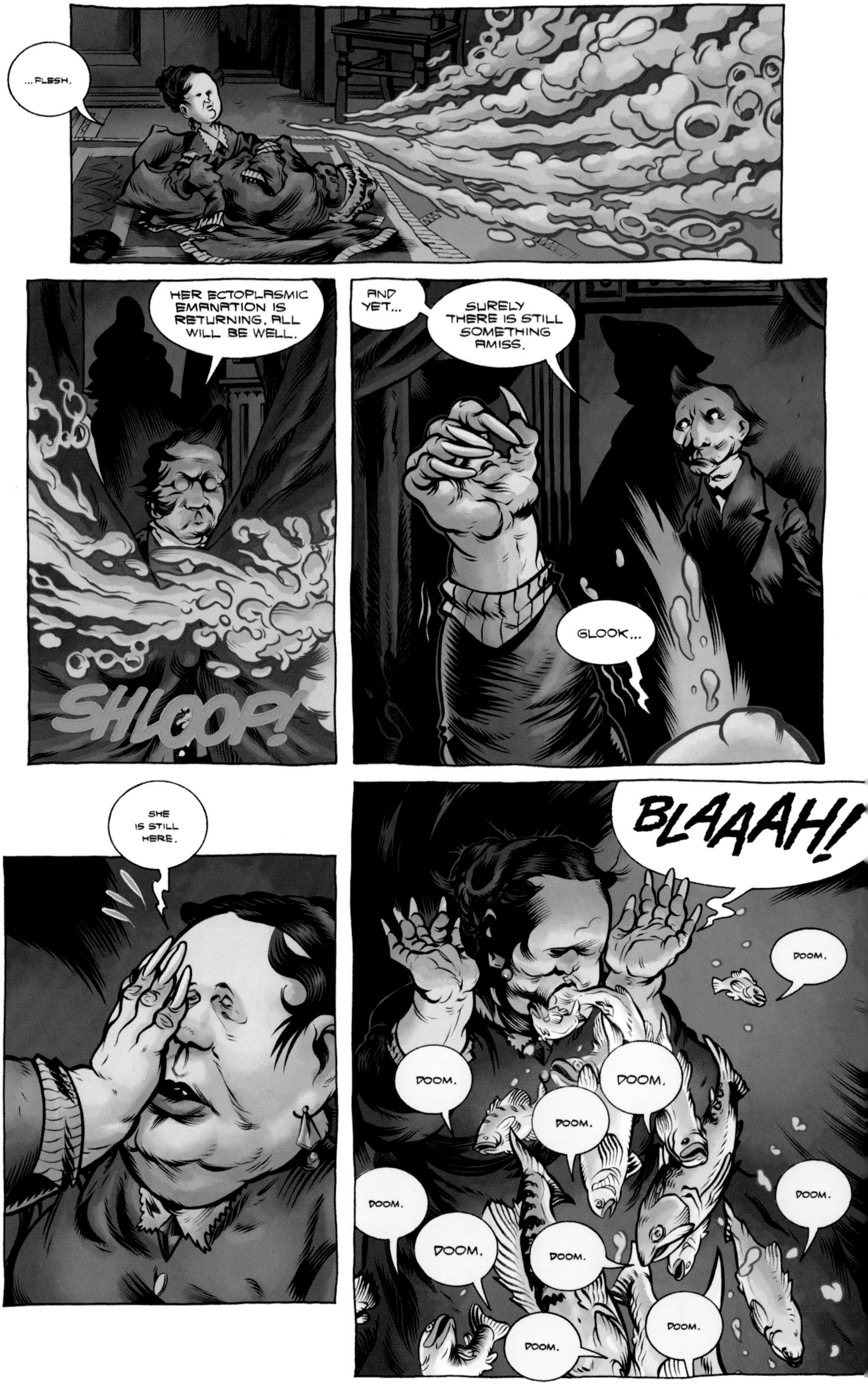
...FLESH.
HER ECTOPLASMIC EMANATION IS RETURNING. ALL WILL BE WELL.
SHLOOP!
AND YET...
SURELY THERE IS STILL SOMETHING AMISS.
GLOOK...
SHE IS STILL HERE.
BLAAAH!
DOOM.
DOOM.
DOOM.
DOOM.
DOOM.
DOOM.
DOOM.
DOOM.
DOOM.
DOOM.
DOOM.

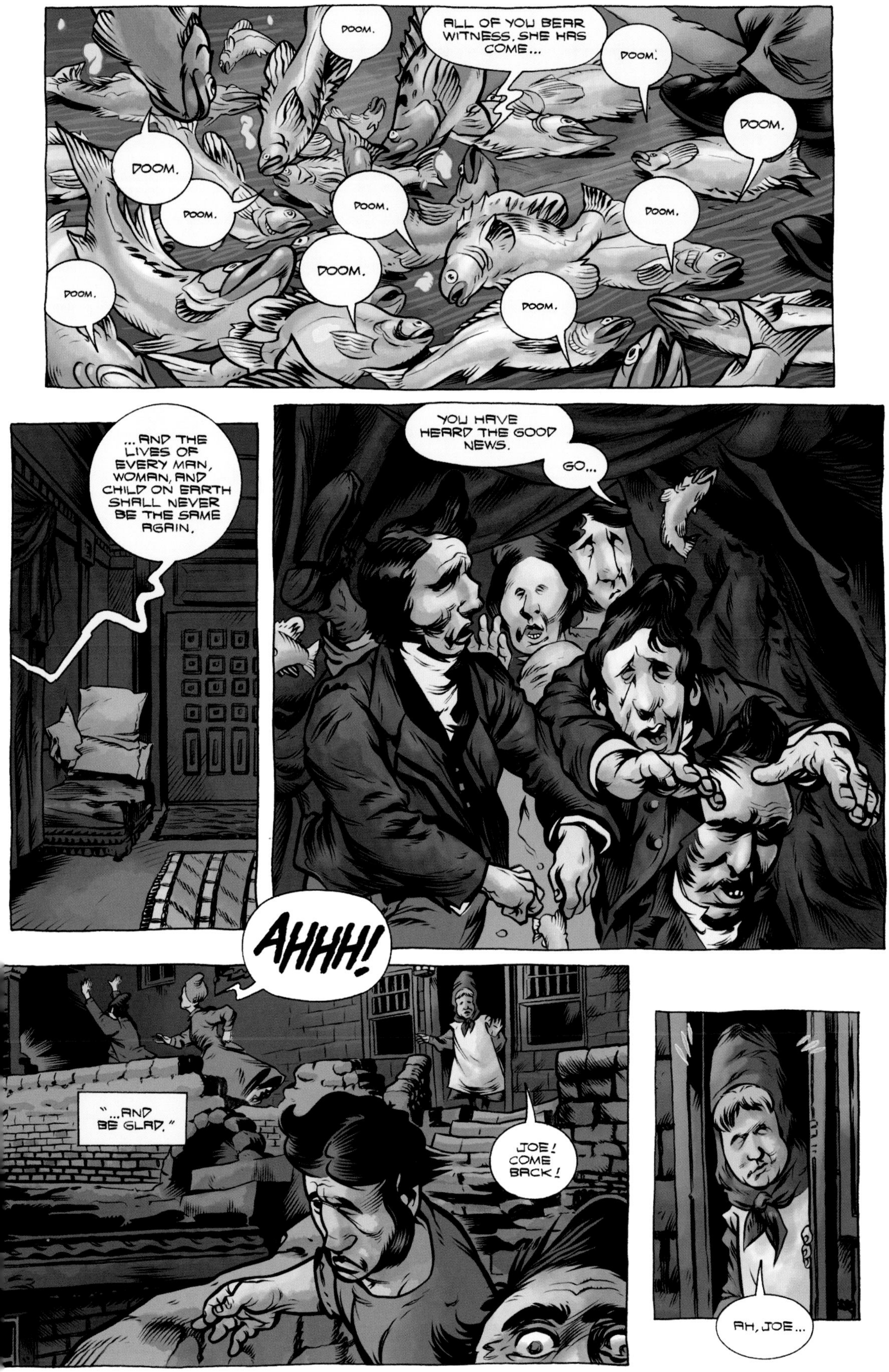
DOOM.
ALL OF YOU BEAR WITNESS. SHE HAS COME...
DOOM.
DOOM.
DOOM.
DOOM.
DOOM.
DOOM.
DOOM.
DOOM.
DOOM.
DOOM.
...AND THE LIVES OF EVERY MAN, WOMAN, AND CHILD ON EARTH SHALL NEVER BE THE SAME AGAIN.
YOU HAVE HEARD THE GOOD NEWS.
GO...
AHHH!
"...AND BE GLAD."
JOE! COME BACK!
AH, JOE...

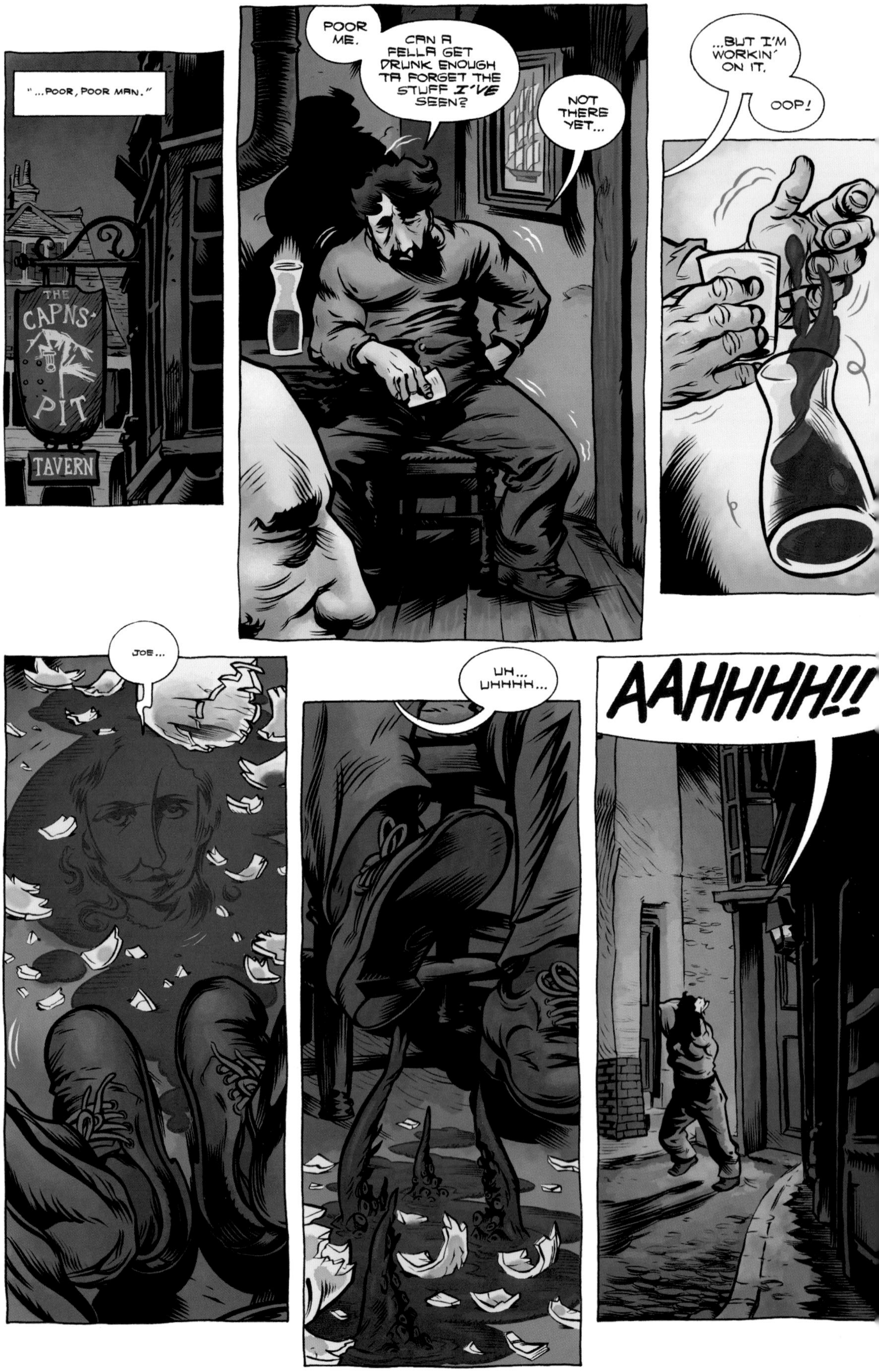
"...POOR, POOR MAN."
THE CAPNS PIT
TAVERN
POOR ME.
CAN A FELLA GET DRUNK ENOUGH TA FORGET THE STUFF *I'VE* SEEN?
NOT THERE YET...
...BUT I'M WORKIN' ON IT.
OOP!
JOE...
UH... UHHHH...
AAHHHH!!

JESUS, I CAN'T TAKE MUCH MORE OF THIS.

WHY ME?

IS IT SOMETHIN' I DONE?

I ALWAYS TRIED TO BE GOOD, BUT THIS CITY'S A HARD PLACE.

I DONE SOME THINGS--

THAT'S IT!!

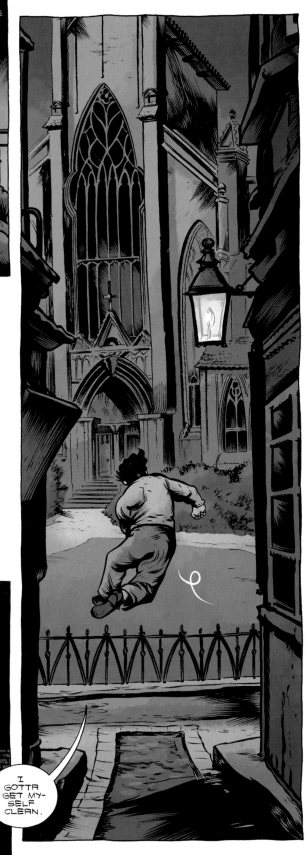

I GOTTA GET MY- SELF CLEAN.

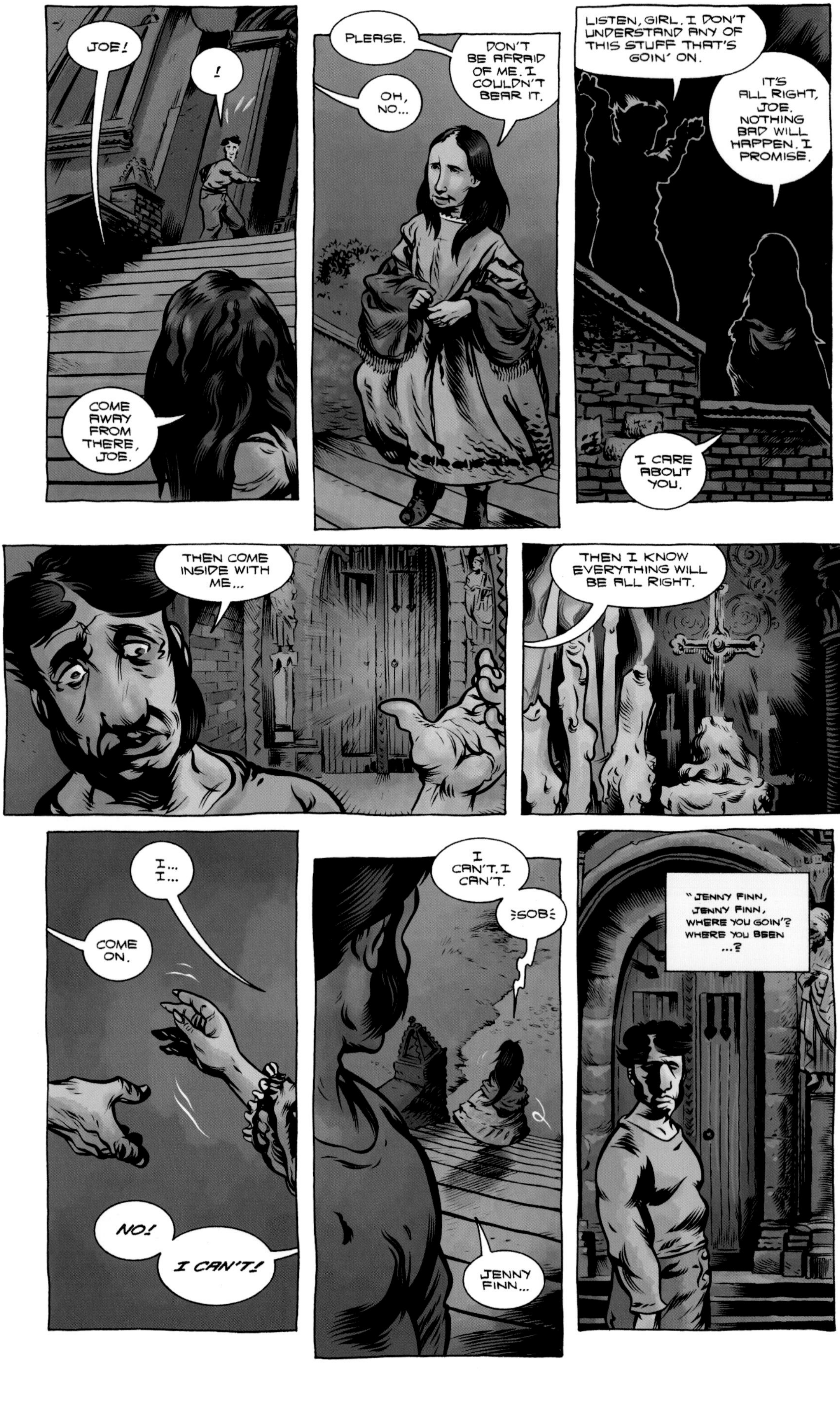

JOE!
!
COME AWAY FROM THERE, JOE.
PLEASE.
OH, NO...
DON'T BE AFRAID OF ME. I COULDN'T BEAR IT.
LISTEN, GIRL. I DON'T UNDERSTAND ANY OF THIS STUFF THAT'S GOIN' ON.
IT'S ALL RIGHT, JOE. NOTHING BAD WILL HAPPEN. I PROMISE.
I CARE ABOUT YOU.
THEN COME INSIDE WITH ME...
THEN I KNOW EVERYTHING WILL BE ALL RIGHT.
I... I...
COME ON.
NO!
I CAN'T!
I CAN'T. I CAN'T.
SOB
JENNY FINN...
"JENNY FINN, JENNY FINN, WHERE YOU GOIN'? WHERE YOU BEEN ...?

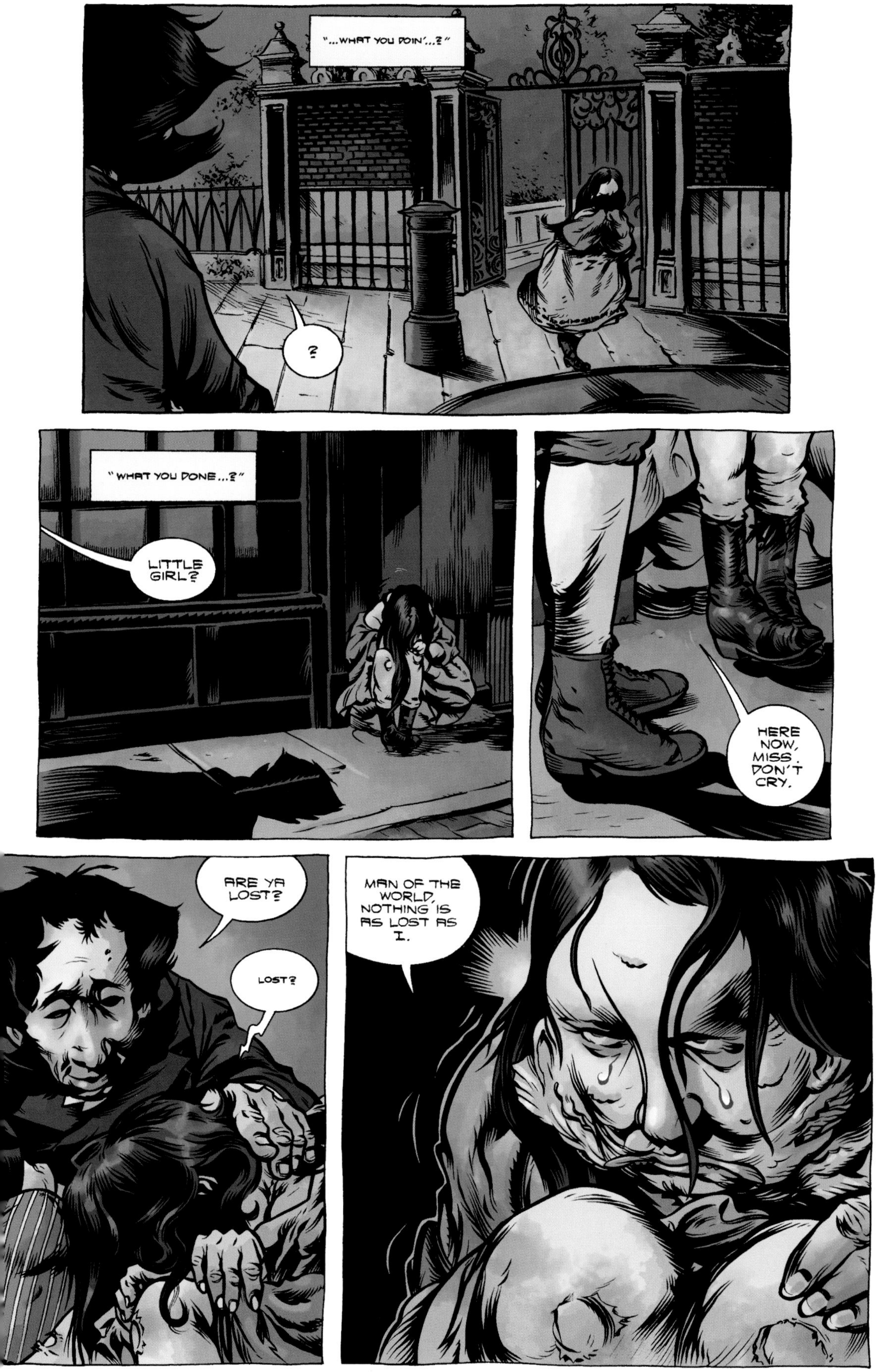
"...WHAT YOU DOIN'...?"
?
"WHAT YOU DONE...?"
LITTLE GIRL?
HERE NOW, MISS. DON'T CRY.
ARE YA LOST?
LOST?
MAN OF THE WORLD, NOTHING IS AS LOST AS I.

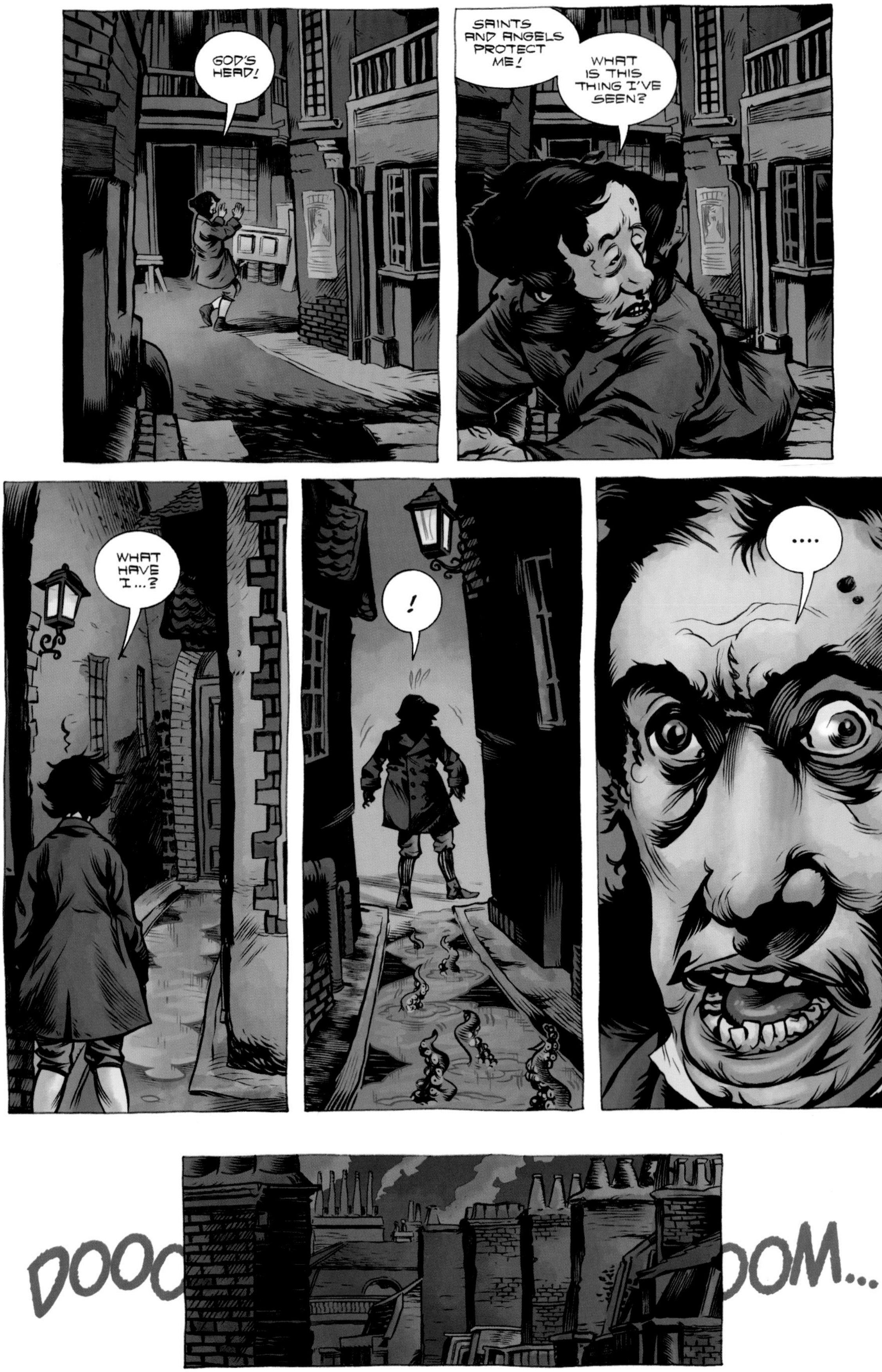
GOD'S HEAD!
SAINTS AND ANGELS PROTECT ME!
WHAT IS THIS THING I'VE SEEN?
WHAT HAVE I...?
!
....
DOOO
OOM...

CHAPTER
THREE

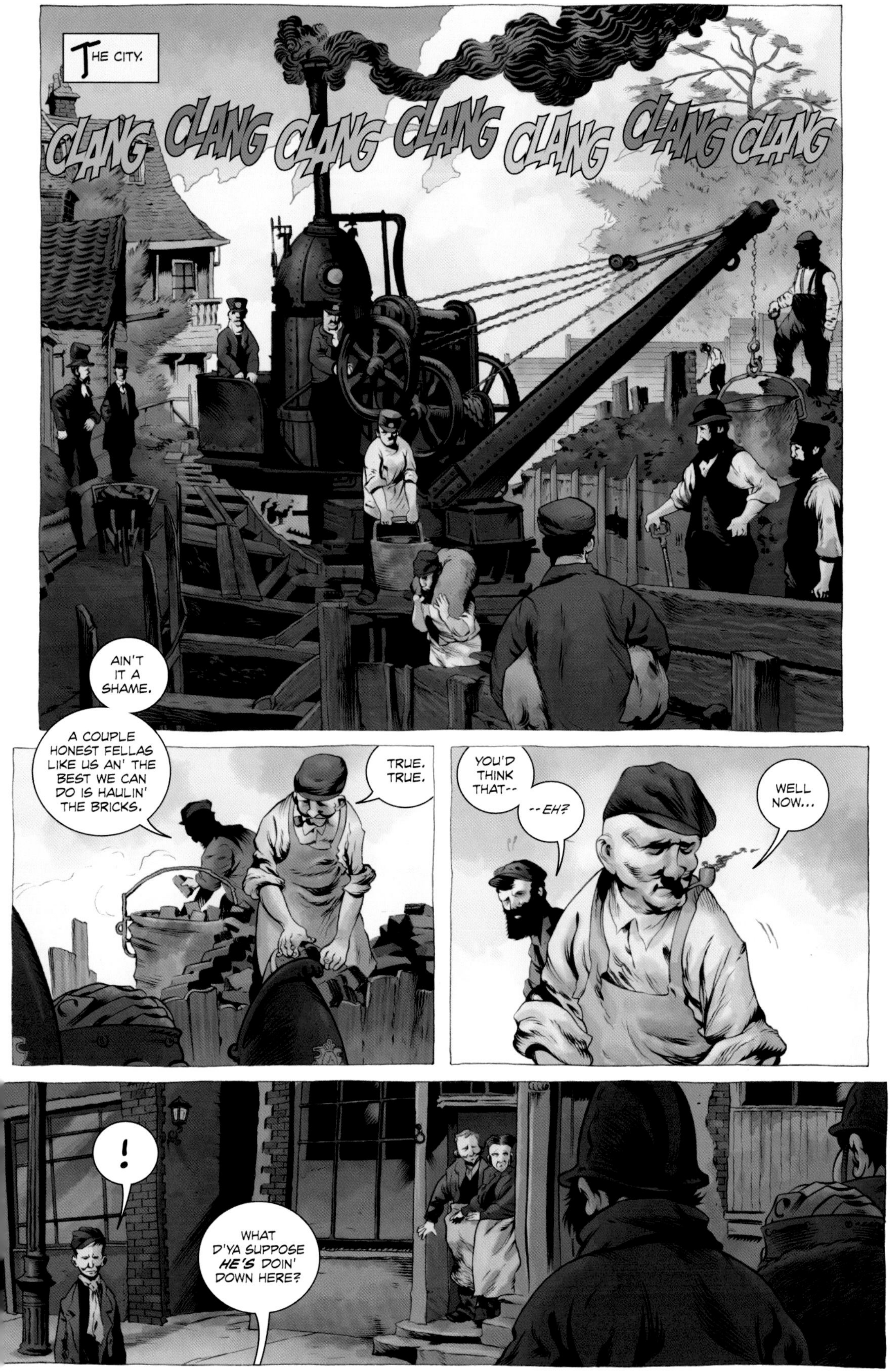
THE CITY.
CLANG CLANG CLANG CLANG CLANG CLANG CLANG
AIN'T IT A SHAME.
A COUPLE HONEST FELLAS LIKE US AN' THE BEST WE CAN DO IS HAULIN' THE BRICKS.
TRUE. TRUE.
YOU'D THINK THAT--
--EH?
WELL NOW...
!
WHAT D'YA SUPPOSE HE'S DOIN' DOWN HERE?

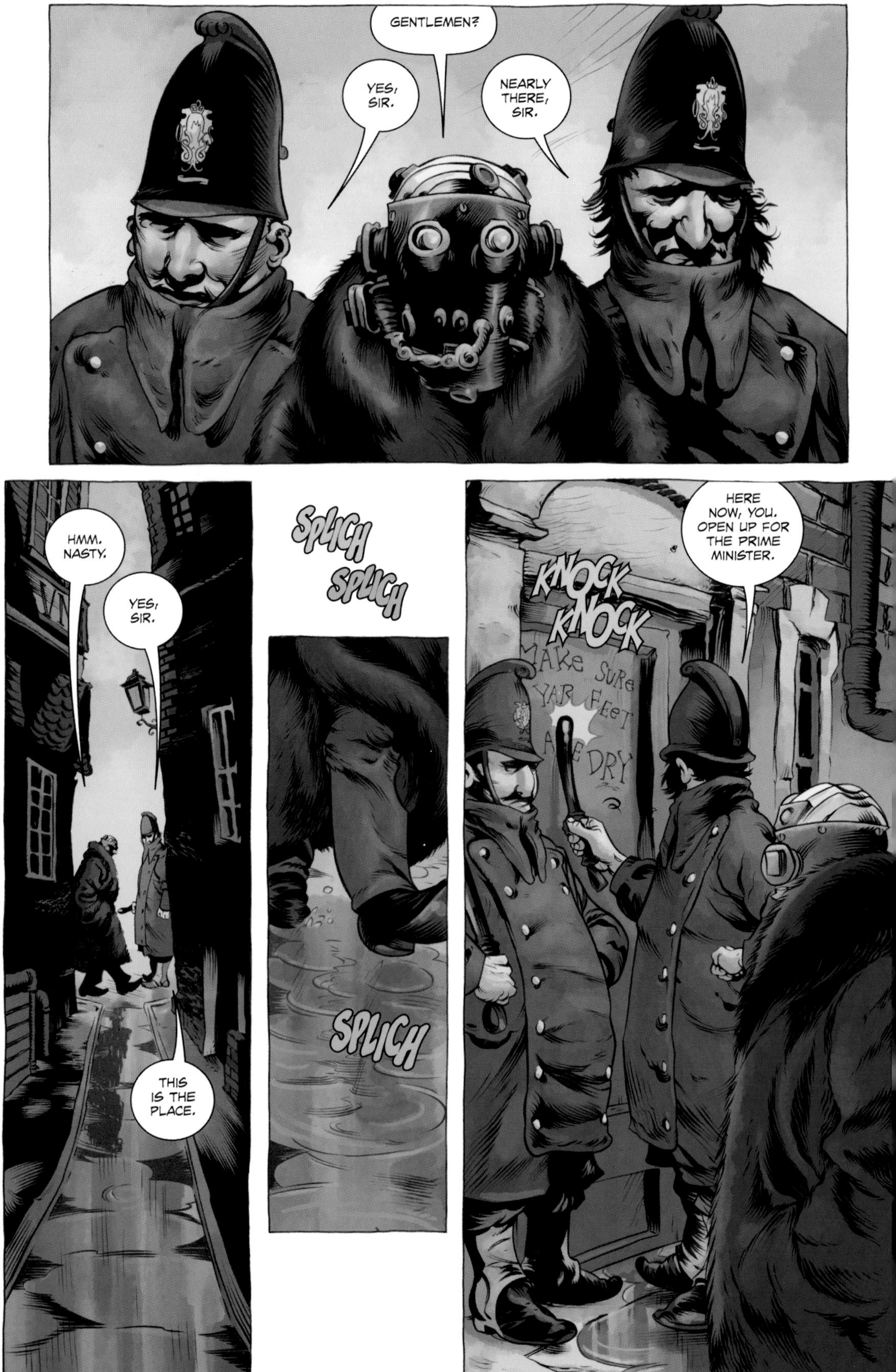
GENTLEMEN?
YES, SIR.
NEARLY THERE, SIR.
HMM. NASTY.
YES, SIR.
THIS IS THE PLACE.
SPLICH
SPLICH
SPLICH
KNOCK
KNOCK
MAKE SURE YAR FEET
DRY
HERE NOW, YOU. OPEN UP FOR THE PRIME MINISTER.

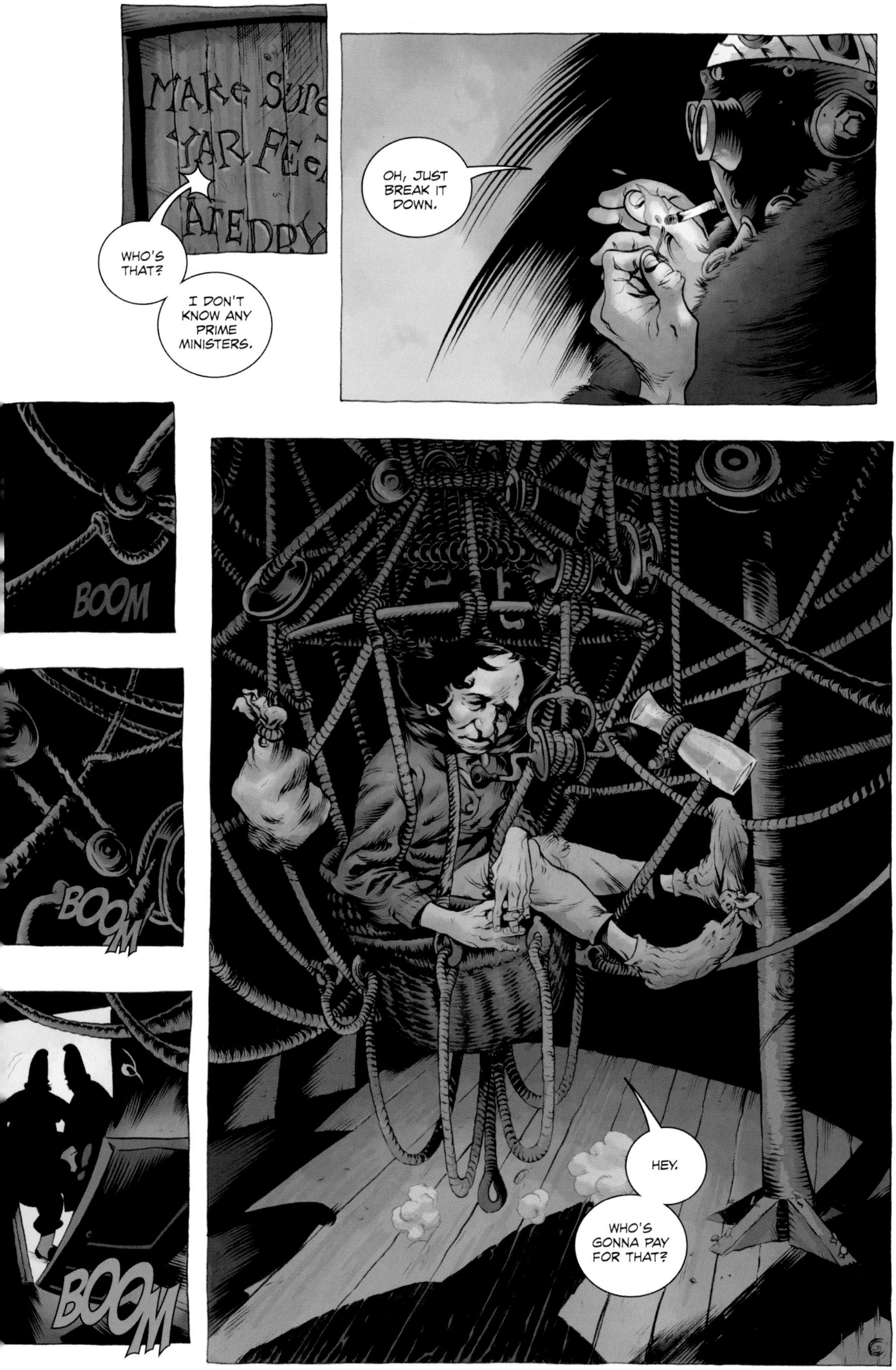
Make Sure
YAR FEE
ArE DRY
WHO'S THAT?
I DON'T KNOW ANY PRIME MINISTERS.
OH, JUST BREAK IT DOWN.
BOOM
BOOM
BOOM
HEY.
WHO'S GONNA PAY FOR THAT?

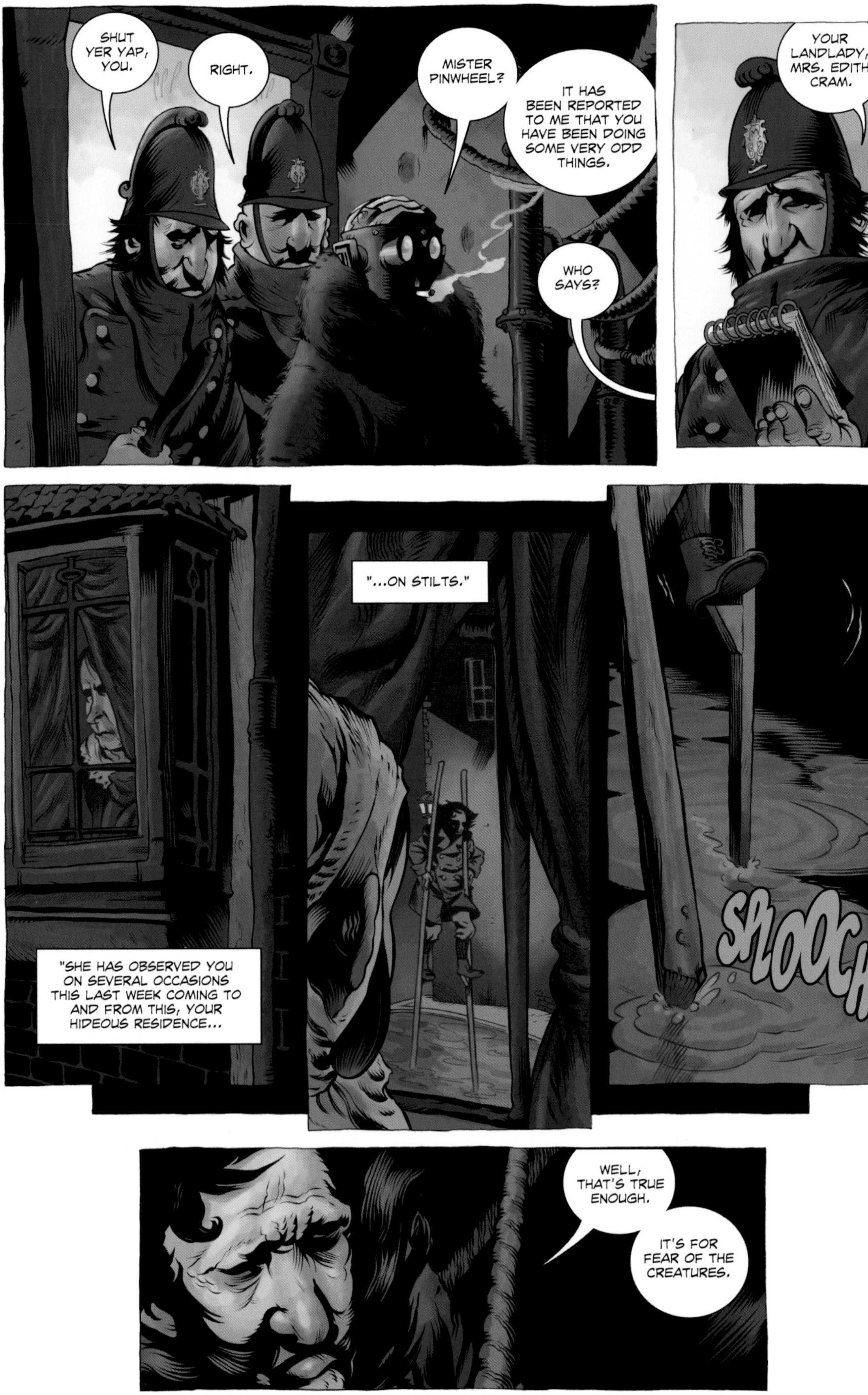
SHUT YER YAP, YOU.
RIGHT.
MISTER PINWHEEL?
IT HAS BEEN REPORTED TO ME THAT YOU HAVE BEEN DOING SOME VERY ODD THINGS.
WHO SAYS?
YOUR LANDLADY, MRS. EDITH CRAM.
"SHE HAS OBSERVED YOU ON SEVERAL OCCASIONS THIS LAST WEEK COMING TO AND FROM THIS, YOUR HIDEOUS RESIDENCE...
"...ON STILTS."
SPLOOCH
WELL, THAT'S TRUE ENOUGH.
IT'S FOR FEAR OF THE CREATURES.

CREATURES? I DON'T LIKE *THAT*.

LUNATIC, EXPLAIN YOURSELF.

SQUEE SQUEE SQUEE

CREATURES. WHAT THE LITTLE GIRL SHOWED ME.

OH, YES. SHE QUITE OPENED MY EYES TO THE DANGER LURKING IN THE PUDDLES.

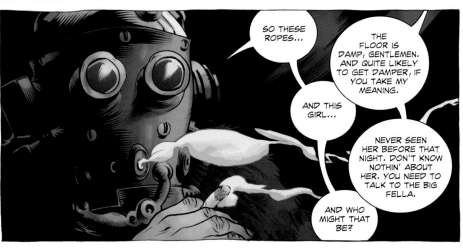

SO THESE ROPES...

THE FLOOR IS DAMP, GENTLEMEN. AND QUITE LIKELY TO GET DAMPER, IF YOU TAKE MY MEANING.

AND THIS GIRL...

NEVER SEEN HER BEFORE THAT NIGHT. DON'T KNOW NOTHIN' ABOUT HER. YOU NEED TO TALK TO THE BIG FELLA.

AND WHO MIGHT THAT BE?

I SEEN HIM AND THE GIRL ARGUING. AND I SEEN *HIM* BEFORE.

HE'S THE HAMMER-MAN...

"...DOWN AT THE SLOP YARD."

MOOOOOO

COME ON, YOU LADIES. EASY DOES IT.

THAT'S NICE. THAT'S NICE.

CLONK

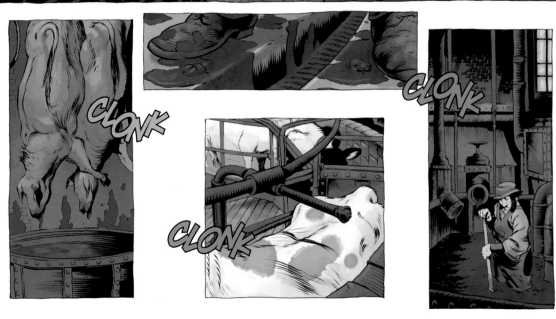

CLONK

CLONK

CLONK

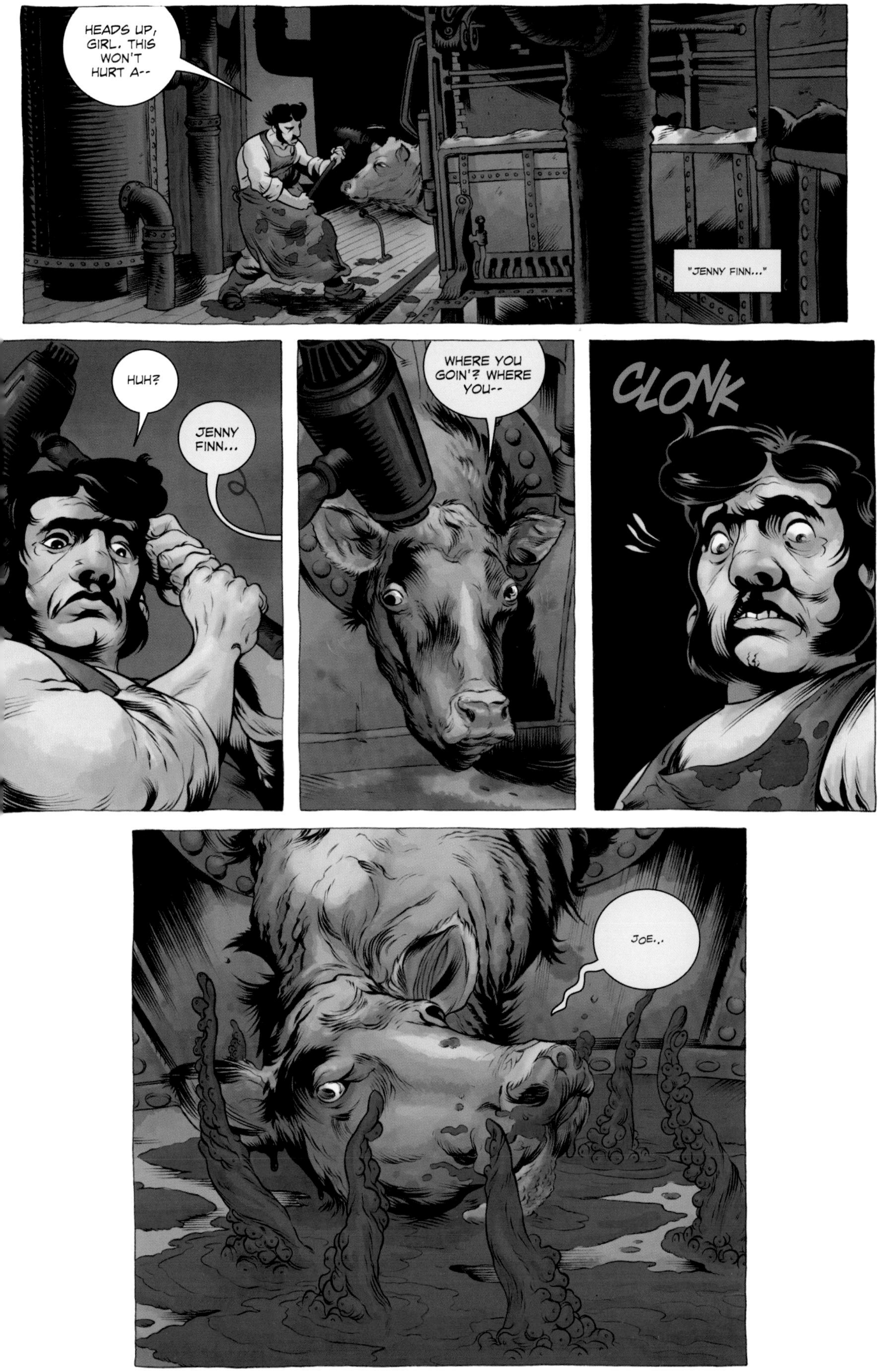
HEADS UP, GIRL. THIS WON'T HURT A--
"JENNY FINN..."
HUH?
JENNY FINN...
WHERE YOU GOIN'? WHERE YOU--
CLONK
JOE..

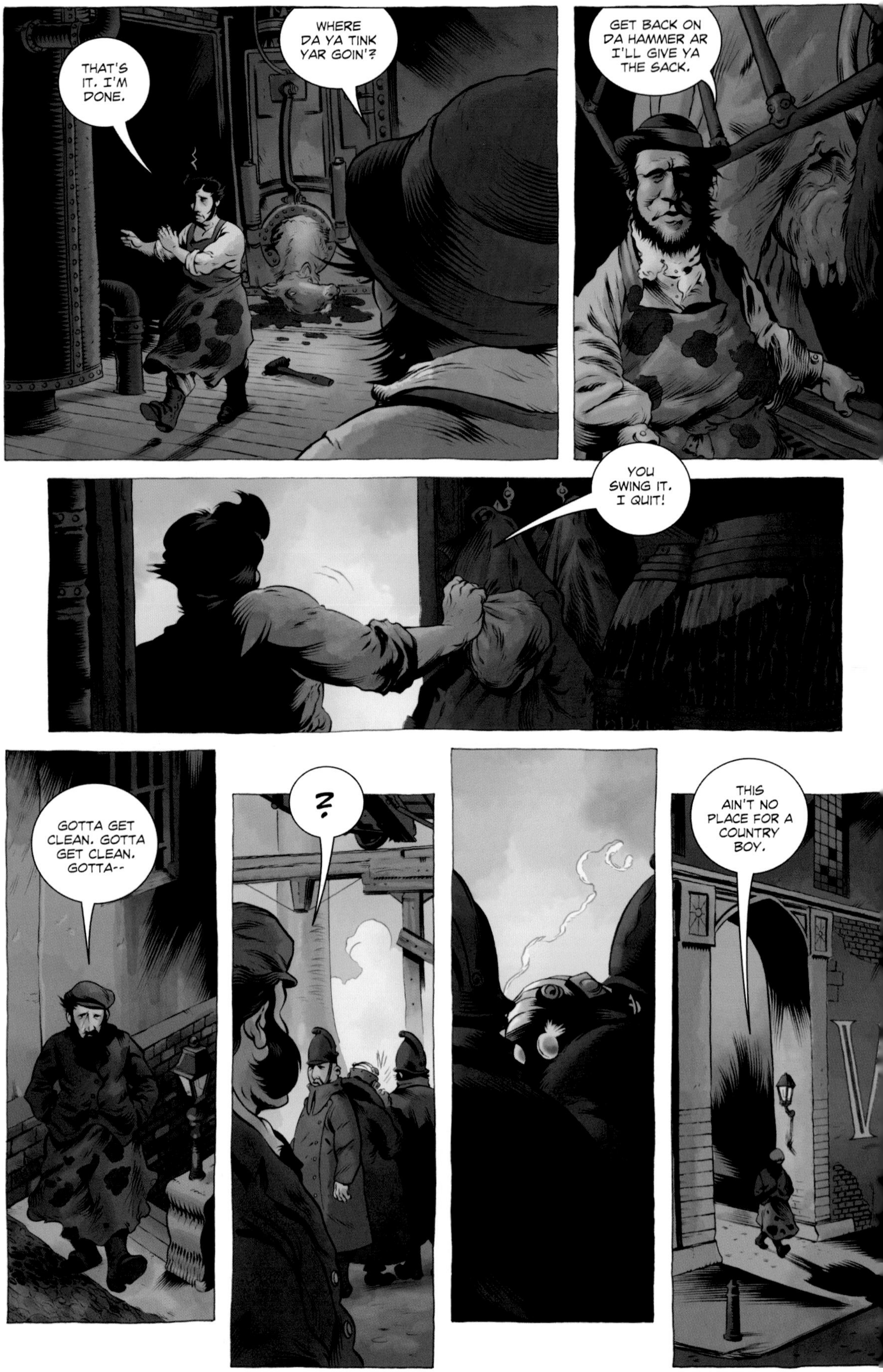
THAT'S IT. I'M DONE.
WHERE DA YA TINK YAR GOIN'?
GET BACK ON DA HAMMER AR I'LL GIVE YA THE SACK.
YOU SWING IT. I QUIT!
GOTTA GET CLEAN. GOTTA GET CLEAN. GOTTA--
?
THIS AIN'T NO PLACE FOR A COUNTRY BOY.

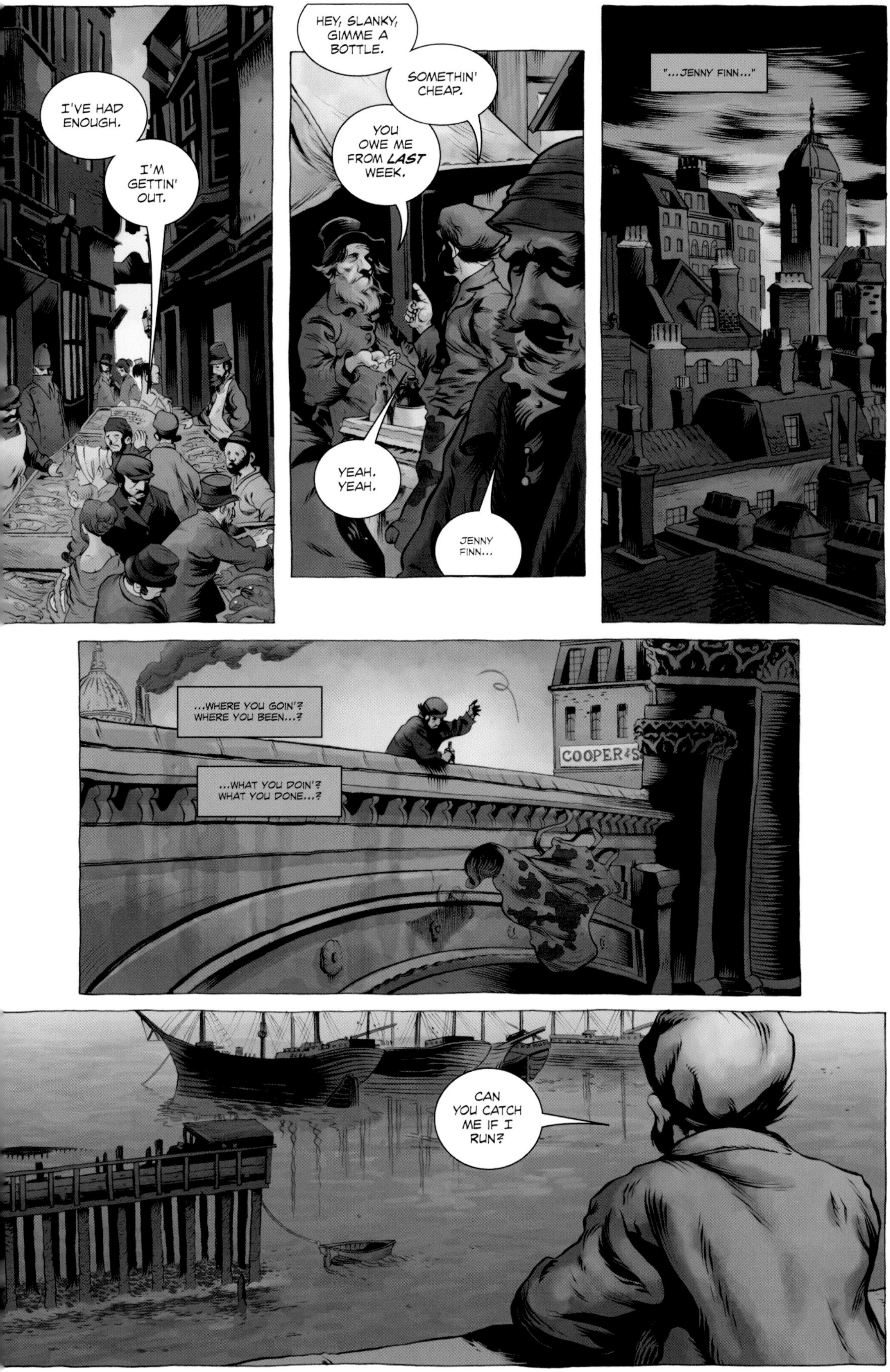
I'VE HAD ENOUGH.
I'M GETTIN' OUT.
HEY, SLANKY, GIMME A BOTTLE.
SOMETHIN' CHEAP.
YOU OWE ME FROM LAST WEEK.
YEAH. YEAH.
JENNY FINN...
"...JENNY FINN..."
...WHERE YOU GOIN'? WHERE YOU BEEN...?
...WHAT YOU DOIN'? WHAT YOU DONE...?
COOPER & S
CAN YOU CATCH ME IF I RUN?

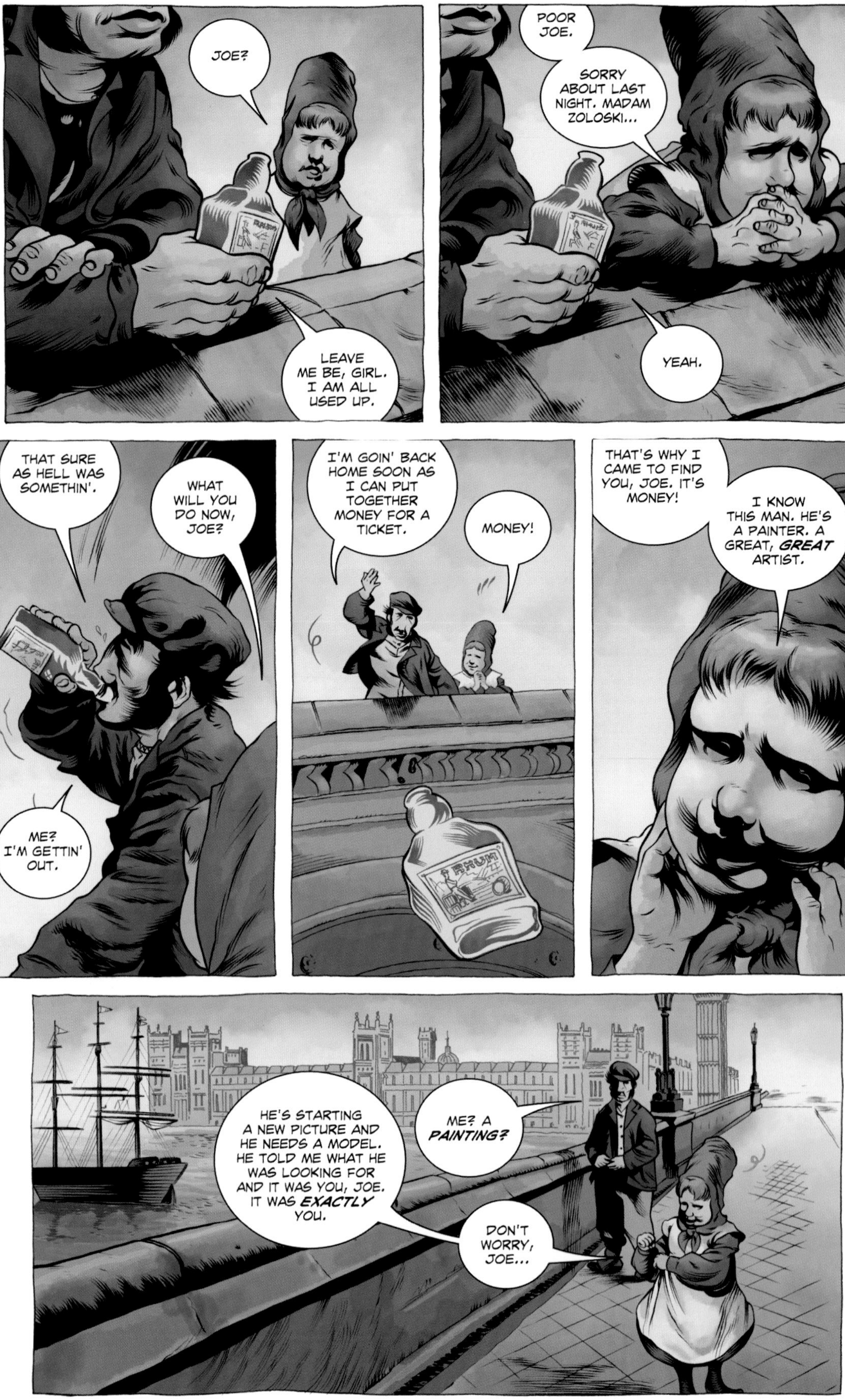
JOE?
LEAVE ME BE, GIRL. I AM ALL USED UP.
POOR JOE.
SORRY ABOUT LAST NIGHT. MADAM ZOLOSKI...
YEAH.
THAT SURE AS HELL WAS SOMETHIN'.
WHAT WILL YOU DO NOW, JOE?
ME? I'M GETTIN' OUT.
I'M GOIN' BACK HOME SOON AS I CAN PUT TOGETHER MONEY FOR A TICKET.
MONEY!
THAT'S WHY I CAME TO FIND YOU, JOE. IT'S MONEY!
I KNOW THIS MAN. HE'S A PAINTER. A GREAT, *GREAT* ARTIST.
HE'S STARTING A NEW PICTURE AND HE NEEDS A MODEL. HE TOLD ME WHAT HE WAS LOOKING FOR AND IT WAS YOU, JOE. IT WAS *EXACTLY* YOU.
ME? A *PAINTING?*
DON'T WORRY, JOE...

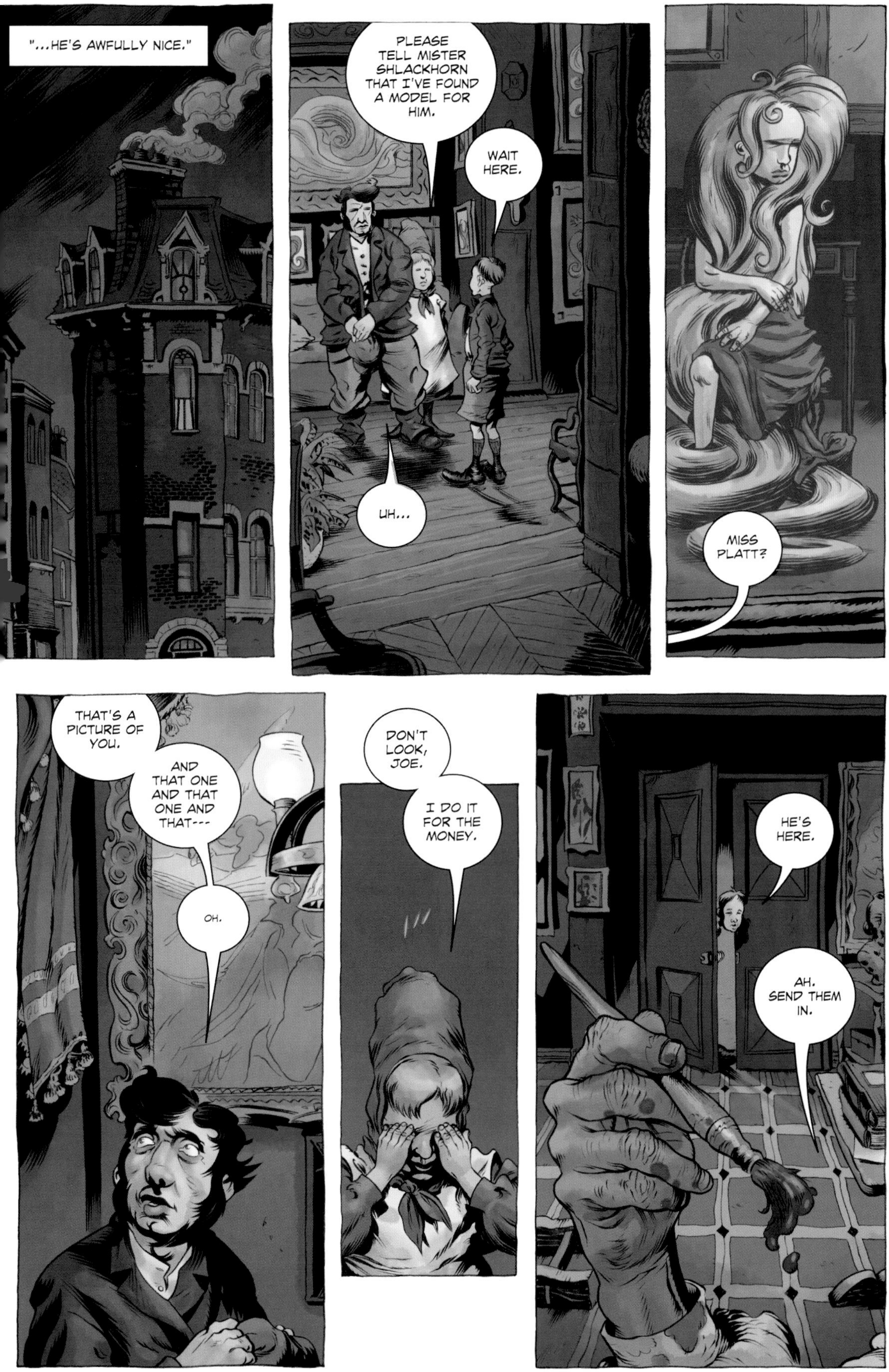
"...HE'S AWFULLY NICE."
PLEASE TELL MISTER SHLACKHORN THAT I'VE FOUND A MODEL FOR HIM.
WAIT HERE.
UH...
MISS PLATT?
THAT'S A PICTURE OF YOU.
AND THAT ONE AND THAT ONE AND THAT---
OH.
DON'T LOOK, JOE.
I DO IT FOR THE MONEY.
HE'S HERE.
AH. SEND THEM IN.

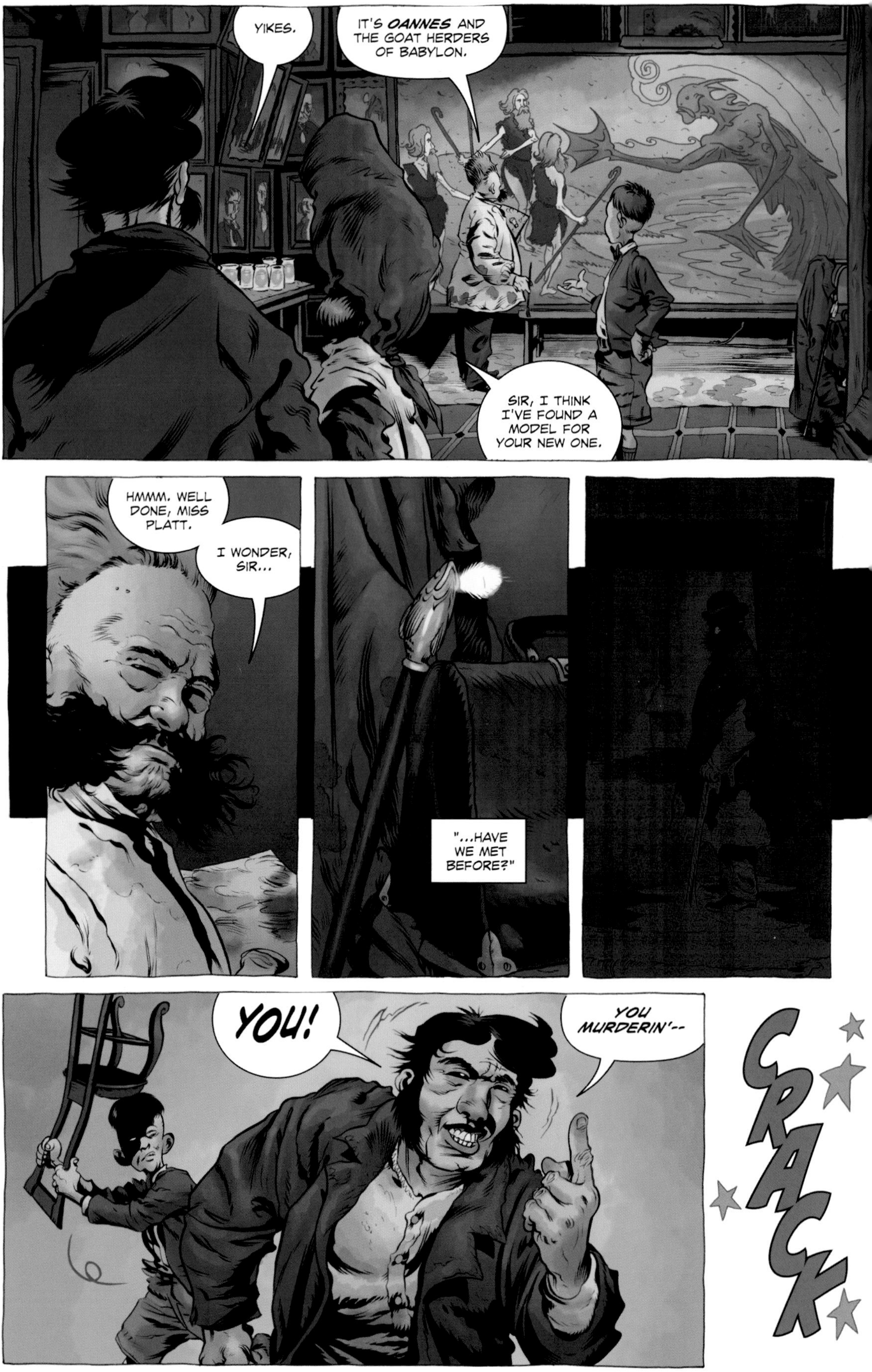
YIKES.
IT'S OANNES AND THE GOAT HERDERS OF BABYLON.
SIR, I THINK I'VE FOUND A MODEL FOR YOUR NEW ONE.
HMMM. WELL DONE, MISS PLATT.
I WONDER, SIR...
"...HAVE WE MET BEFORE?"
YOU!
YOU MURDERIN'--
CRACK

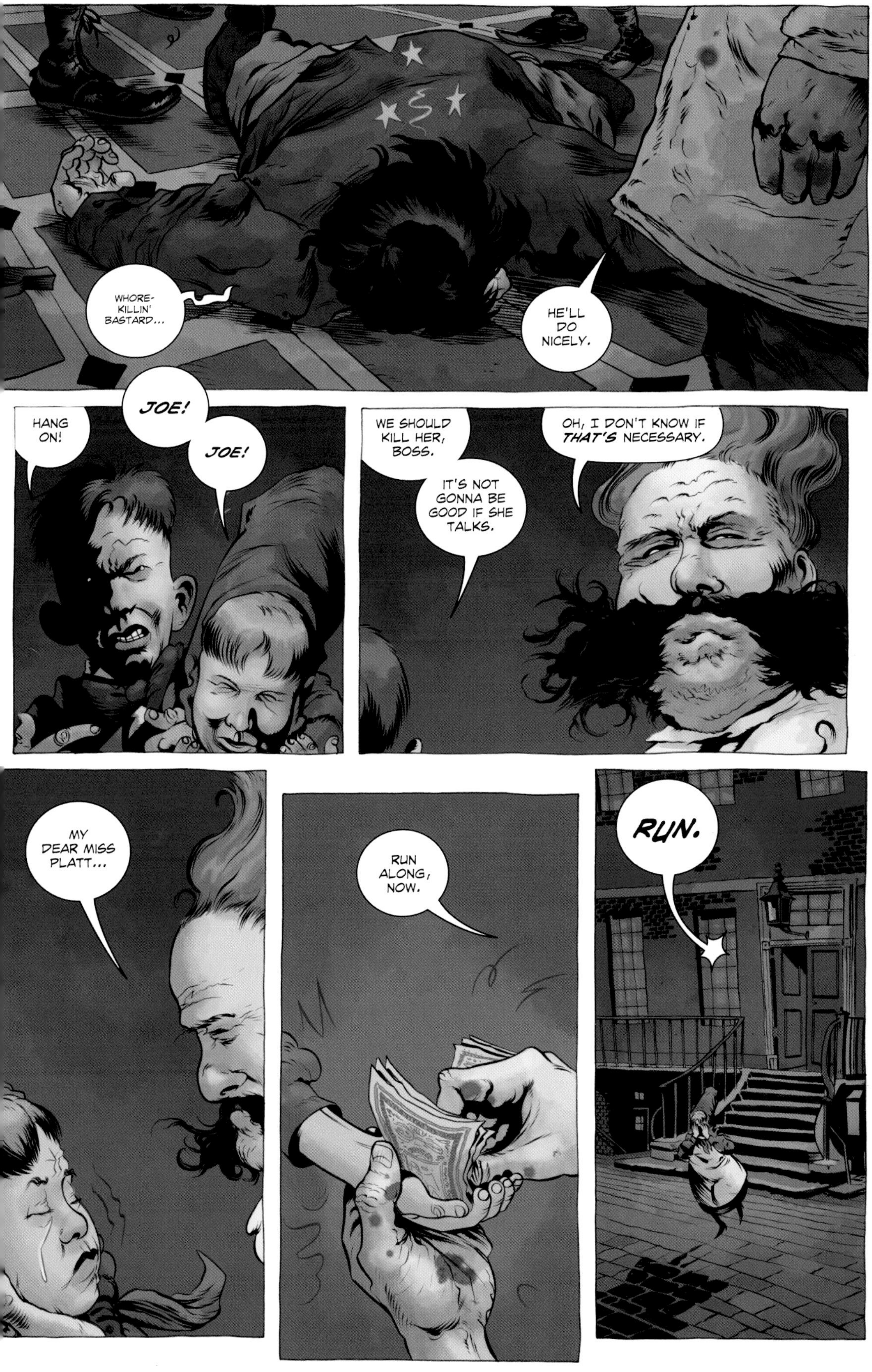

WHORE-KILLIN' BASTARD...
HE'LL DO NICELY.
HANG ON!
JOE!
JOE!
WE SHOULD KILL HER, BOSS.
IT'S NOT GONNA BE GOOD IF SHE TALKS.
OH, I DON'T KNOW IF *THAT'S* NECESSARY.
MY DEAR MISS PLATT...
RUN ALONG, NOW.
RUN.

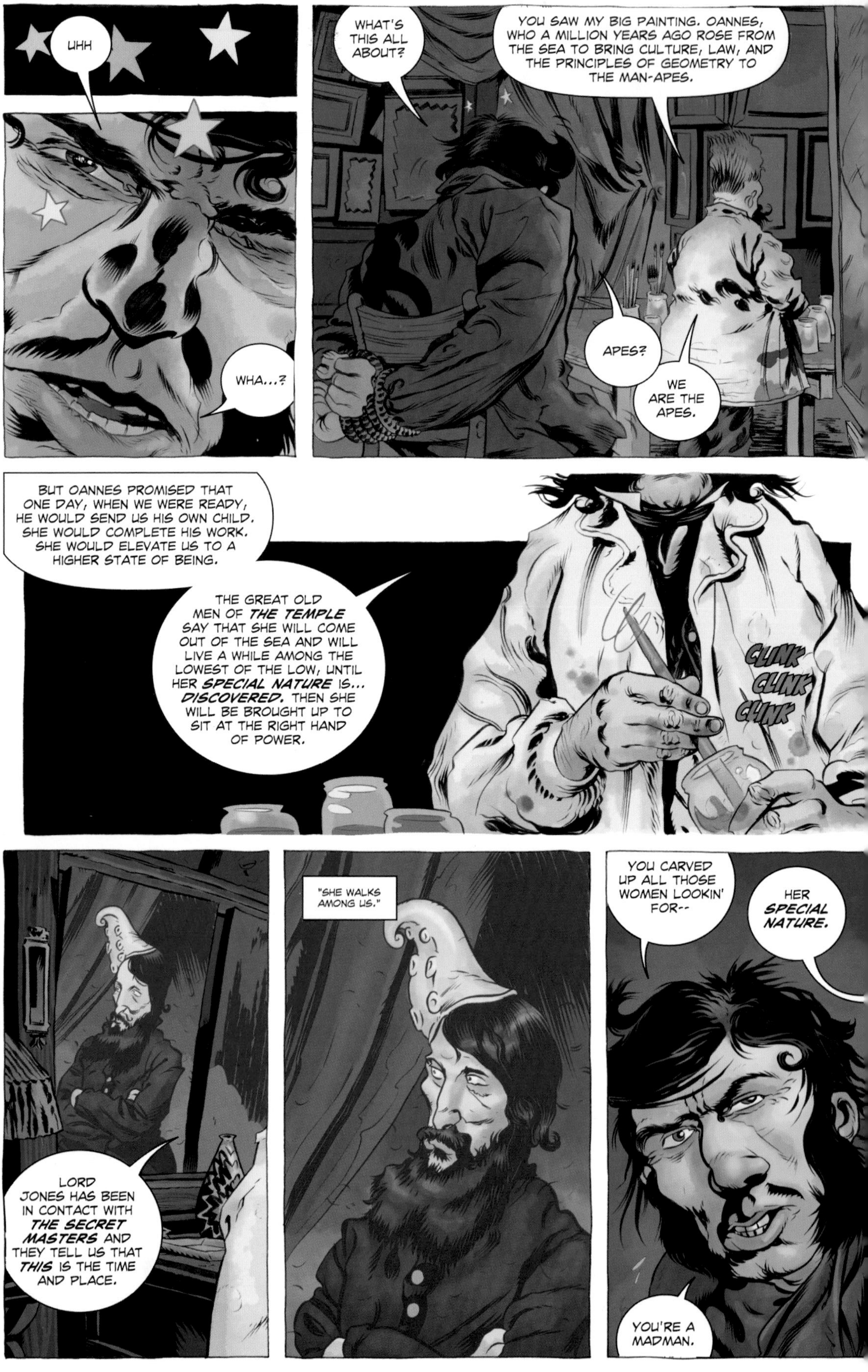
UHH
WHA...?
WHAT'S THIS ALL ABOUT?
YOU SAW MY BIG PAINTING. OANNES, WHO A MILLION YEARS AGO ROSE FROM THE SEA TO BRING CULTURE, LAW, AND THE PRINCIPLES OF GEOMETRY TO THE MAN-APES.
APES?
WE ARE THE APES.
BUT OANNES PROMISED THAT ONE DAY, WHEN WE WERE READY, HE WOULD SEND US HIS OWN CHILD. SHE WOULD COMPLETE HIS WORK. SHE WOULD ELEVATE US TO A HIGHER STATE OF BEING.
THE GREAT OLD MEN OF THE TEMPLE SAY THAT SHE WILL COME OUT OF THE SEA AND WILL LIVE A WHILE AMONG THE LOWEST OF THE LOW, UNTIL HER SPECIAL NATURE IS... DISCOVERED. THEN SHE WILL BE BROUGHT UP TO SIT AT THE RIGHT HAND OF POWER.
CLINK
CLINK
CLINK
LORD JONES HAS BEEN IN CONTACT WITH THE SECRET MASTERS AND THEY TELL US THAT THIS IS THE TIME AND PLACE.
"SHE WALKS AMONG US."
YOU CARVED UP ALL THOSE WOMEN LOOKIN' FOR--
HER SPECIAL NATURE.
YOU'RE A MADMAN.

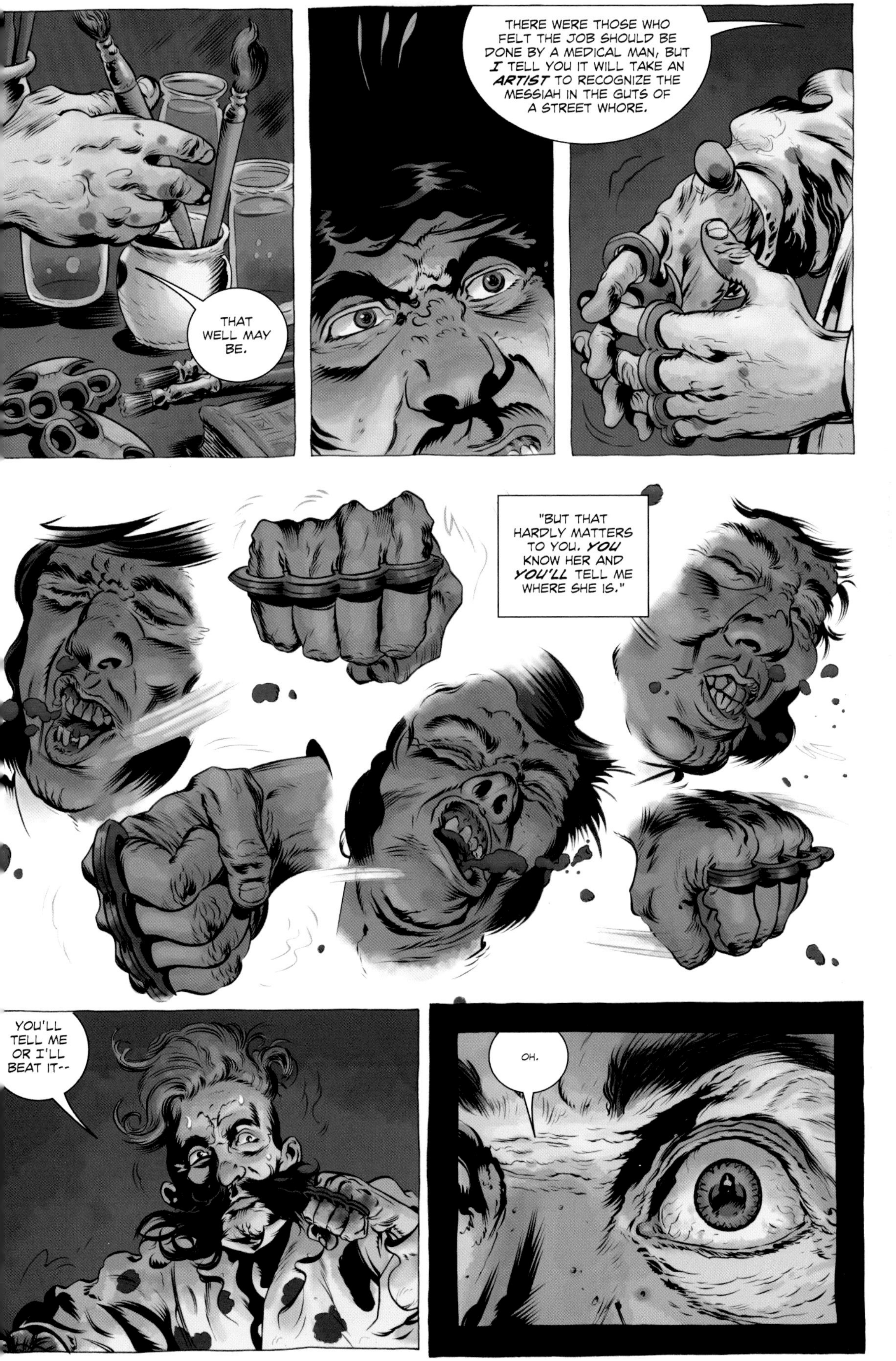
THERE WERE THOSE WHO FELT THE JOB SHOULD BE DONE BY A MEDICAL MAN, BUT I TELL YOU IT WILL TAKE AN ARTIST TO RECOGNIZE THE MESSIAH IN THE GUTS OF A STREET WHORE.
THAT WELL MAY BE.
"BUT THAT HARDLY MATTERS TO YOU. YOU KNOW HER AND YOU'LL TELL ME WHERE SHE IS."
YOU'LL TELL ME OR I'LL BEAT IT--
OH.

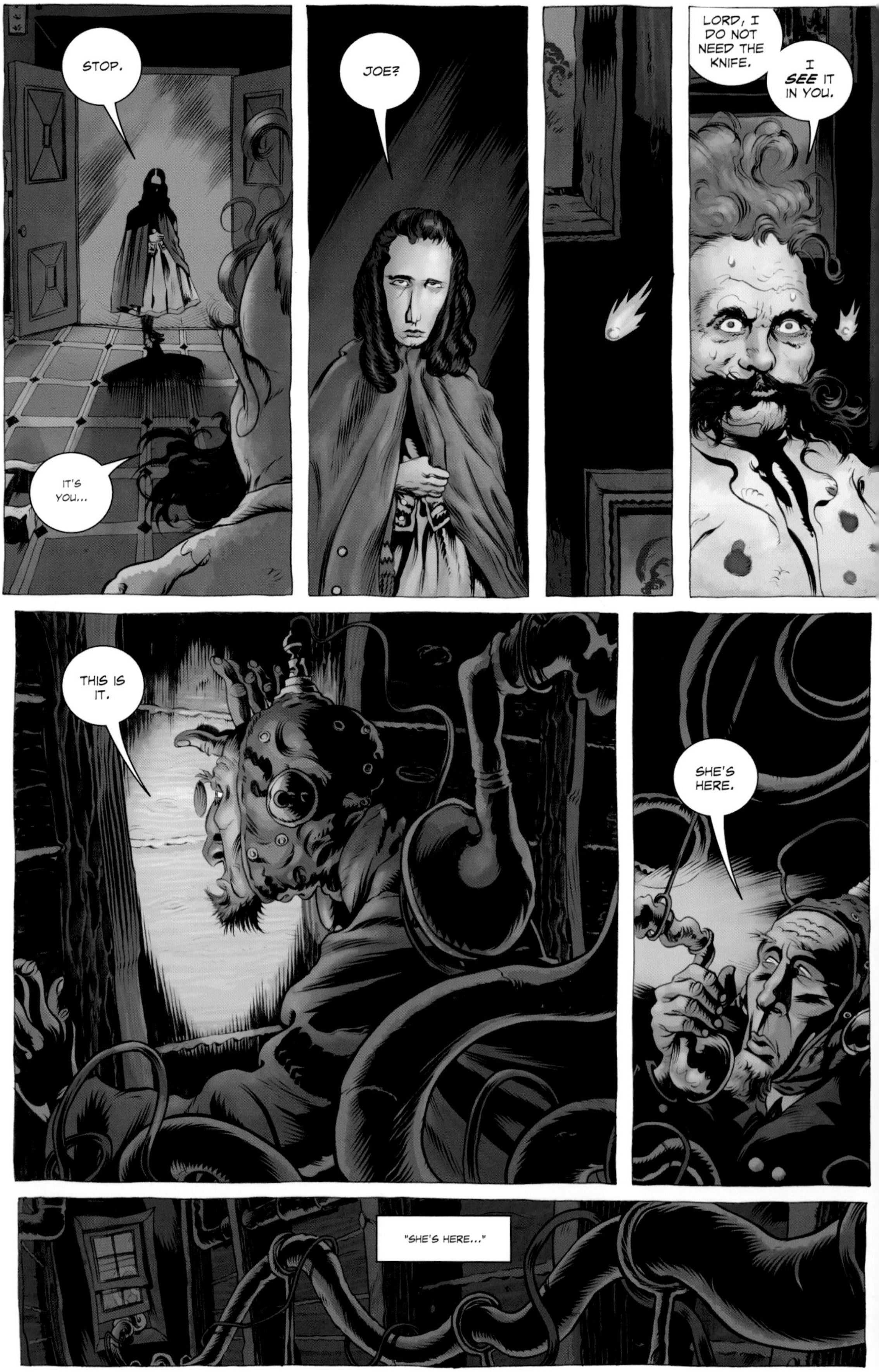
STOP.
IT'S YOU...
JOE?
LORD, I DO NOT NEED THE KNIFE.
I SEE IT IN YOU.
THIS IS IT.
SHE'S HERE.
"SHE'S HERE..."

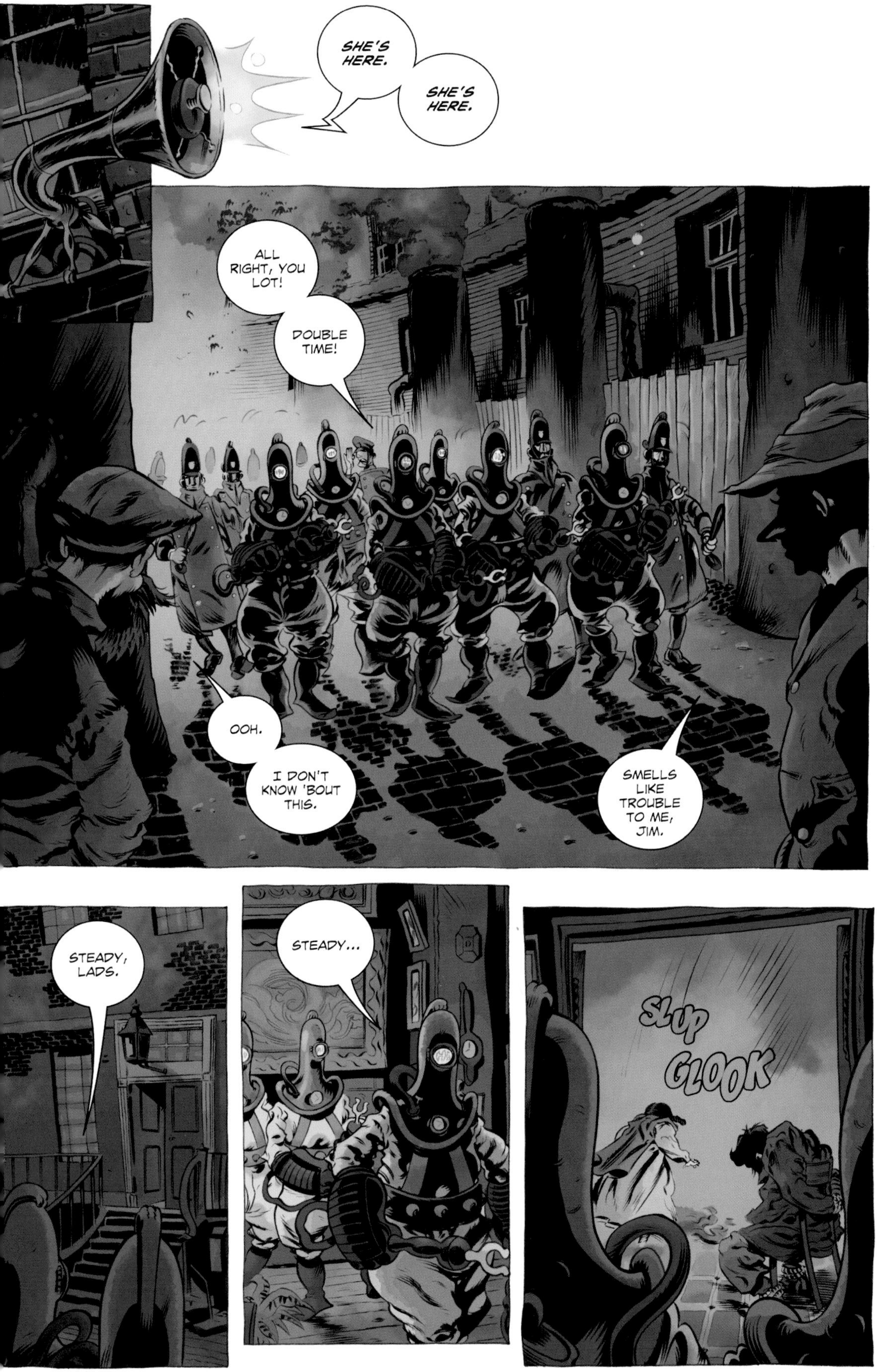
SHE'S HERE.
SHE'S HERE.
ALL RIGHT, YOU LOT!
DOUBLE TIME!
OOH.
I DON'T KNOW 'BOUT THIS.
SMELLS LIKE TROUBLE TO ME, JIM.
STEADY, LADS.
STEADY...
SLUP
GLOOK

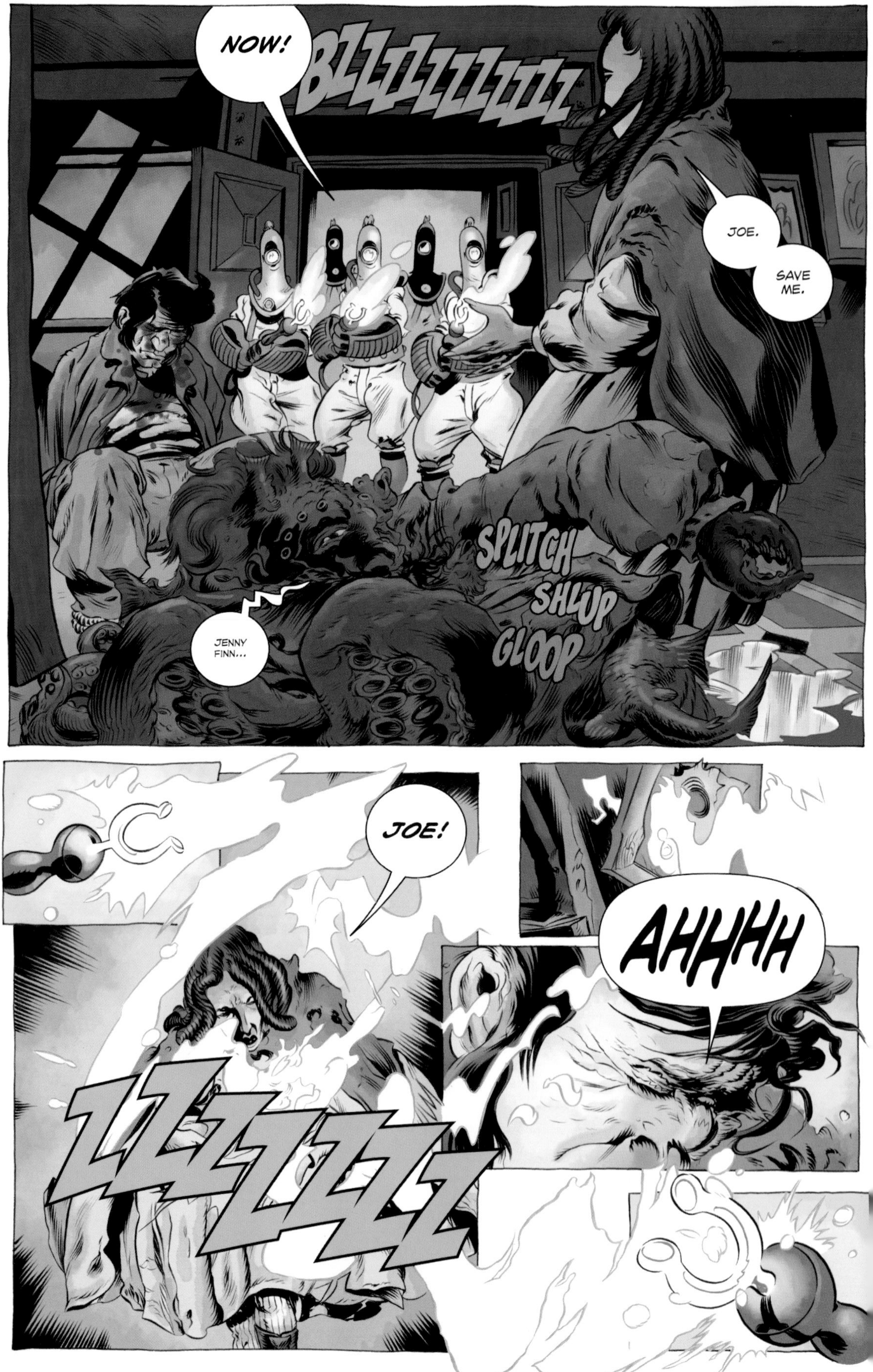
NOW!
BZZZZZZZZZZZ
JOE.
SAVE ME.
SPLITCH
SHLUP
GLOOP
JENNY FINN...
JOE!
AHHHH
ZZZZZZ

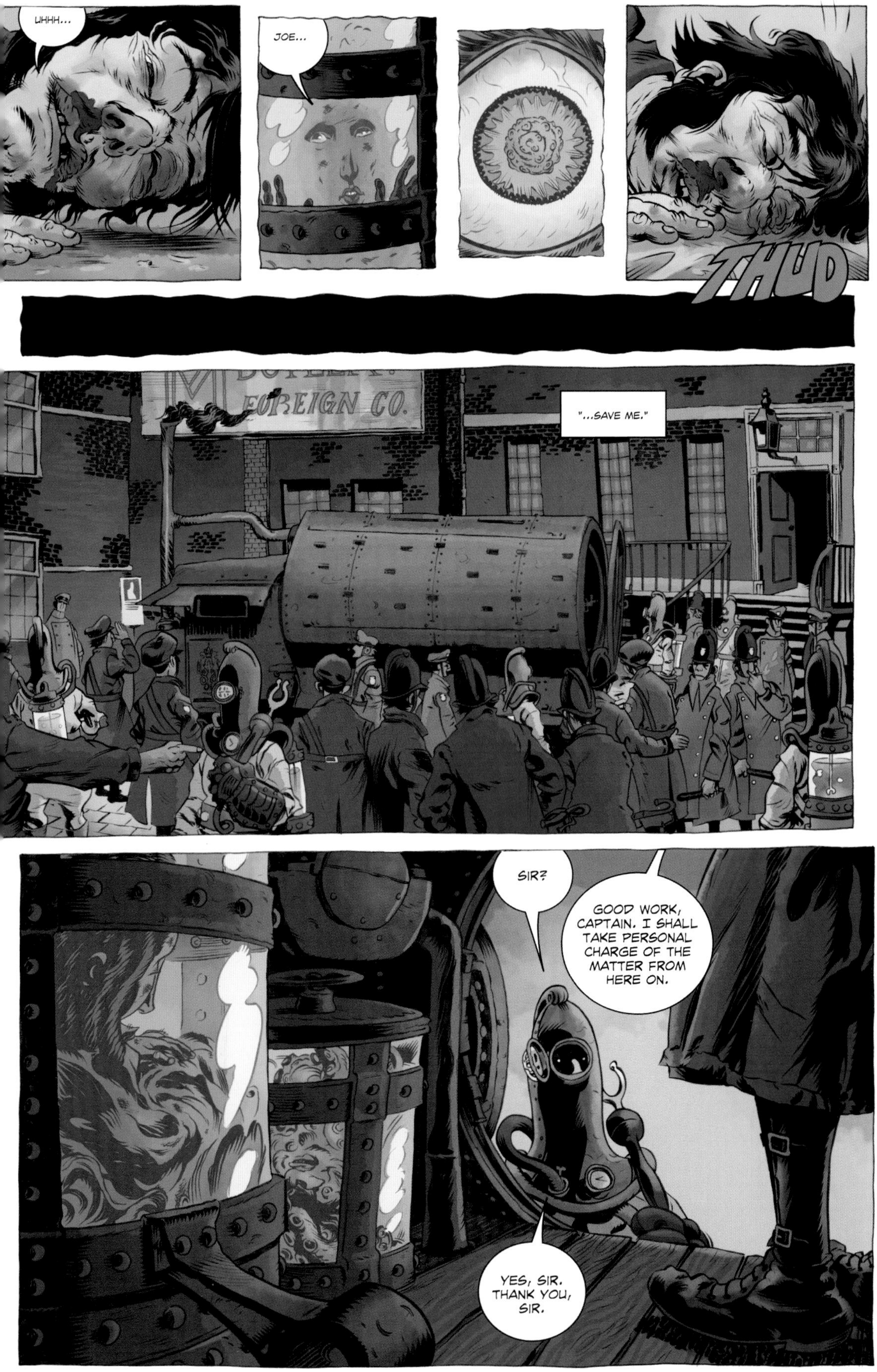

UHHH...
JOE...
THUD
FOREIGN CO.
"...SAVE ME."
SIR?
GOOD WORK, CAPTAIN. I SHALL TAKE PERSONAL CHARGE OF THE MATTER FROM HERE ON.
YES, SIR. THANK YOU, SIR.

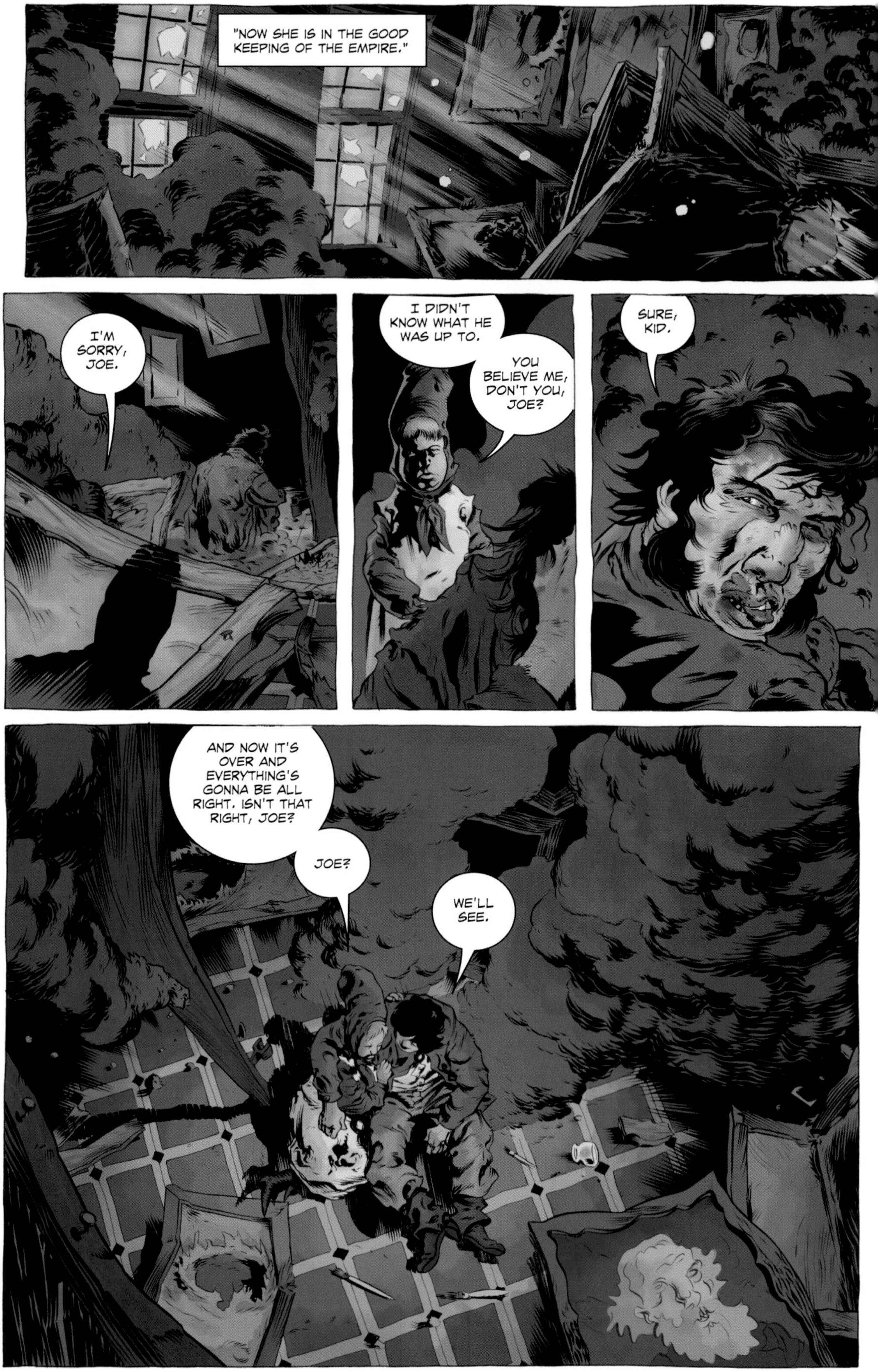
"NOW SHE IS IN THE GOOD KEEPING OF THE EMPIRE."
I'M SORRY, JOE.
I DIDN'T KNOW WHAT HE WAS UP TO.
YOU BELIEVE ME, DON'T YOU, JOE?
SURE, KID.
AND NOW IT'S OVER AND EVERYTHING'S GONNA BE ALL RIGHT. ISN'T THAT RIGHT, JOE?
JOE?
WE'LL SEE.

CHAPTER
FOUR

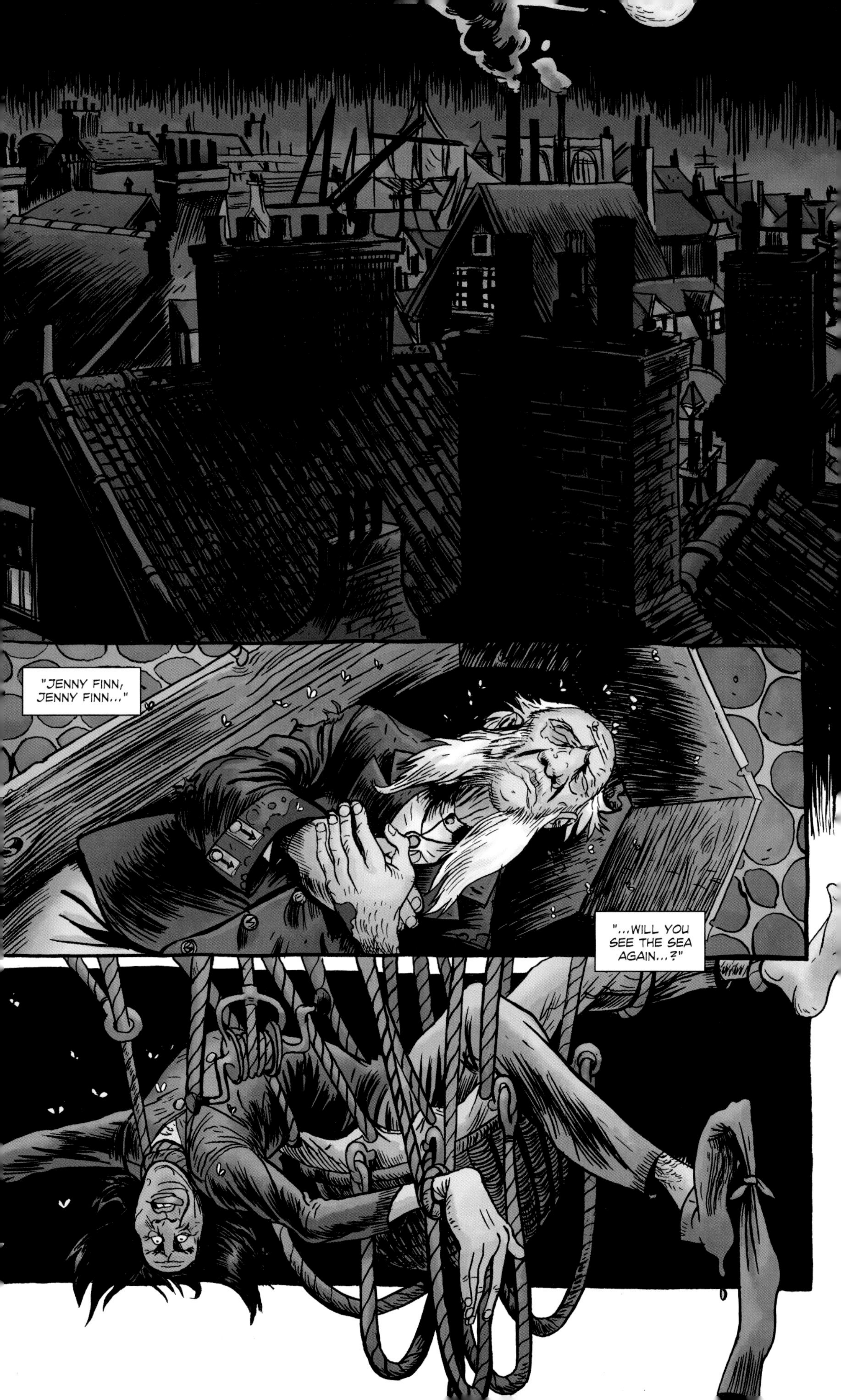
"JENNY FINN,
JENNY FINN..."
"...WILL YOU
SEE THE SEA
AGAIN...?"

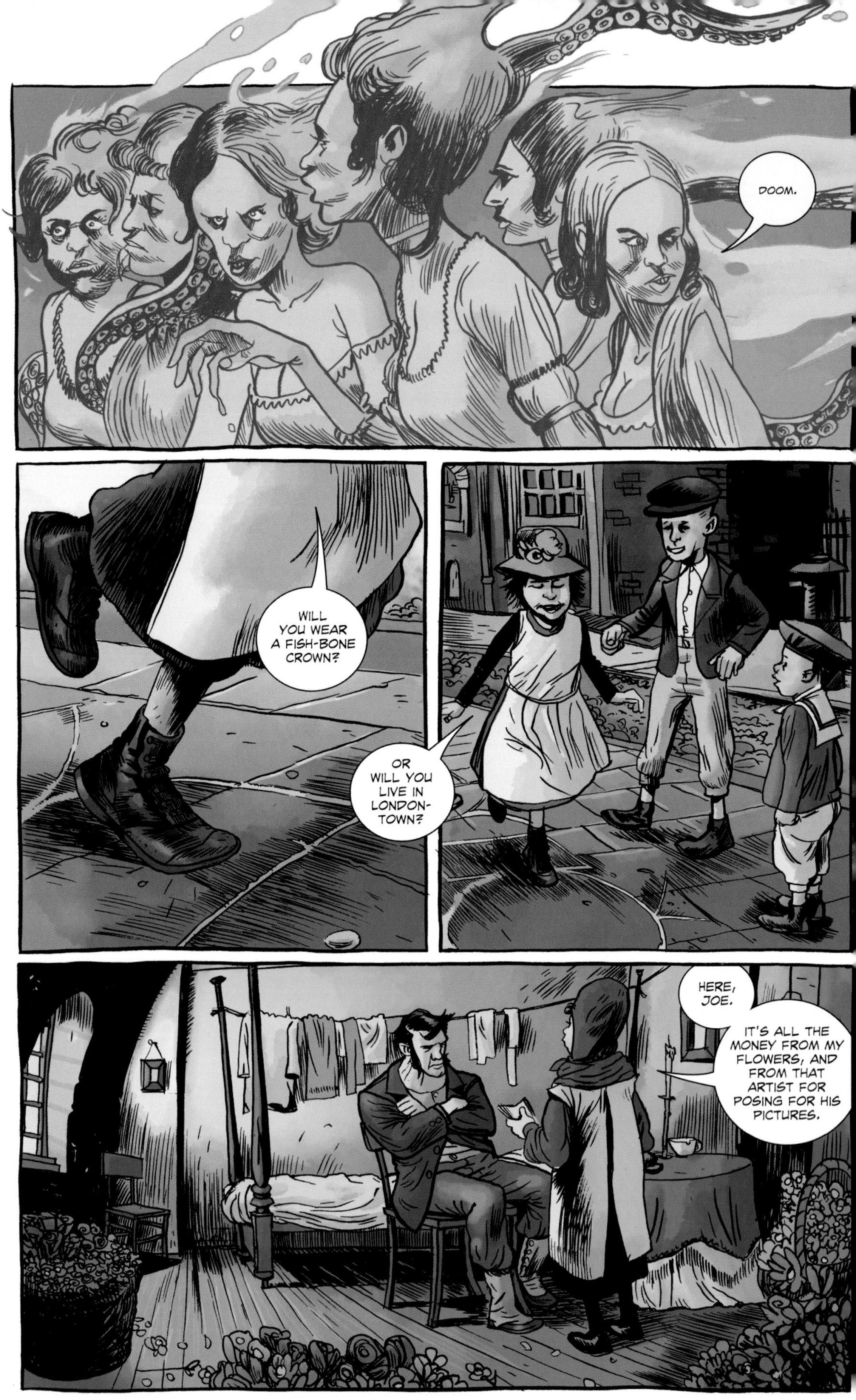
DOOM.
WILL YOU WEAR A FISH-BONE CROWN?
OR WILL YOU LIVE IN LONDON-TOWN?
HERE, JOE.
IT'S ALL THE MONEY FROM MY FLOWERS, AND FROM THAT ARTIST FOR POSING FOR HIS PICTURES.

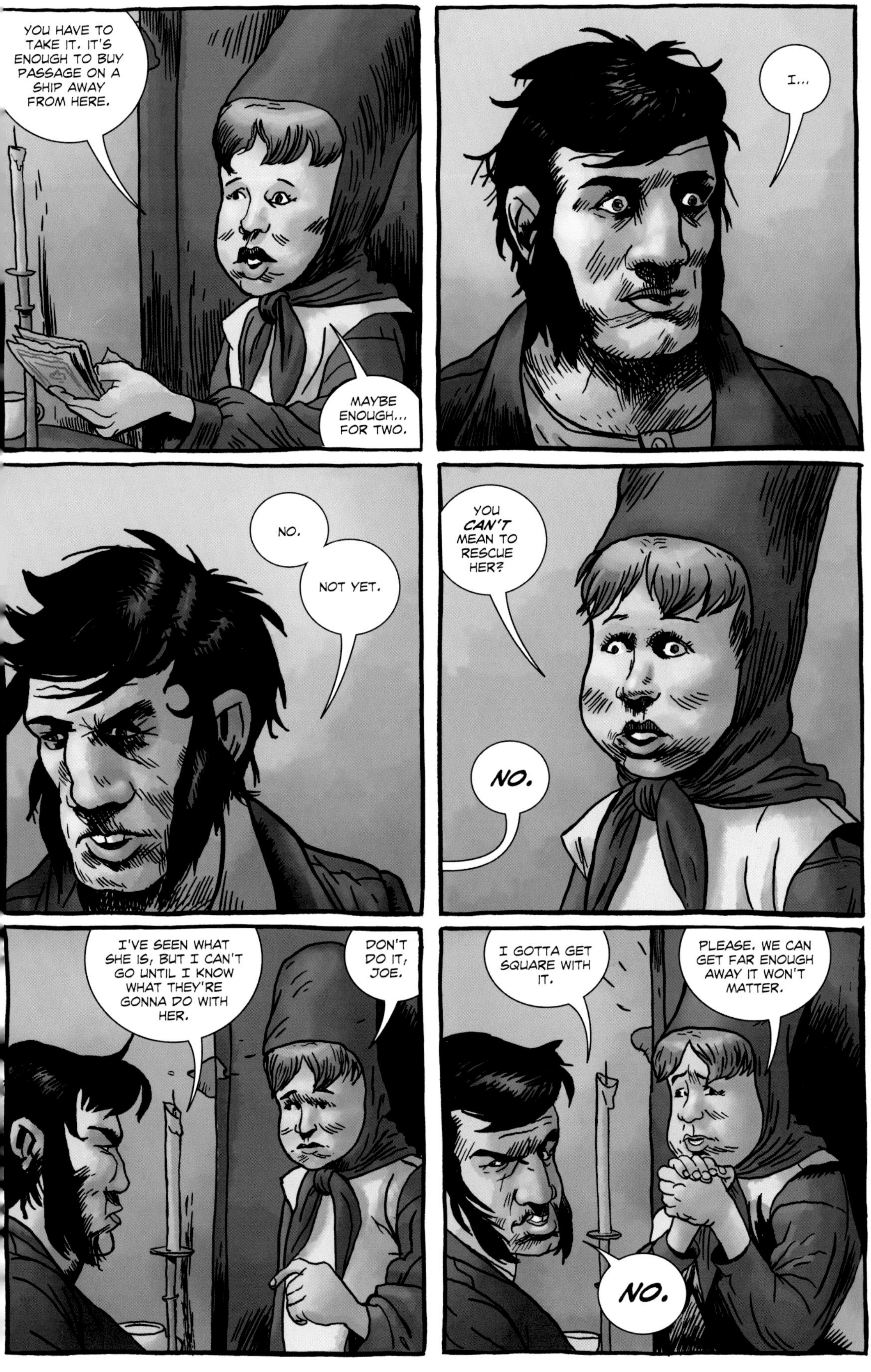

YOU HAVE TO TAKE IT. IT'S ENOUGH TO BUY PASSAGE ON A SHIP AWAY FROM HERE.
MAYBE ENOUGH... FOR TWO.
I...
NO.
NOT YET.
YOU *CAN'T* MEAN TO RESCUE HER?
NO.
I'VE SEEN WHAT SHE IS, BUT I CAN'T GO UNTIL I KNOW WHAT THEY'RE GONNA DO WITH HER.
DON'T DO IT, JOE.
I GOTTA GET SQUARE WITH IT.
PLEASE. WE CAN GET FAR ENOUGH AWAY IT WON'T MATTER.
NO.

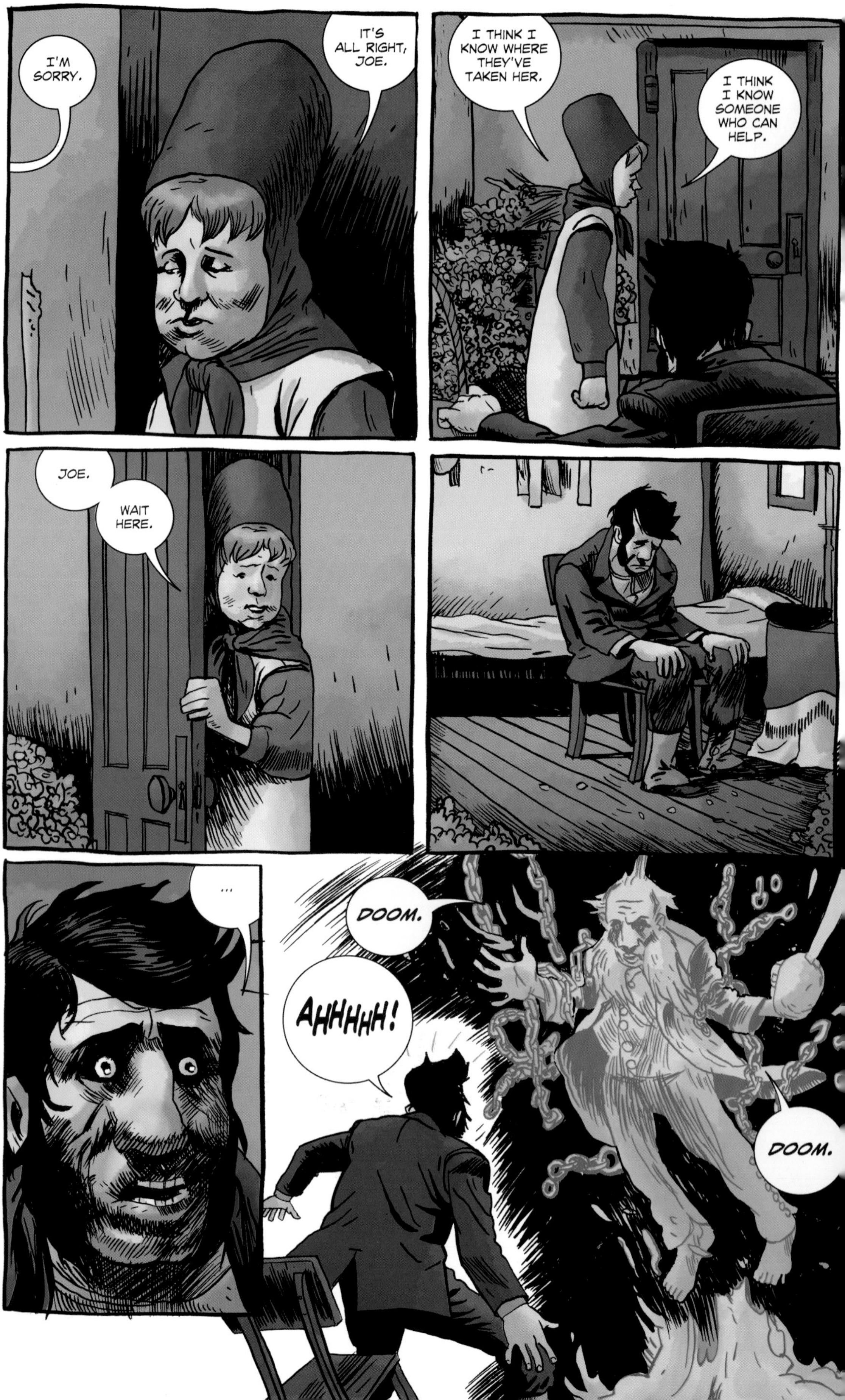
I'M SORRY.
IT'S ALL RIGHT, JOE.
I THINK I KNOW WHERE THEY'VE TAKEN HER.
I THINK I KNOW SOMEONE WHO CAN HELP.
JOE.
WAIT HERE.
...
DOOM.
AHHHHH!
DOOM.

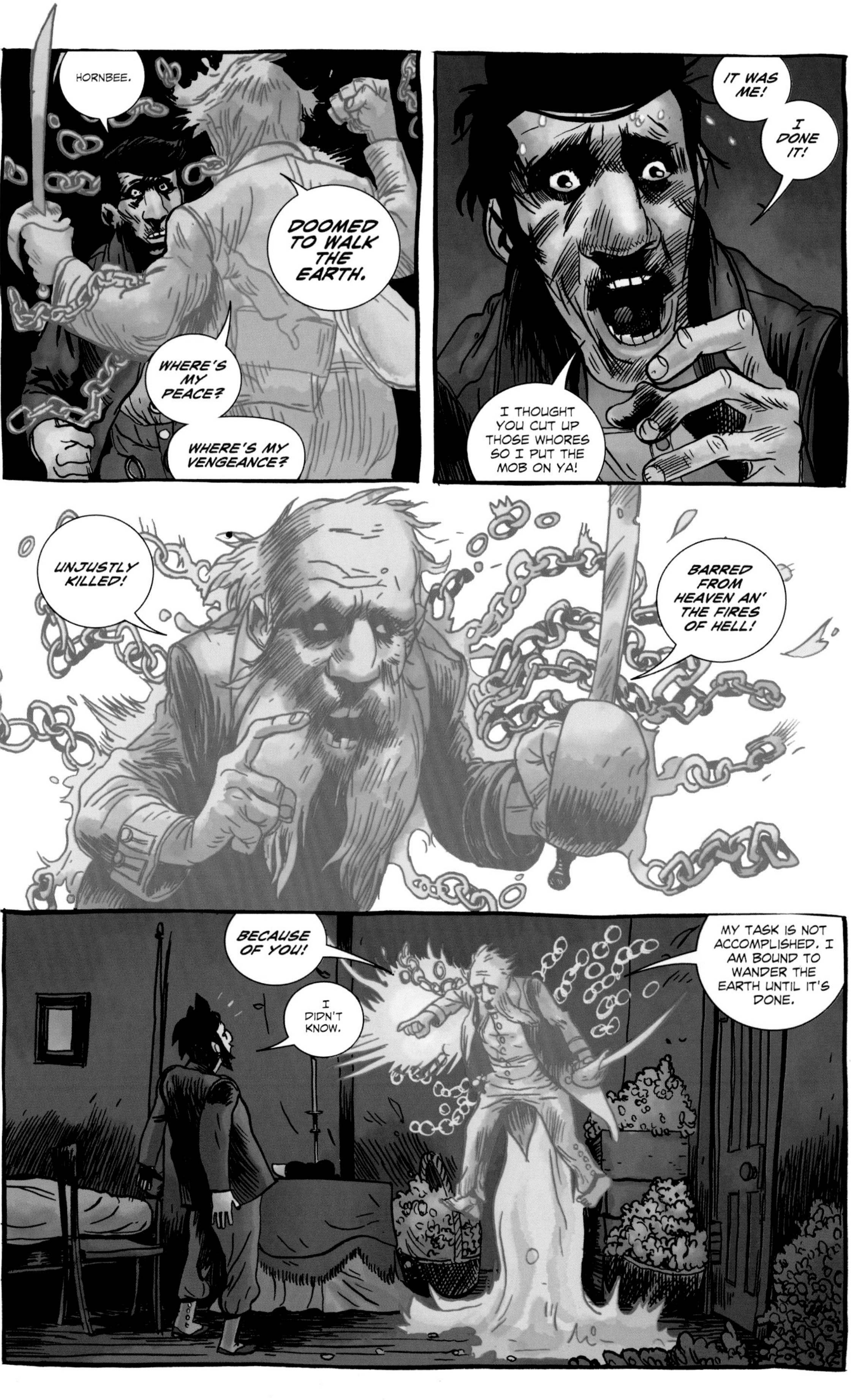
HORNBEE.
DOOMED TO WALK THE EARTH.
WHERE'S MY PEACE?
WHERE'S MY VENGEANCE?
IT WAS ME!
I DONE IT!
I THOUGHT YOU CUT UP THOSE WHORES SO I PUT THE MOB ON YA!
UNJUSTLY KILLED!
BARRED FROM HEAVEN AN' THE FIRES OF HELL!
BECAUSE OF YOU!
I DIDN'T KNOW.
MY TASK IS NOT ACCOMPLISHED. I AM BOUND TO WANDER THE EARTH UNTIL IT'S DONE.

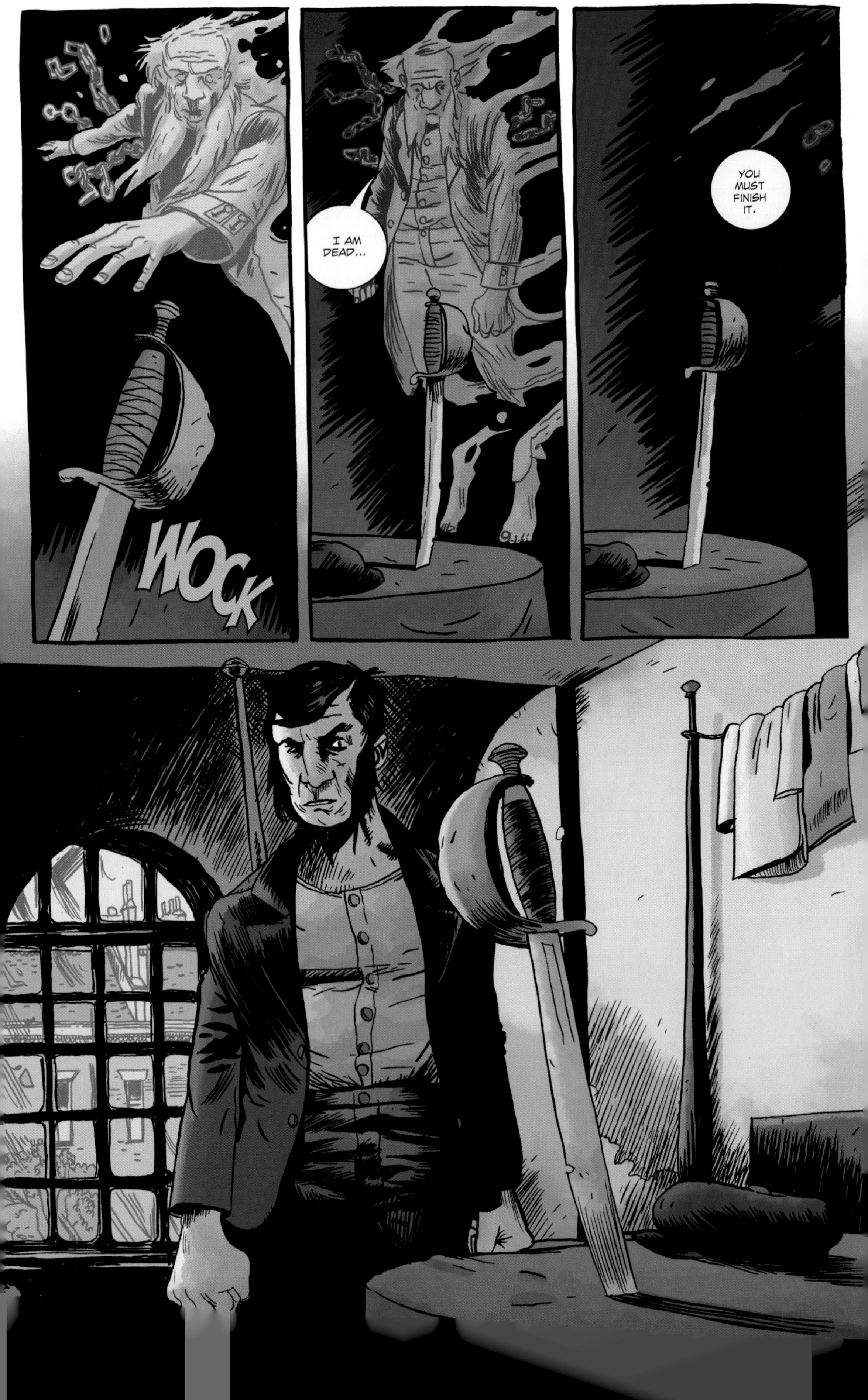

WOCK
I AM DEAD...
YOU MUST FINISH IT.

YEAH, I SEEN HER WHEN THEY BROUGHT HER IN LAST NIGHT...

TOOK HER STRAIGHT UP TO ONE OF THE CLOSED WARDS ON THE TOP FLOOR. AND ALL MORNING ALL SORTS OF FANCY GENTLEMEN HAVE BEEN GOING UP THERE.

THEY DON'T LET NO REGULAR PEOPLE ON THAT TOP FLOOR.

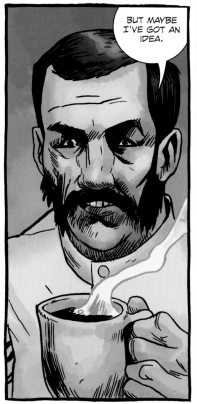

BUT MAYBE I'VE GOT AN IDEA.

JOE?

YEAH...

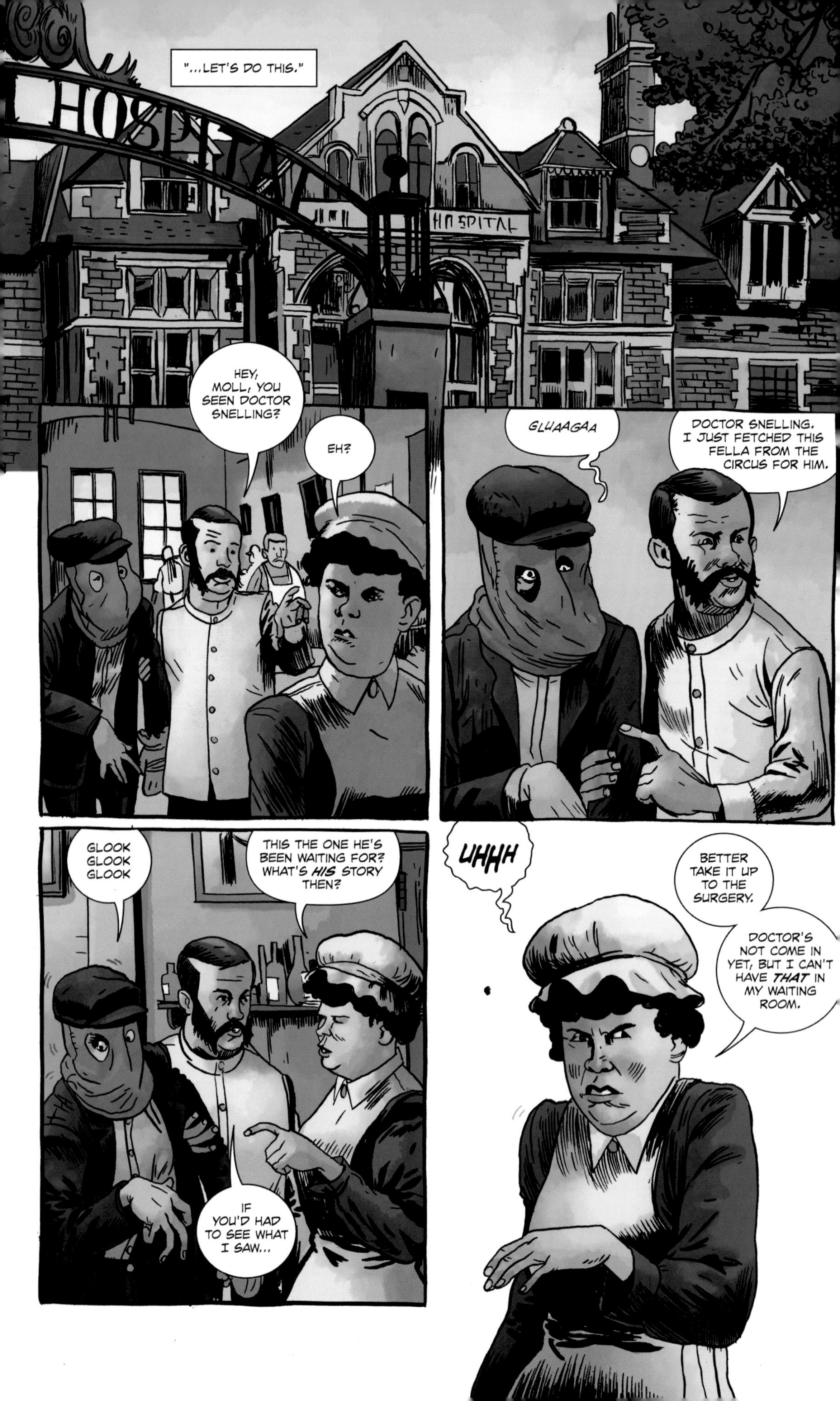
"...LET'S DO THIS."
HOSPITAL
HOSPITAL
HEY, MOLL, YOU SEEN DOCTOR SNELLING?
EH?
GLUAAGAA
DOCTOR SNELLING. I JUST FETCHED THIS FELLA FROM THE CIRCUS FOR HIM.
GLOOK GLOOK GLOOK
THIS THE ONE HE'S BEEN WAITING FOR? WHAT'S HIS STORY THEN?
IF YOU'D HAD TO SEE WHAT I SAW...
UHHH
BETTER TAKE IT UP TO THE SURGERY.
DOCTOR'S NOT COME IN YET, BUT I CAN'T HAVE THAT IN MY WAITING ROOM.

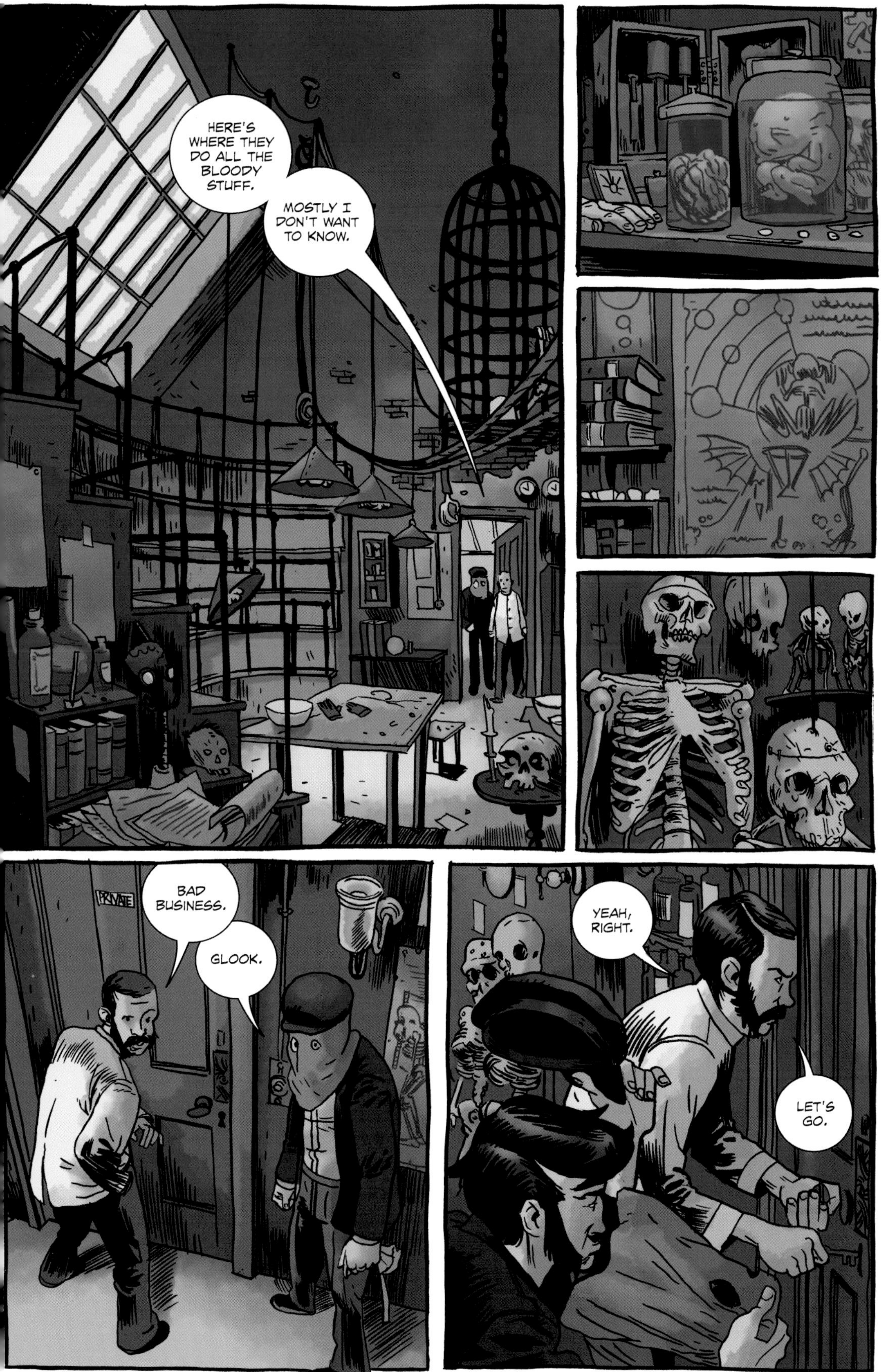
HERE'S WHERE THEY DO ALL THE BLOODY STUFF.
MOSTLY I DON'T WANT TO KNOW.
PRIVATE
BAD BUSINESS.
GLOOK.
YEAH, RIGHT.
LET'S GO.

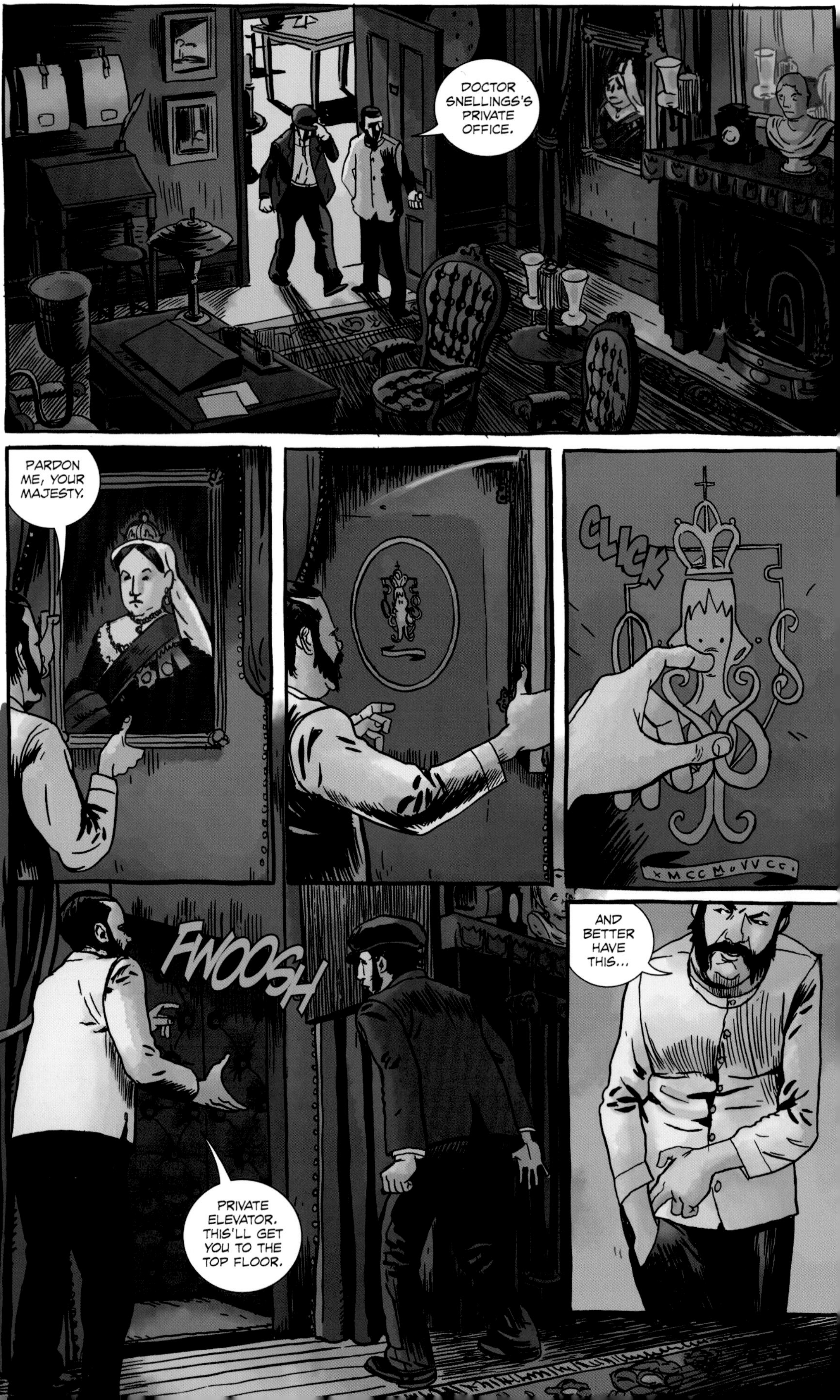
DOCTOR SNELLINGS'S PRIVATE OFFICE.
PARDON ME, YOUR MAJESTY.
CLICK
xMCCMoVVCC.
FWOOSH
PRIVATE ELEVATOR. THIS'LL GET YOU TO THE TOP FLOOR.
AND BETTER HAVE THIS...

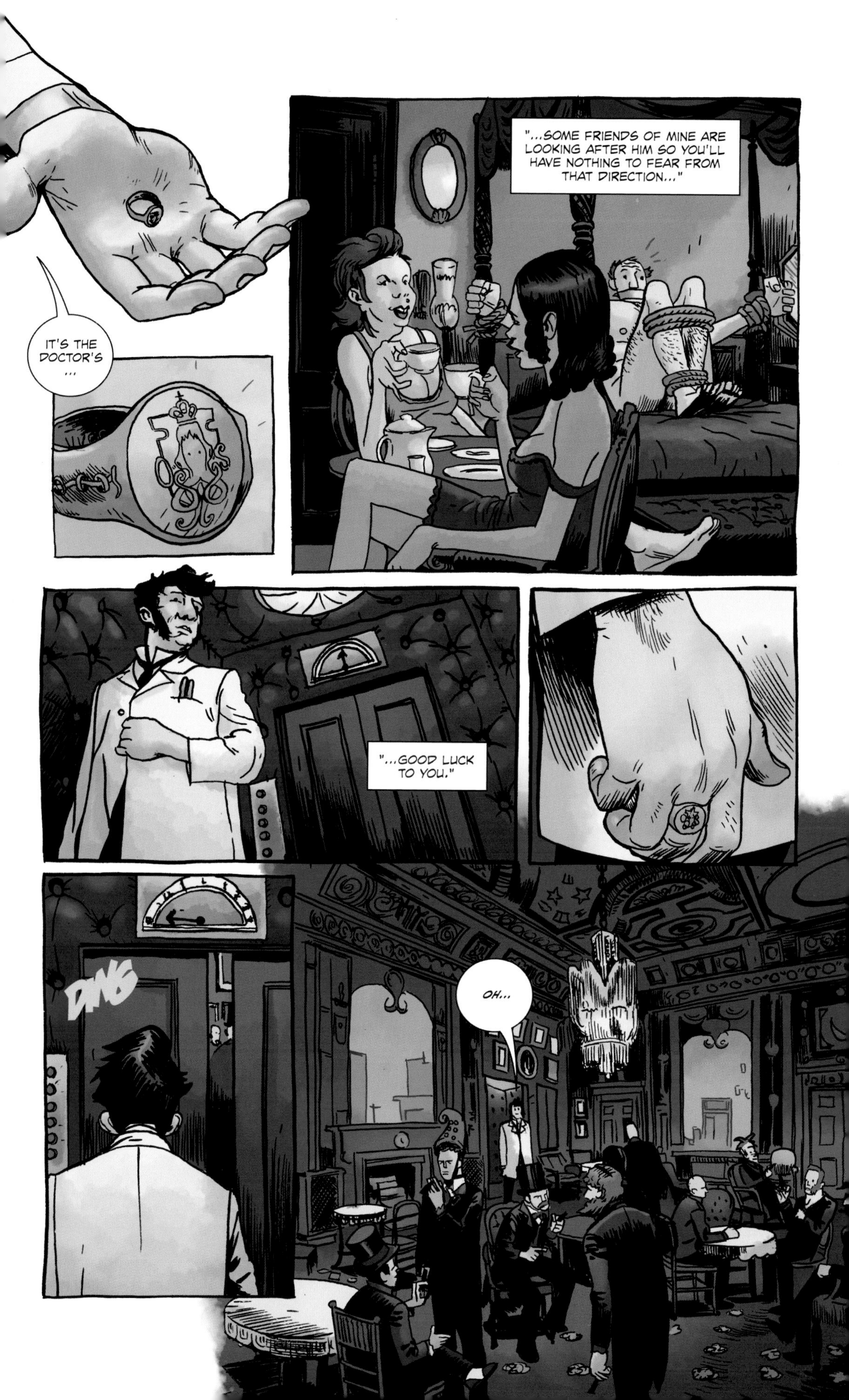
IT'S THE DOCTOR'S ...
"...SOME FRIENDS OF MINE ARE LOOKING AFTER HIM SO YOU'LL HAVE NOTHING TO FEAR FROM THAT DIRECTION..."
"...GOOD LUCK TO YOU."
DING
OH...

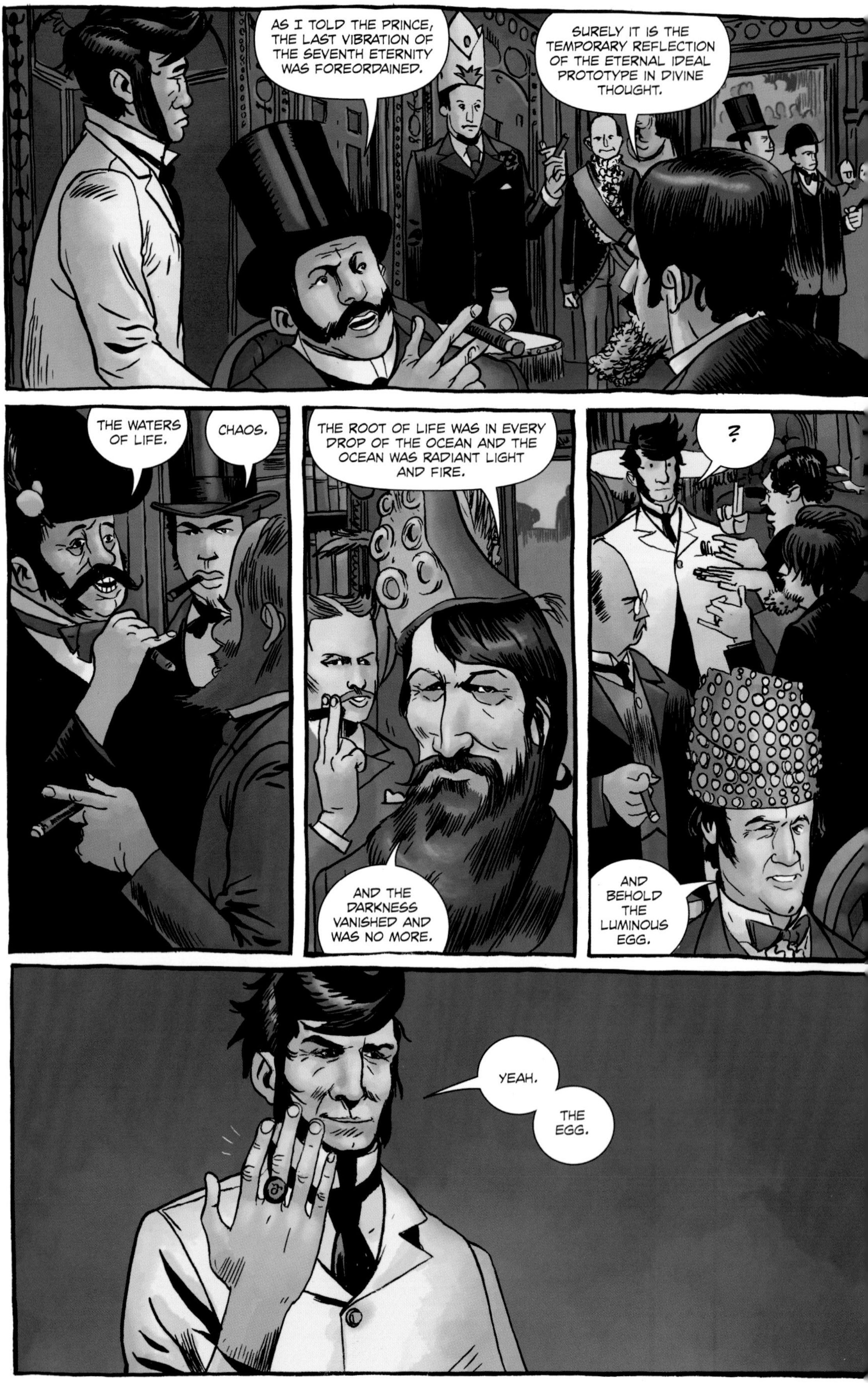
AS I TOLD THE PRINCE, THE LAST VIBRATION OF THE SEVENTH ETERNITY WAS FOREORDAINED.
SURELY IT IS THE TEMPORARY REFLECTION OF THE ETERNAL IDEAL PROTOTYPE IN DIVINE THOUGHT.
THE WATERS OF LIFE.
CHAOS.
THE ROOT OF LIFE WAS IN EVERY DROP OF THE OCEAN AND THE OCEAN WAS RADIANT LIGHT AND FIRE.
AND THE DARKNESS VANISHED AND WAS NO MORE.
?
AND BEHOLD THE LUMINOUS EGG.
YEAH.
THE EGG.

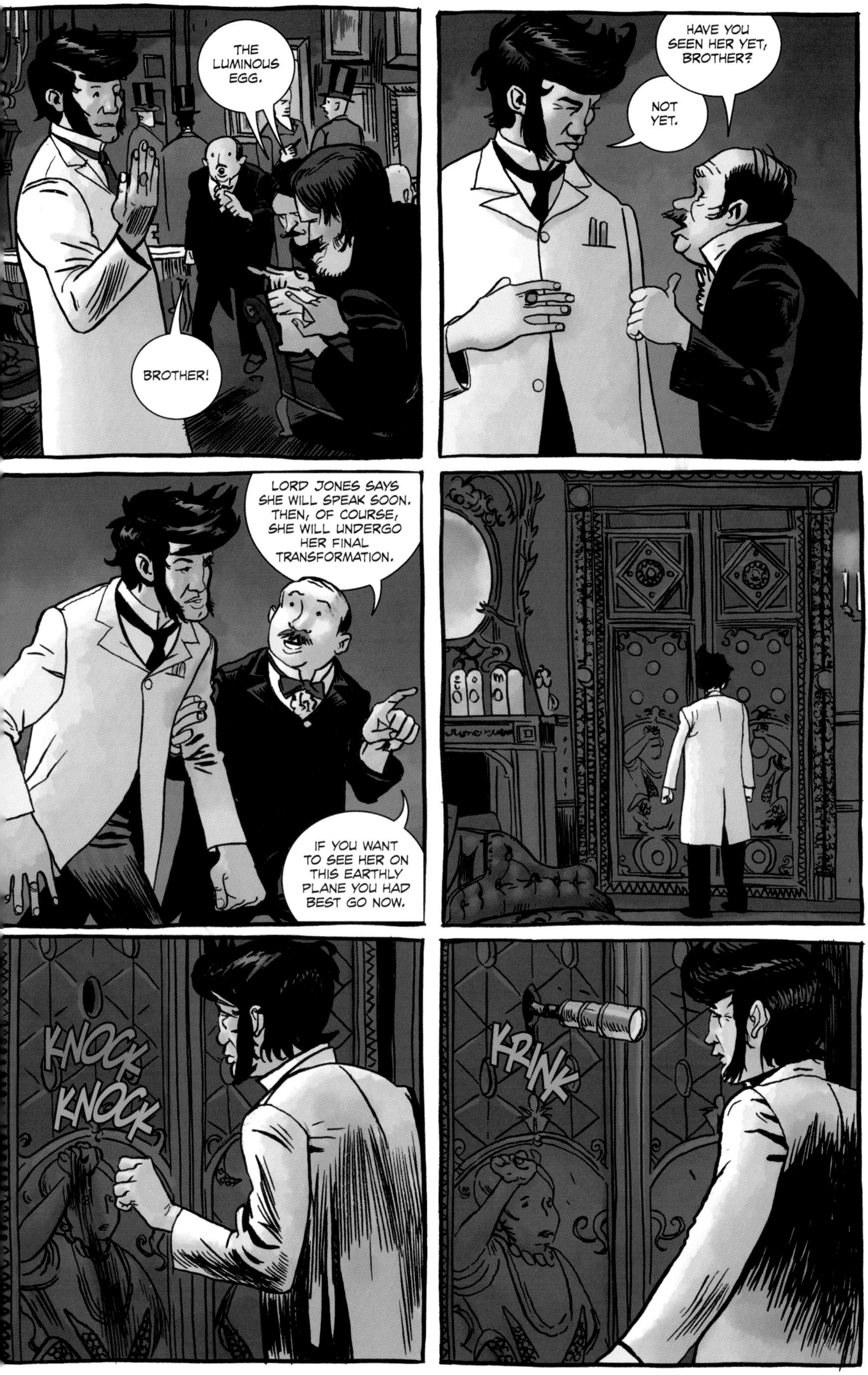
THE LUMINOUS EGG.
BROTHER!
HAVE YOU SEEN HER YET, BROTHER?
NOT YET.
LORD JONES SAYS SHE WILL SPEAK SOON. THEN, OF COURSE, SHE WILL UNDERGO HER FINAL TRANSFORMATION.
IF YOU WANT TO SEE HER ON THIS EARTHLY PLANE YOU HAD BEST GO NOW.
KNOCK KNOCK
KRINK

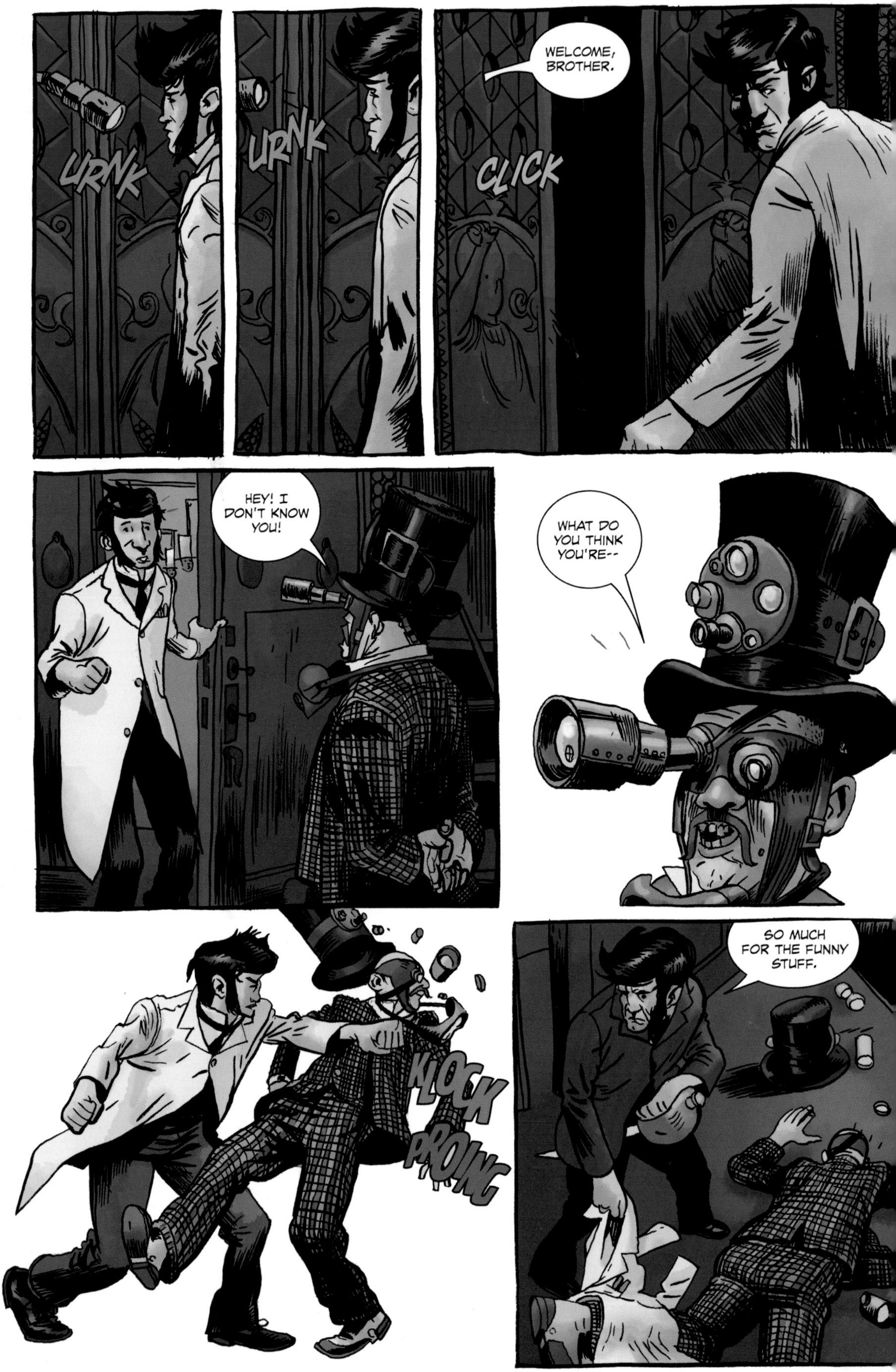
URNK
URNK
WELCOME, BROTHER.
CLICK
HEY! I DON'T KNOW YOU!
WHAT DO YOU THINK YOU'RE--
KLOCK
PROING
SO MUCH FOR THE FUNNY STUFF.

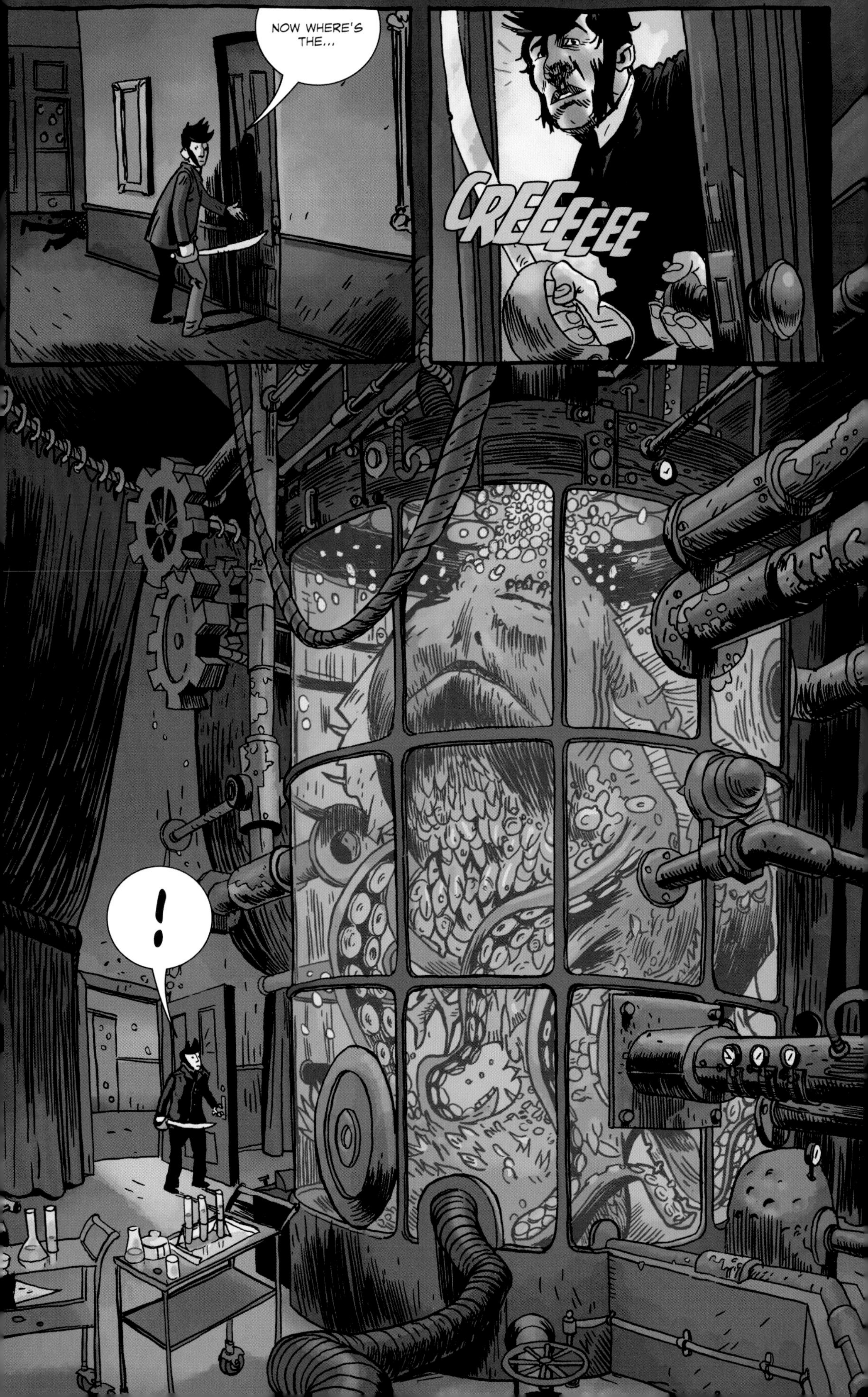
NOW WHERE'S THE...
CREEEEEEE
!

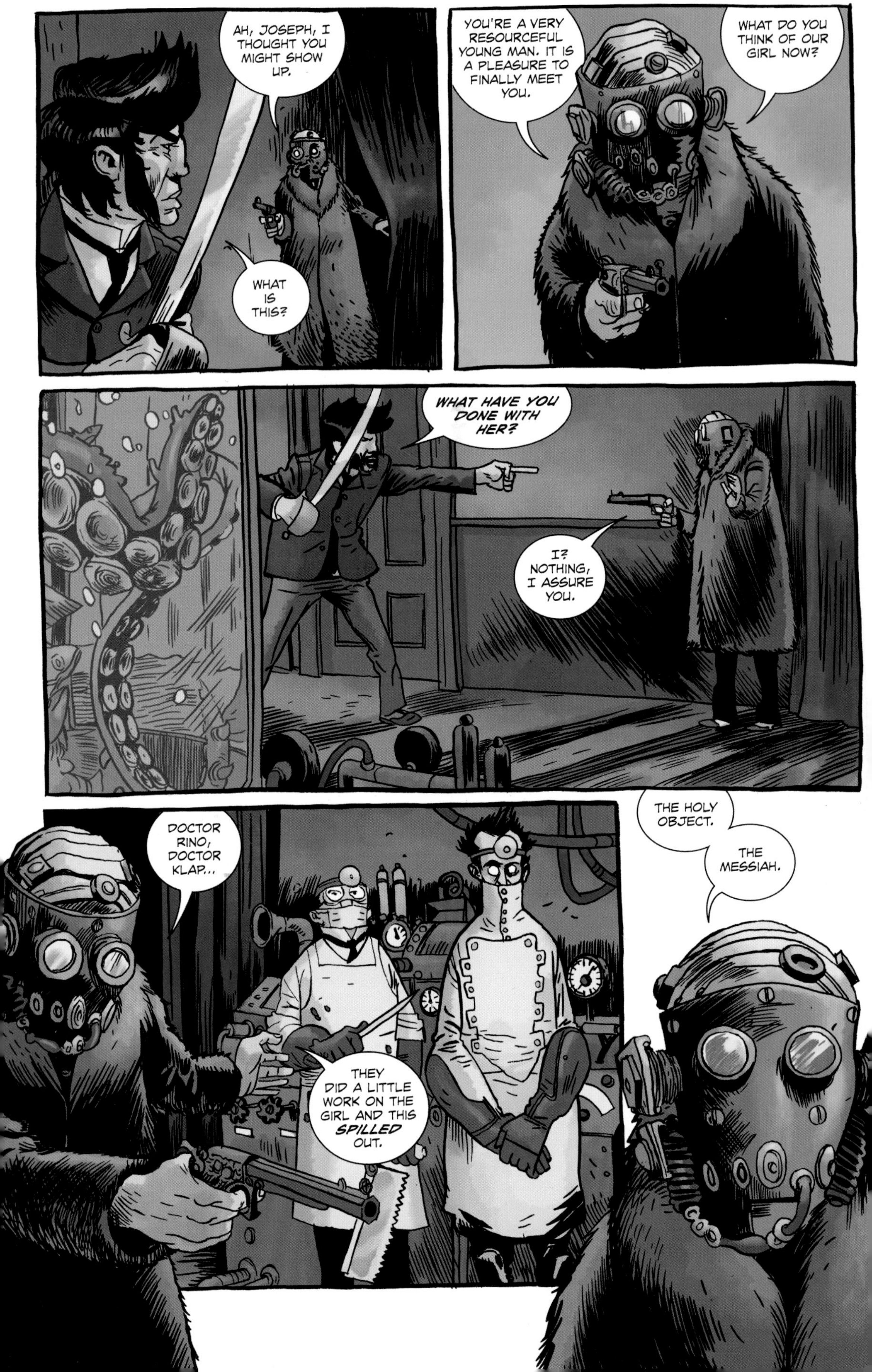
AH, JOSEPH, I THOUGHT YOU MIGHT SHOW UP.
WHAT IS THIS?
YOU'RE A VERY RESOURCEFUL YOUNG MAN. IT IS A PLEASURE TO FINALLY MEET YOU.
WHAT DO YOU THINK OF OUR GIRL NOW?
WHAT HAVE YOU DONE WITH HER?
I? NOTHING, I ASSURE YOU.
DOCTOR RINO, DOCTOR KLAP...
THEY DID A LITTLE WORK ON THE GIRL AND THIS SPILLED OUT.
THE HOLY OBJECT.
THE MESSIAH.

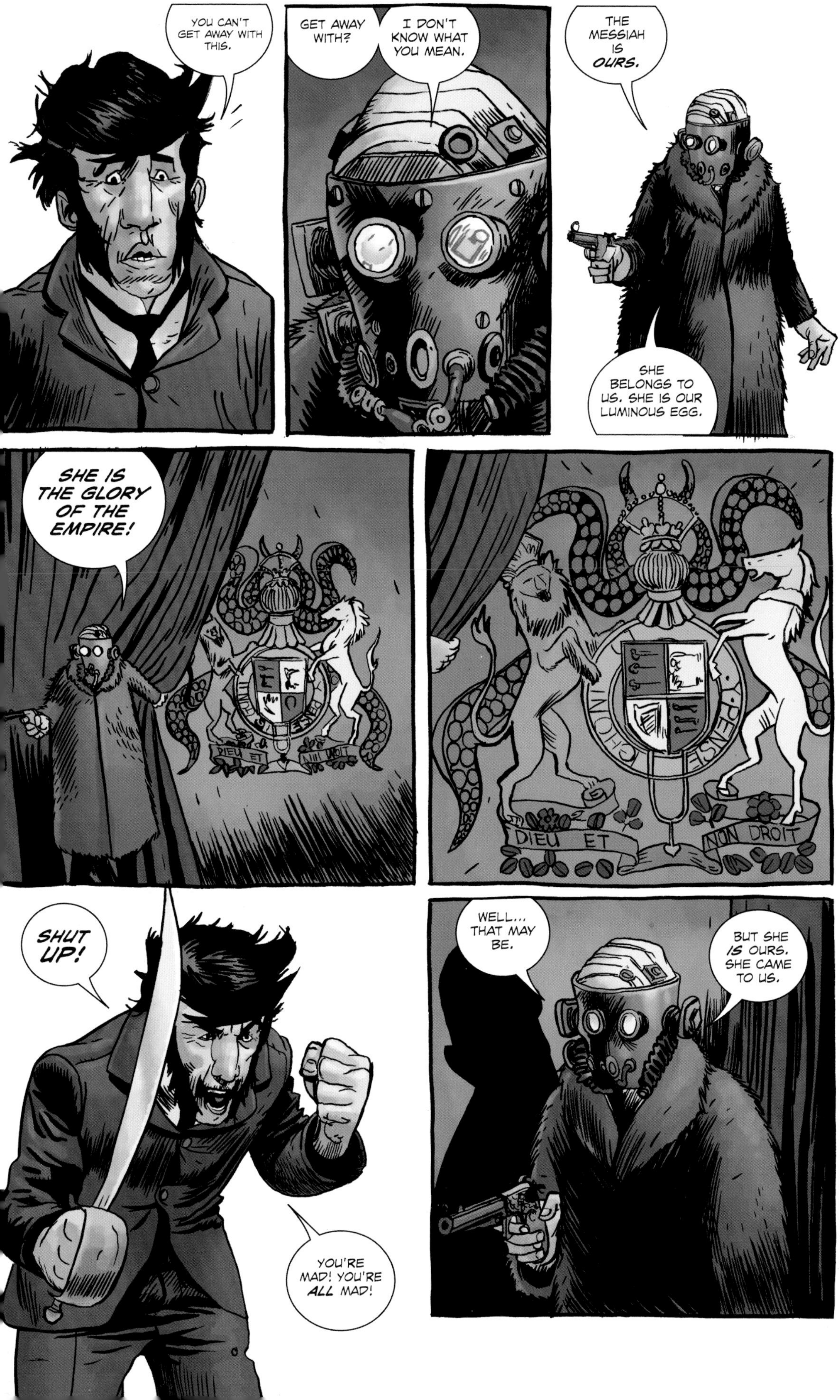

YOU CAN'T GET AWAY WITH THIS.
GET AWAY WITH?
I DON'T KNOW WHAT YOU MEAN.
THE MESSIAH IS *OURS.*
SHE BELONGS TO US. SHE IS OUR LUMINOUS EGG.
SHE IS THE GLORY OF THE EMPIRE!
DIEU ET MON DROIT
DIEU ET NON DROIT
SHUT UP!
YOU'RE MAD! YOU'RE *ALL* MAD!
WELL... THAT MAY BE.
BUT SHE *IS* OURS. SHE CAME TO US.

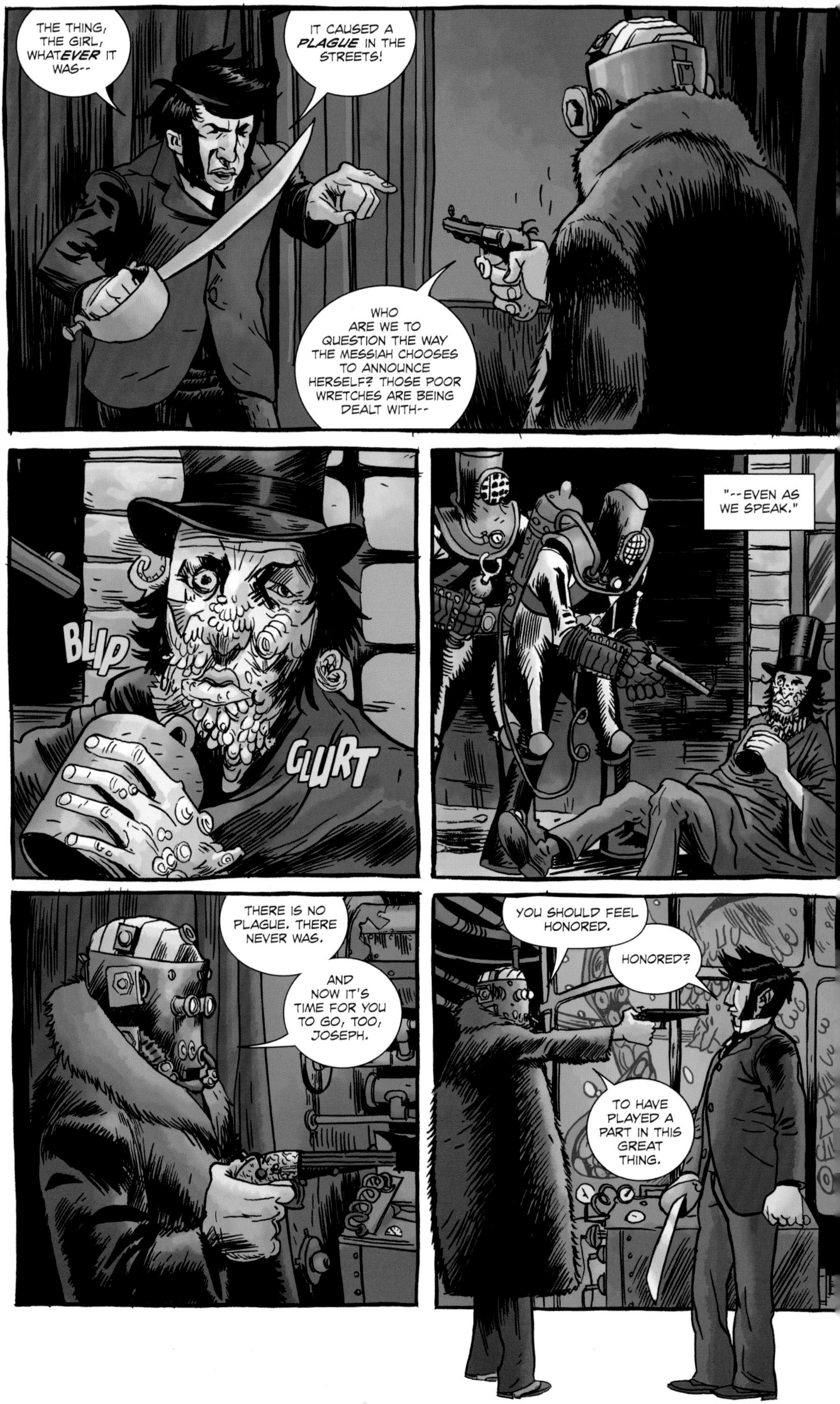
THE THING, THE GIRL, WHATEVER IT WAS--
IT CAUSED A PLAGUE IN THE STREETS!
WHO ARE WE TO QUESTION THE WAY THE MESSIAH CHOOSES TO ANNOUNCE HERSELF? THOSE POOR WRETCHES ARE BEING DEALT WITH--
BLIP
GLURT
"--EVEN AS WE SPEAK."
THERE IS NO PLAGUE. THERE NEVER WAS.
AND NOW IT'S TIME FOR YOU TO GO, TOO, JOSEPH.
YOU SHOULD FEEL HONORED.
HONORED?
TO HAVE PLAYED A PART IN THIS GREAT THING.

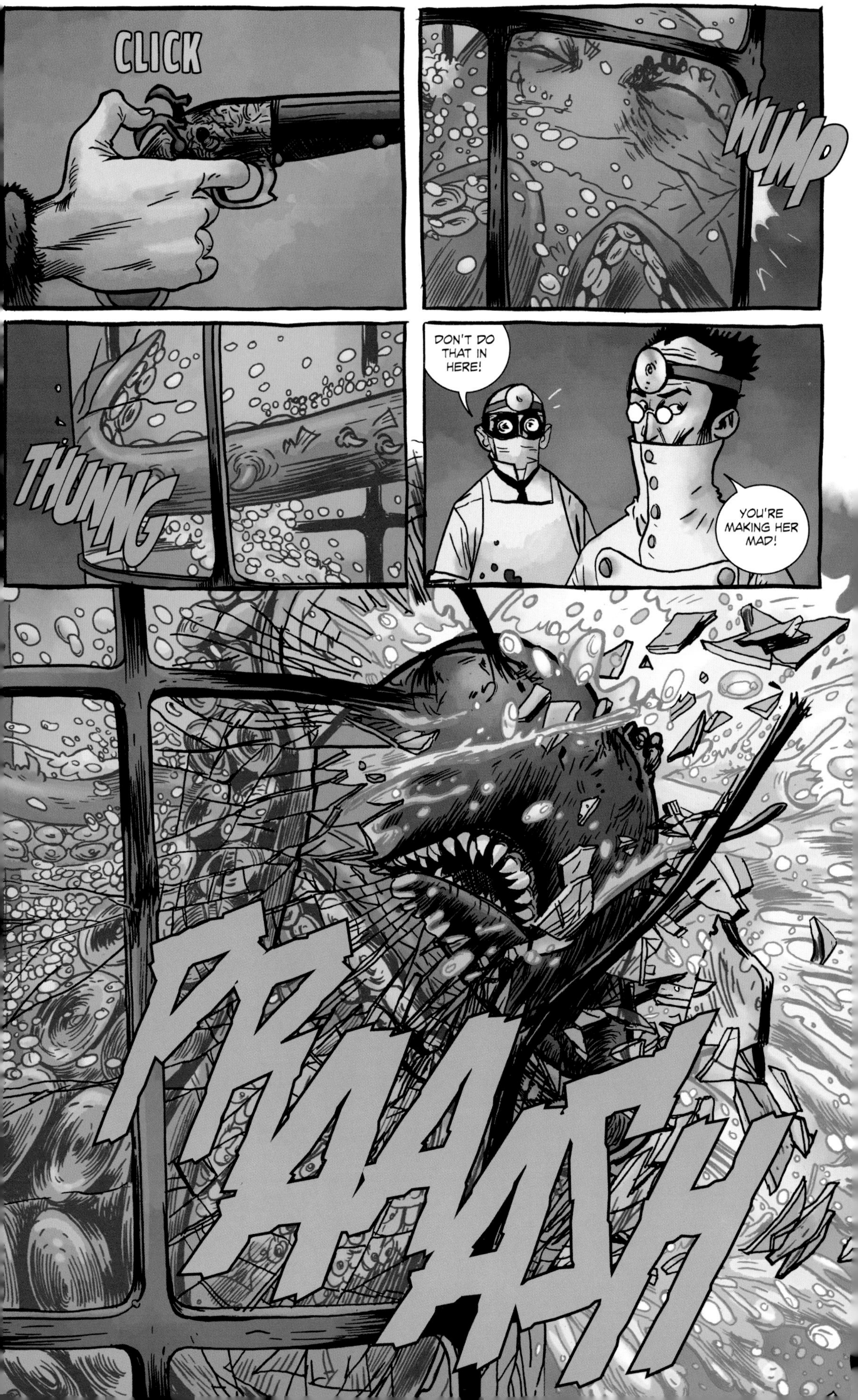
CLICK
WUMP
THUNNG
DON'T DO THAT IN HERE!
YOU'RE MAKING HER MAD!
KRAAASH

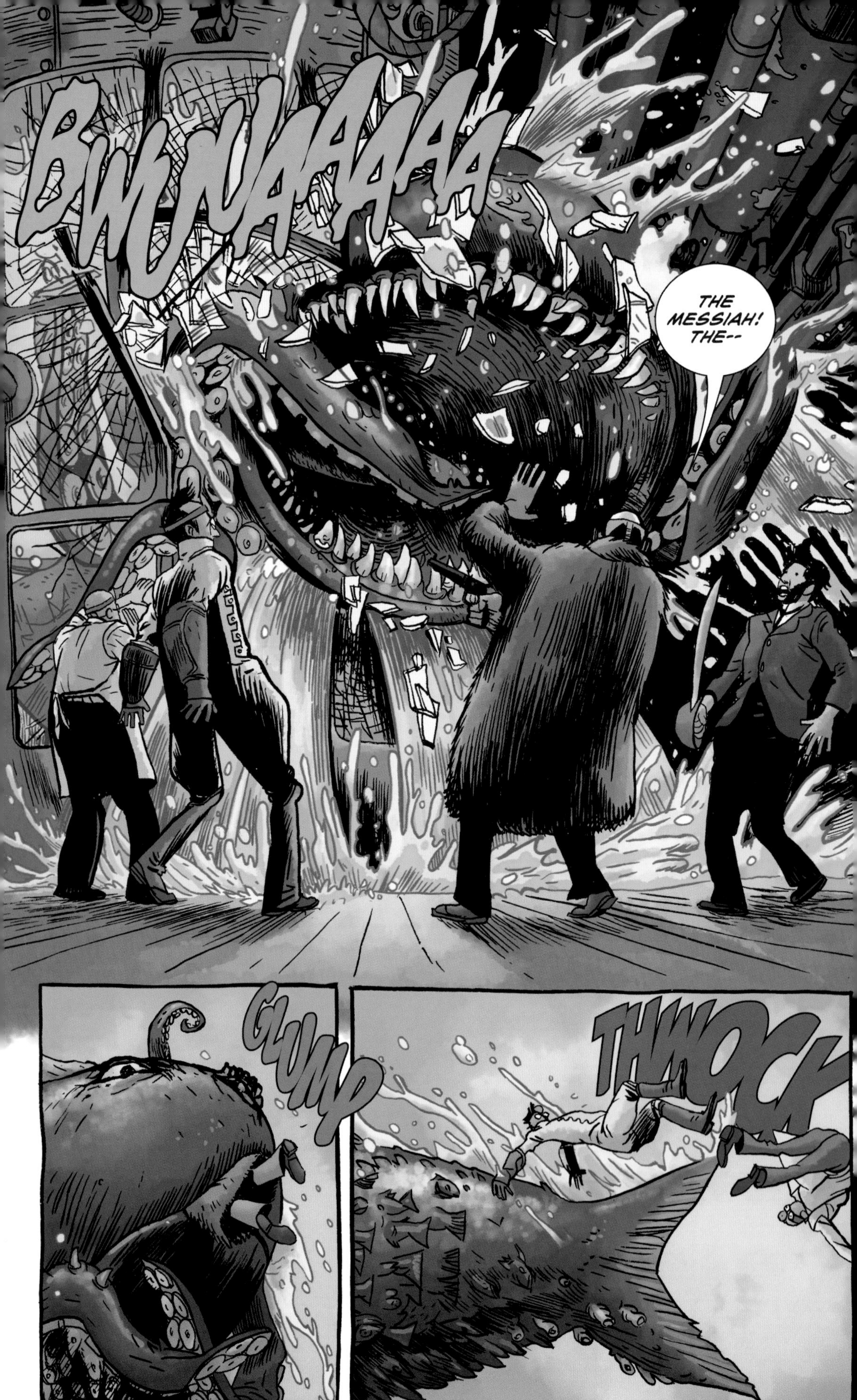
BWUAAAAA
THE MESSIAH! THE--
GLUMP
THWOCK

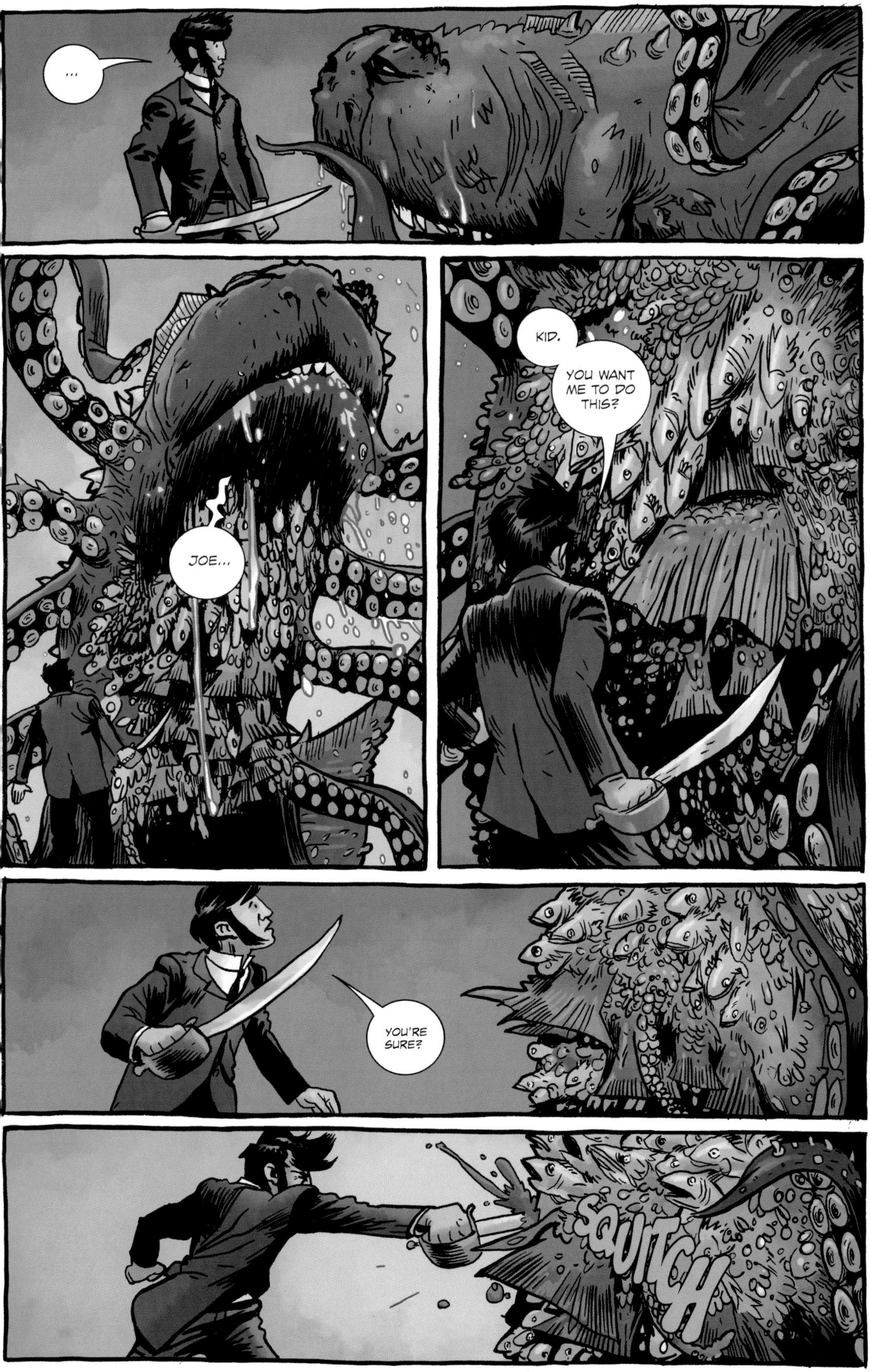
...
JOE...
KID.
YOU WANT ME TO DO THIS?
YOU'RE SURE?
SQUITCH

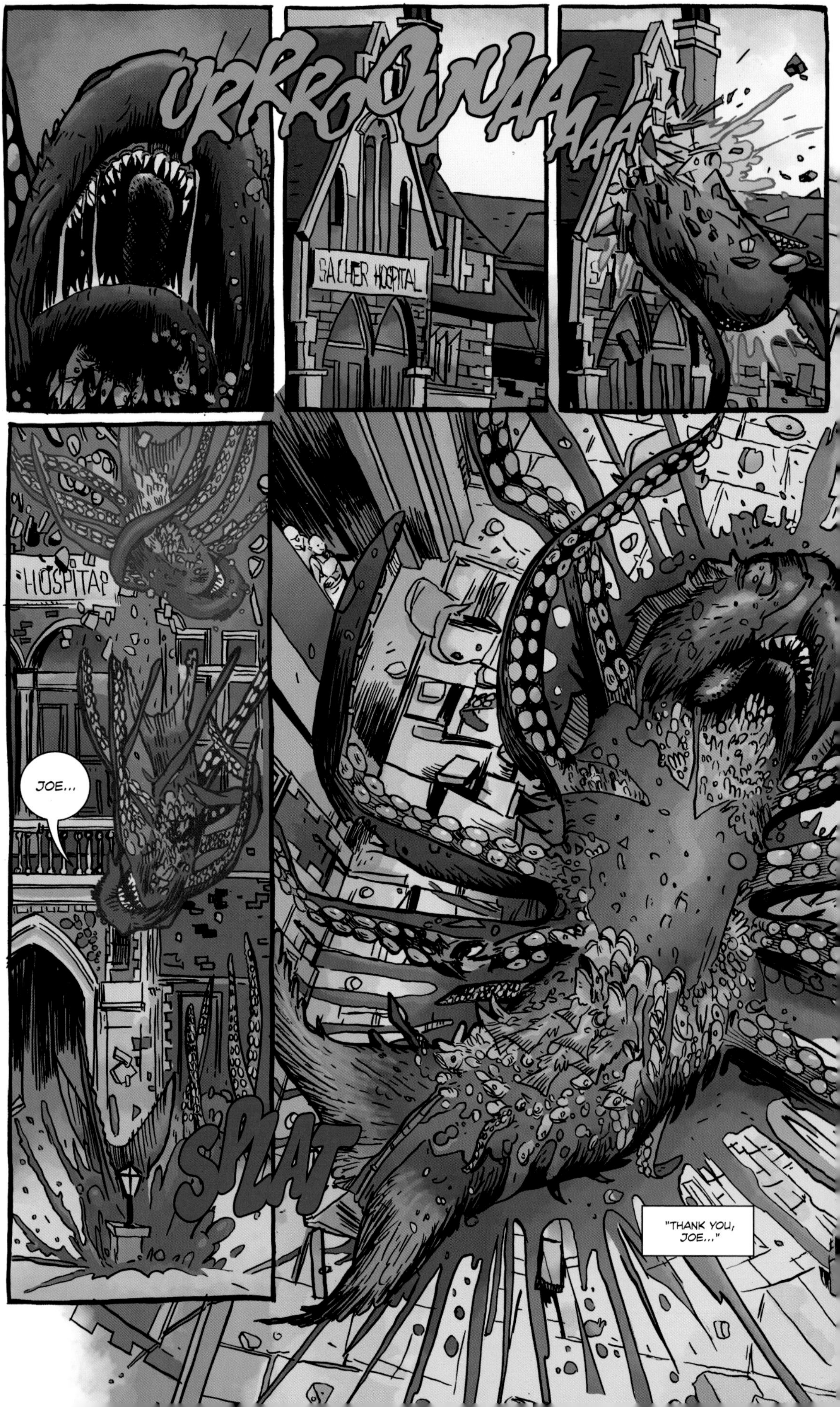
URRROOUUAAAAAA
SACHER HOSPITAL
HOSPITAL
JOE...
SPLAT
"THANK YOU, JOE..."

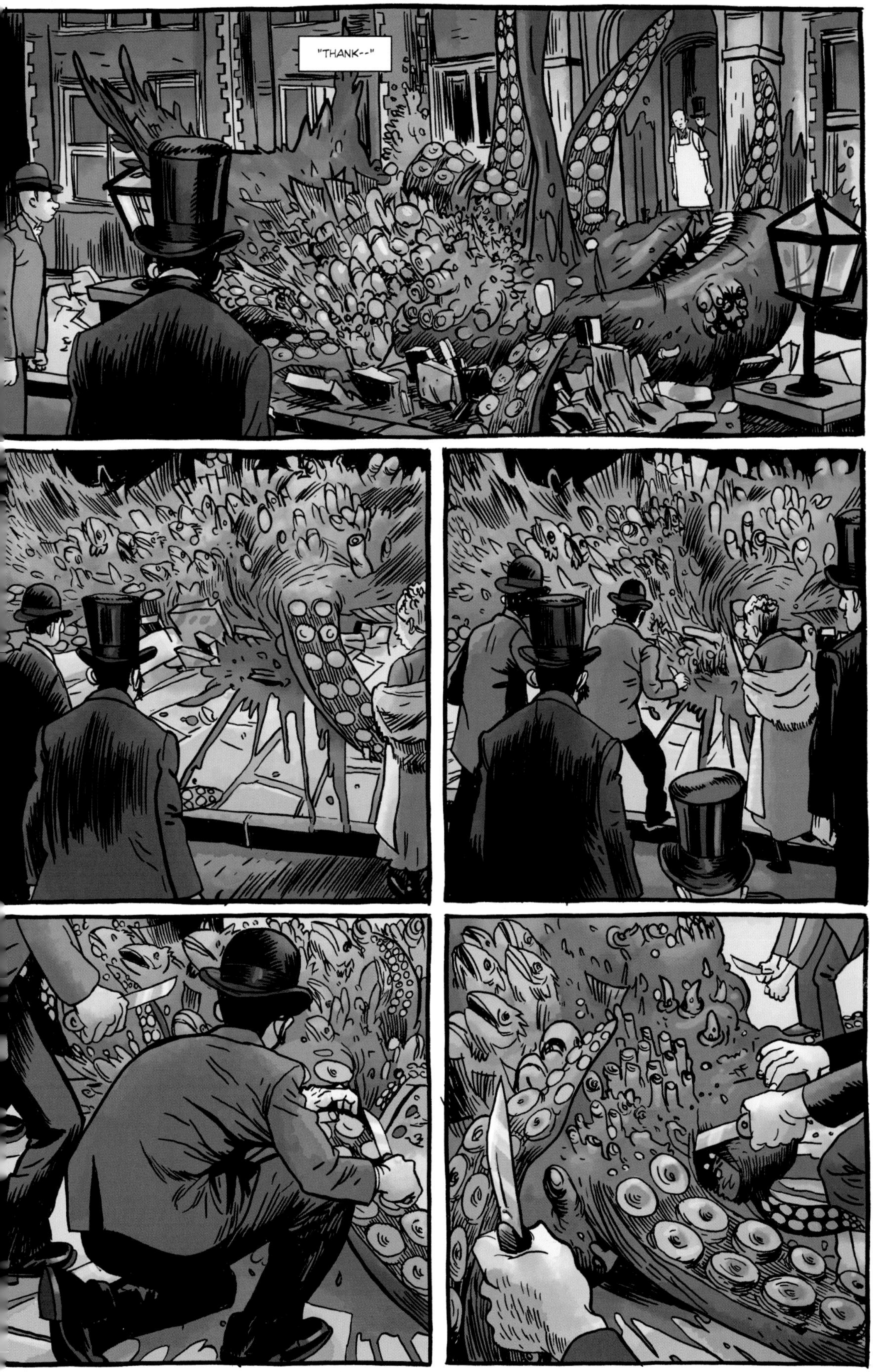
"THANK--"

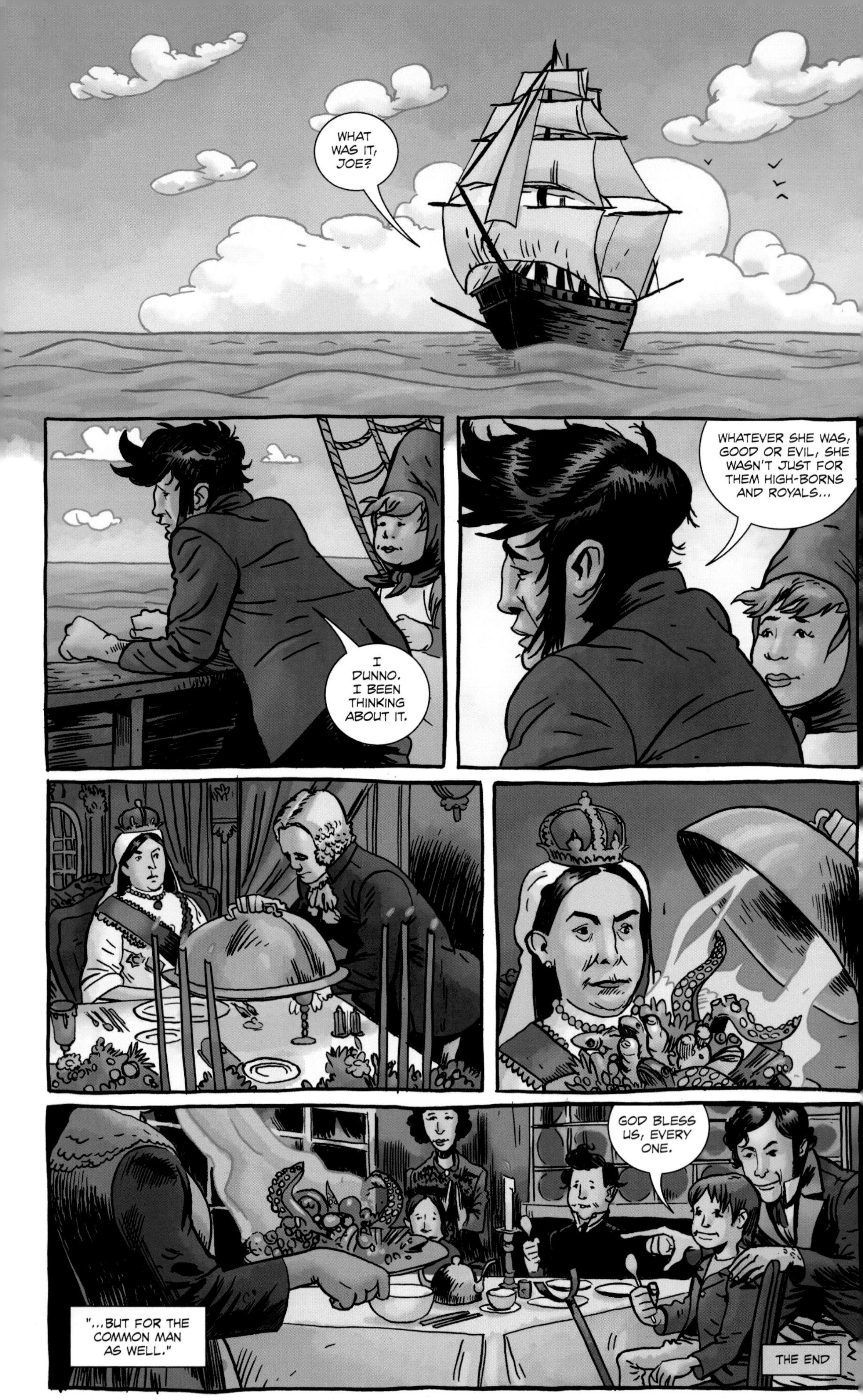

WHAT WAS IT, JOE?
I DUNNO. I BEEN THINKING ABOUT IT.
WHATEVER SHE WAS, GOOD OR EVIL, SHE WASN'T JUST FOR THEM HIGH-BORNS AND ROYALS...
"...BUT FOR THE COMMON MAN AS WELL."
GOD BLESS US, EVERY ONE.
THE END

JENNY FINN

SKETCHBOOK
Notes by Troy Nixey

Where do I begin with a project that's had so many lives? How about with color? *Jenny Finn* was always intended to end up in color. True story, no word of a lie. Some have brazenly scoffed at the suggestion, manners be damned, but it's true! From the beginning *Jenny Finn* was meant to be collected in color. The reasons it didn't happen all those years ago aren't important; what is important is you're holding the book as it was meant to be, and I couldn't be happier. Seeing Dave Stewart's work on the series is like experiencing it for the first time again, but nearly twenty years after it was created.

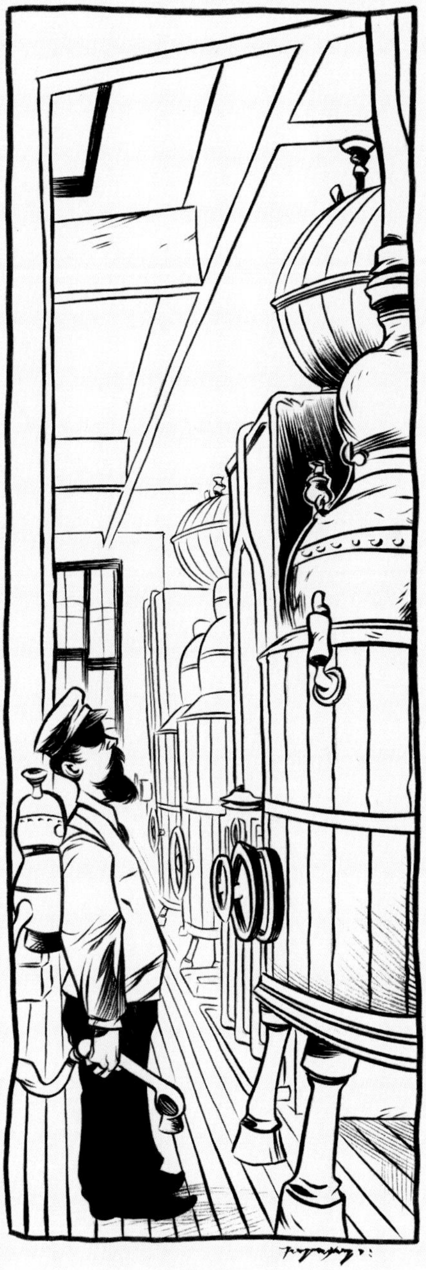

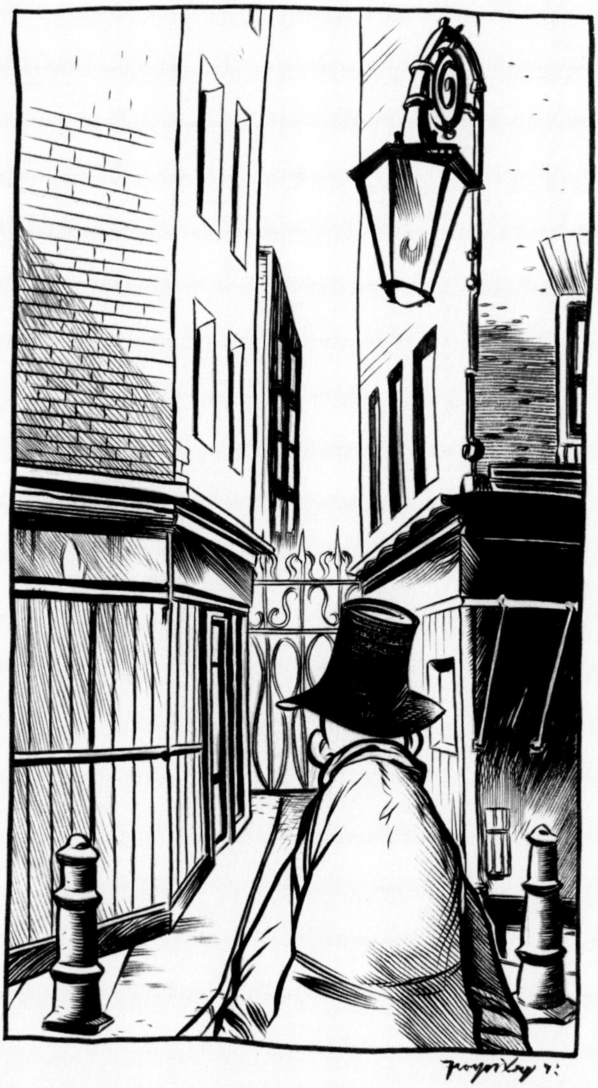

The creation of *Jenny* is an exciting tale—well, for me anyway. Mike has always
been a huge inspiration; his mug belongs on the Mount Rushmore of comics
along with Herge, Kirby, Eisner, and Moebius. So you could have knocked me
over with a feather when Mike agreed to collaborate on a project. He asked what
I wanted to draw and the answer to that is contained in this here extras section.
Instead of a simple response, I filled a sketchbook of some of the weirdest images
I could think of. Clearly there was a Victorian theme throughout; I was obsessed
with drawing anything from that time period in the late 90s and early 2000s . . .
who am I fooling, I'm still obsessed with drawing antiquities, old architecture,
ill-fitting wool suits, heavy dresses, and of course adding monsters to the mix.
That pretty much sums up what you see here. I mailed the sketchbook full of
drawings to Mike. I have never been more worried about art in the mail. Hahaha.
Mike went to work streamlining the menagerie of monstrosity that lived within
the coil-bound sketchbook, and what came out of it was the nucleus for *Jenny*.
At this point I was still very susceptible to feathers and being knocked down. But
there was work to be done and much black ink to be laid down.

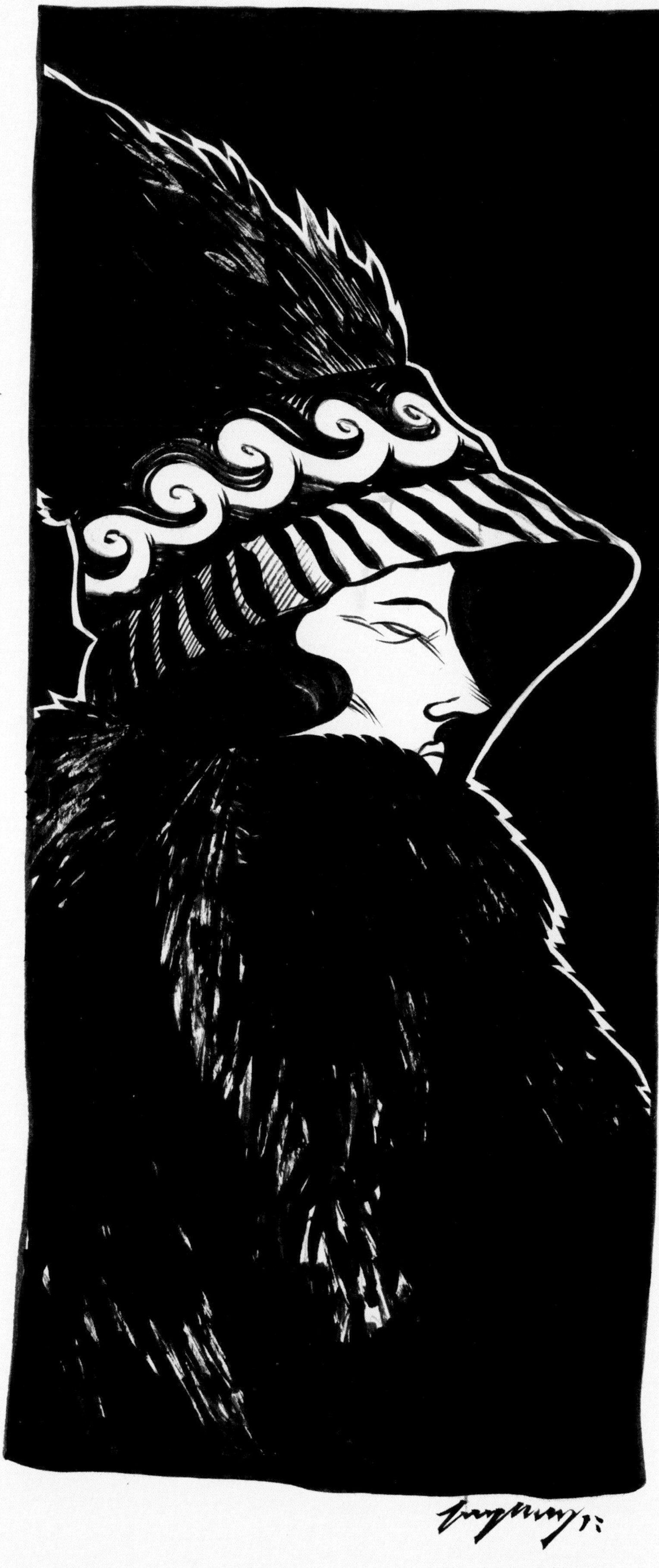

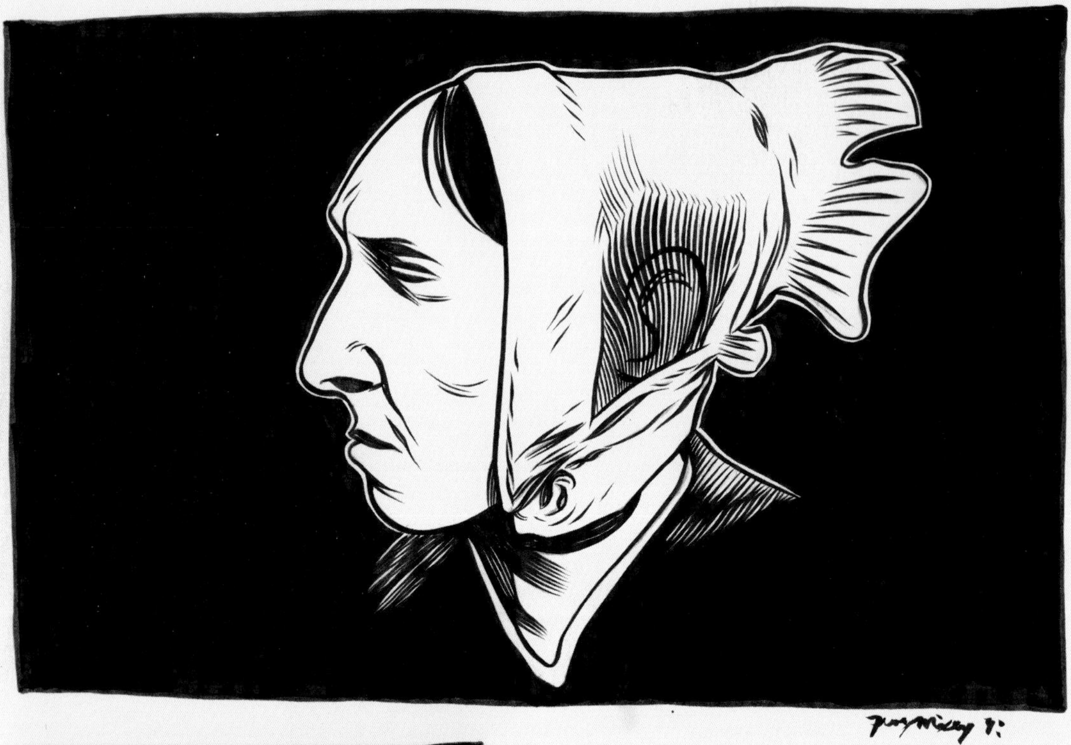

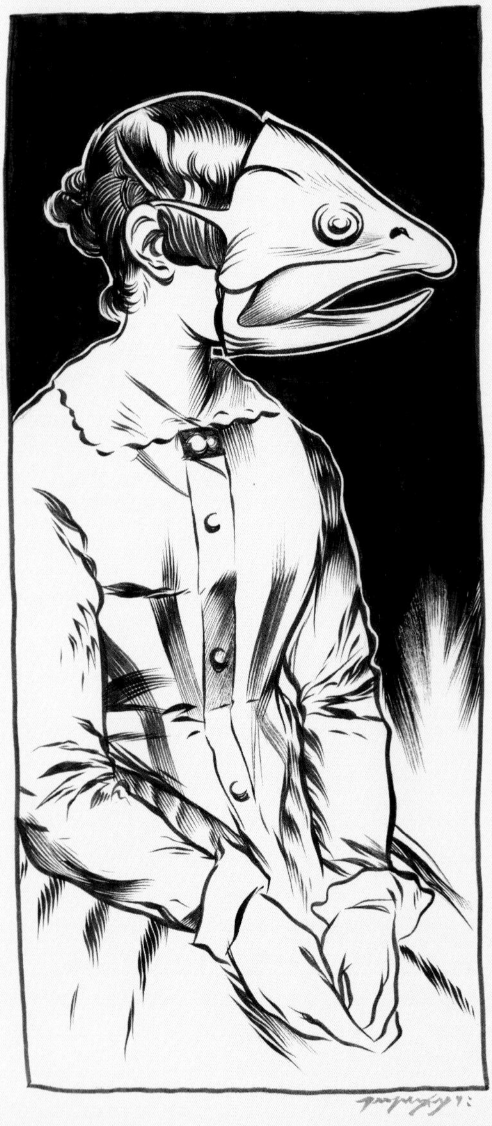

Mike is a wonderful collaborator. He's very open to the sharing of ideas, with the best idea winning even if it isn't his. It's all about the story. An invaluable lesson. I learned a lot working with Mike on *Jenny*. I also learned that I obsess over lines. Holy moly! I used to maintain a death grip on those poor Winsor & Newton series seven, size zero brushes! There were a few ups and downs along the way, but I'm really proud of this miniseries even though I didn't draw the fourth issue (that's the down I mentioned). I'll save that tale for another day, but I want to thank Farel for swooping in and saving the day. He did a tremendous job and I'll always appreciate how he and Mike carried *Jenny* to the finish line.

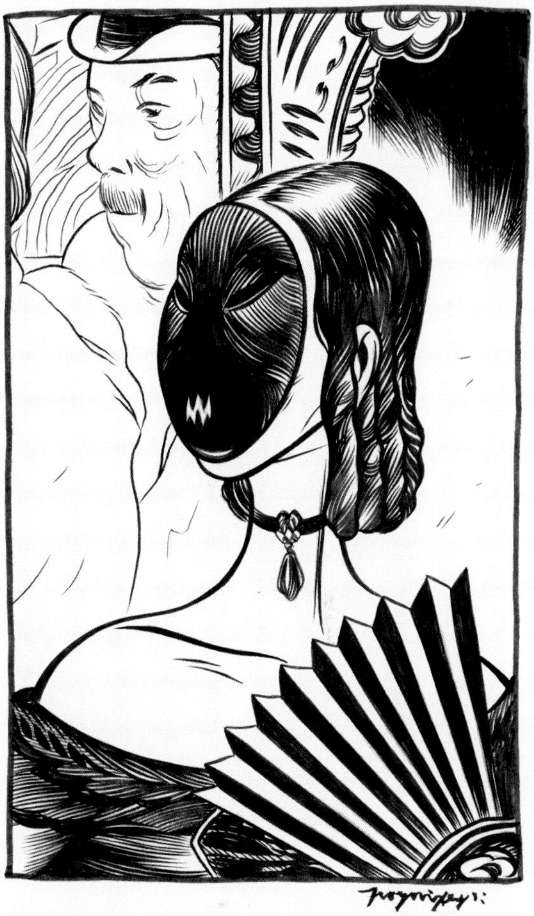

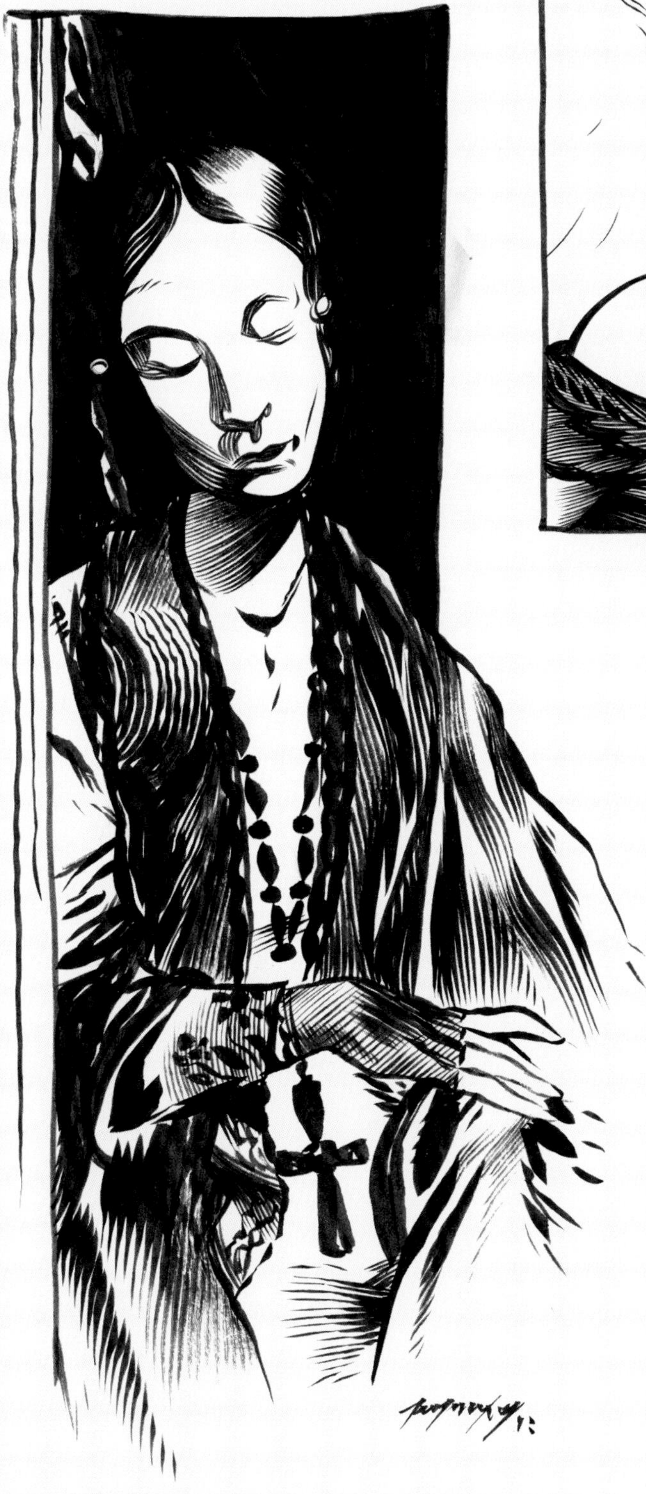

It's fun seeing how many of the drawings from the sketchbook made it as ideas in the series. The Prime Minister, for instance, was used exactly how I drew him. Of course, he was just a weirdo Victorian with a helmet when I created him; it was Mike's genius to make him the PM. There are few designs that didn't make it into *JF*. Perhaps a sequel? Hahahaha . . . just kidding. Seriously though, thanks everyone; I hope you enjoyed the book as it was always meant to be, in color. I know I do.

From somewhere in Canada,
Troy

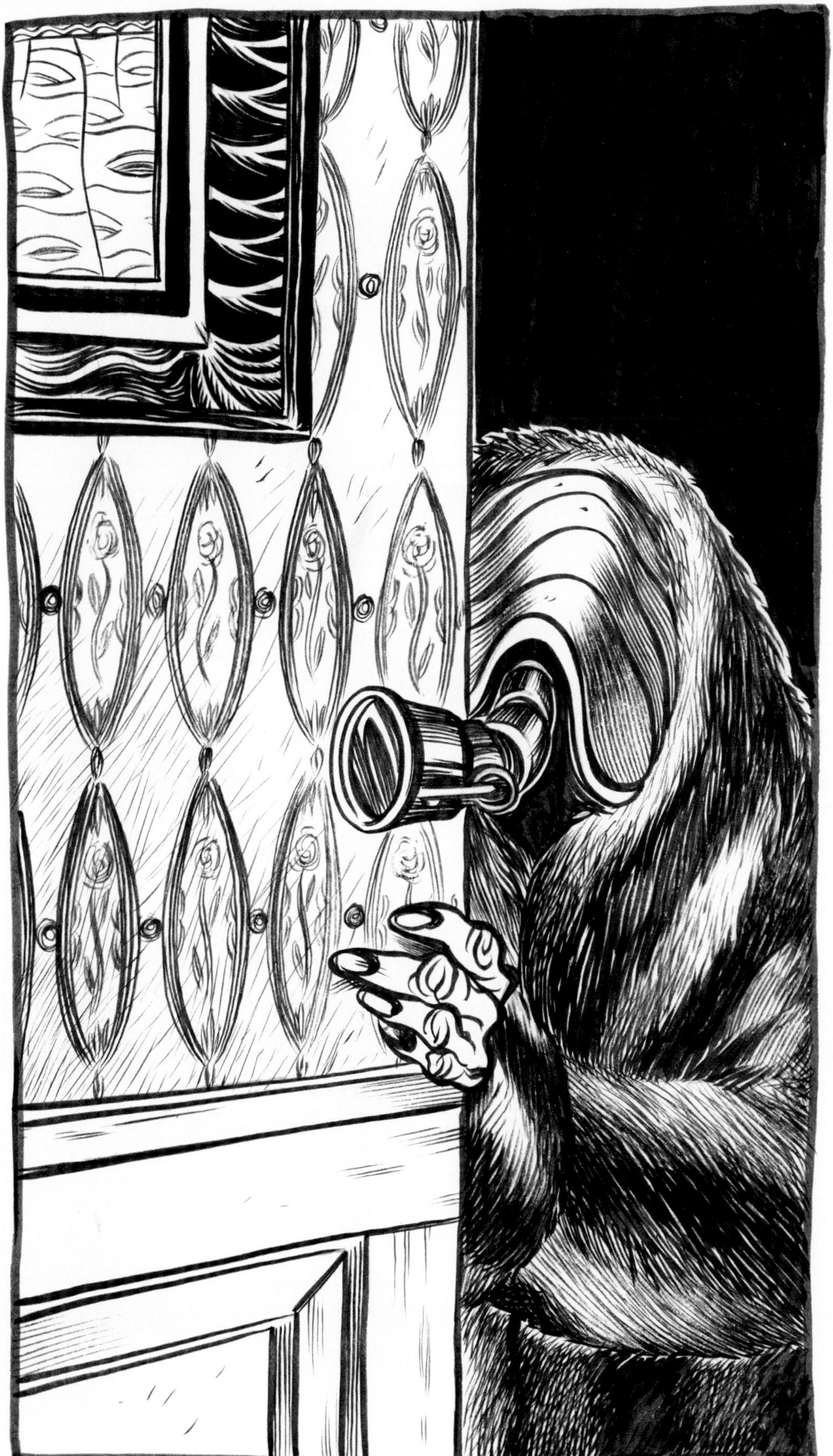

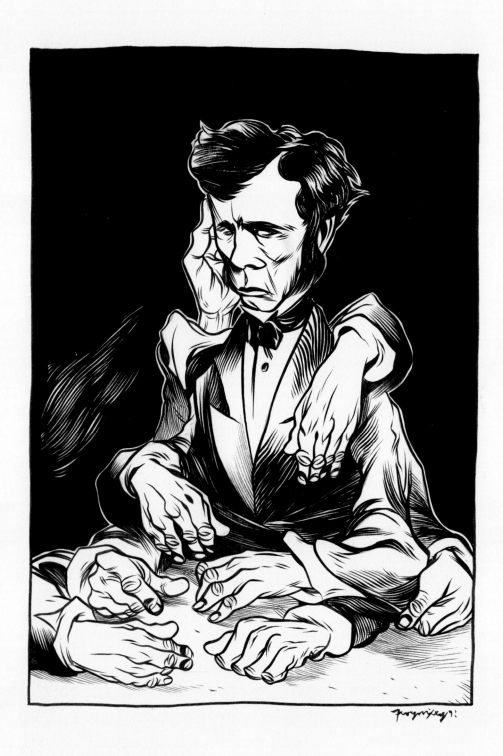

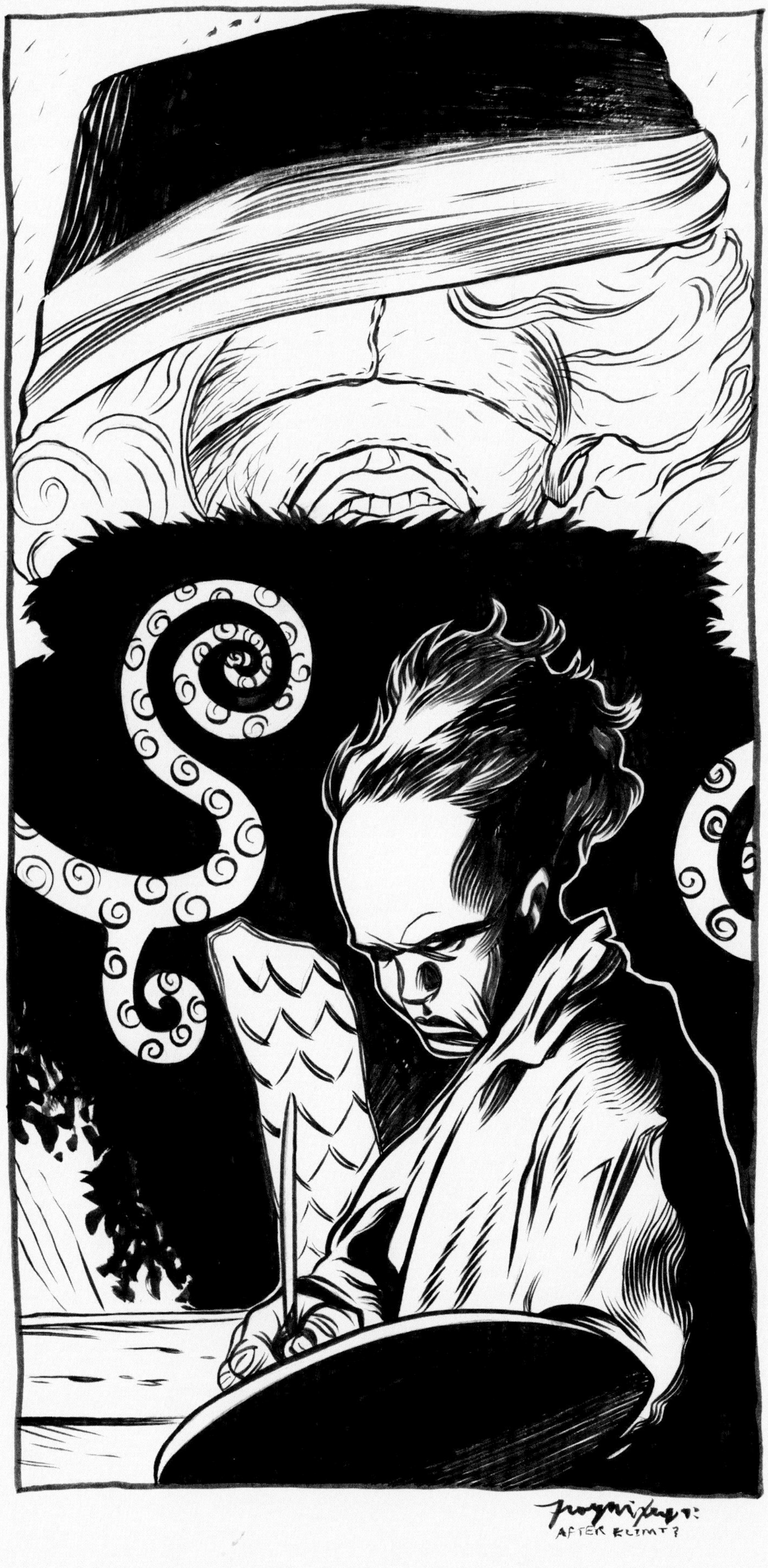
AFTER KLIMT?

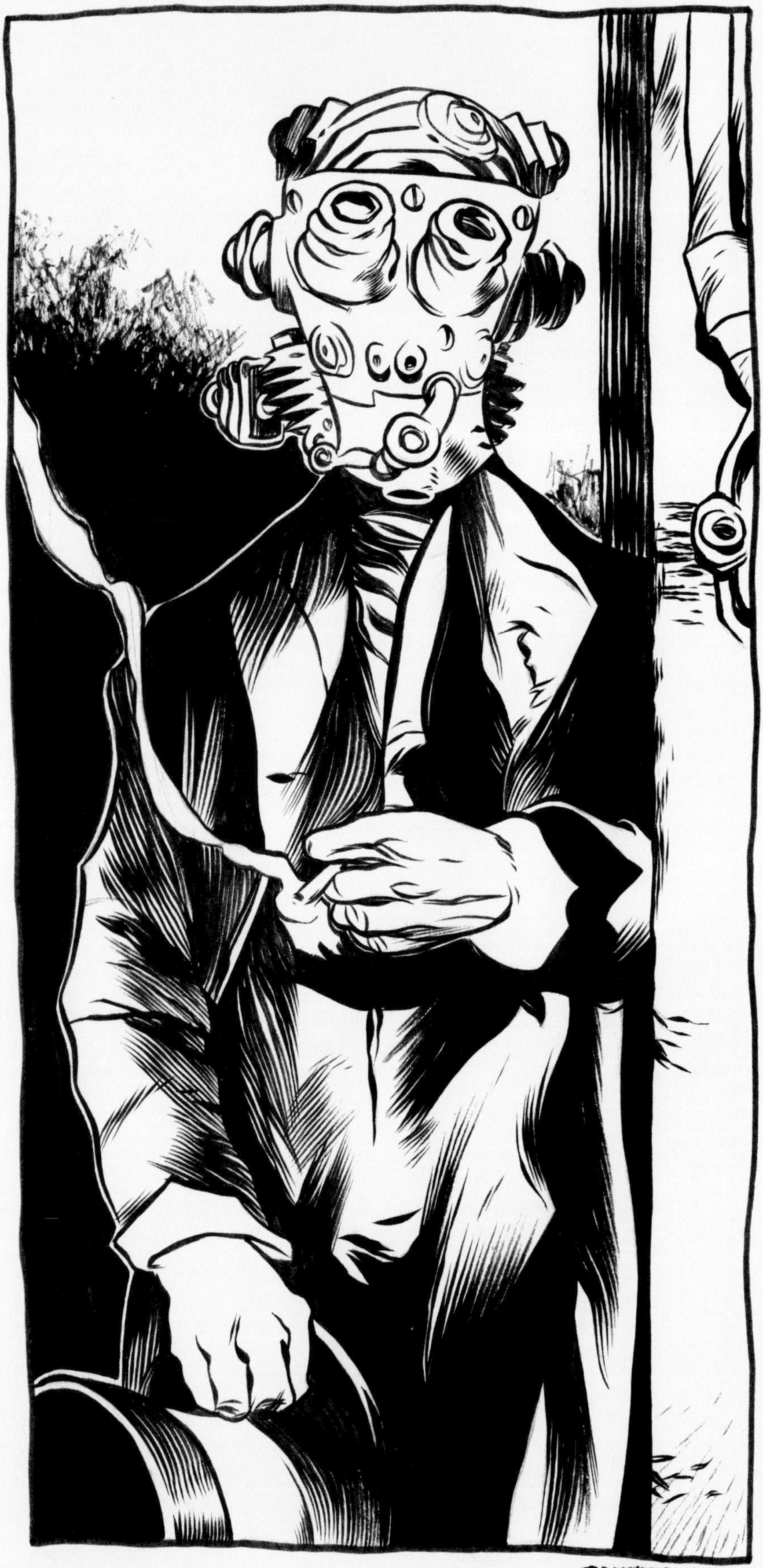

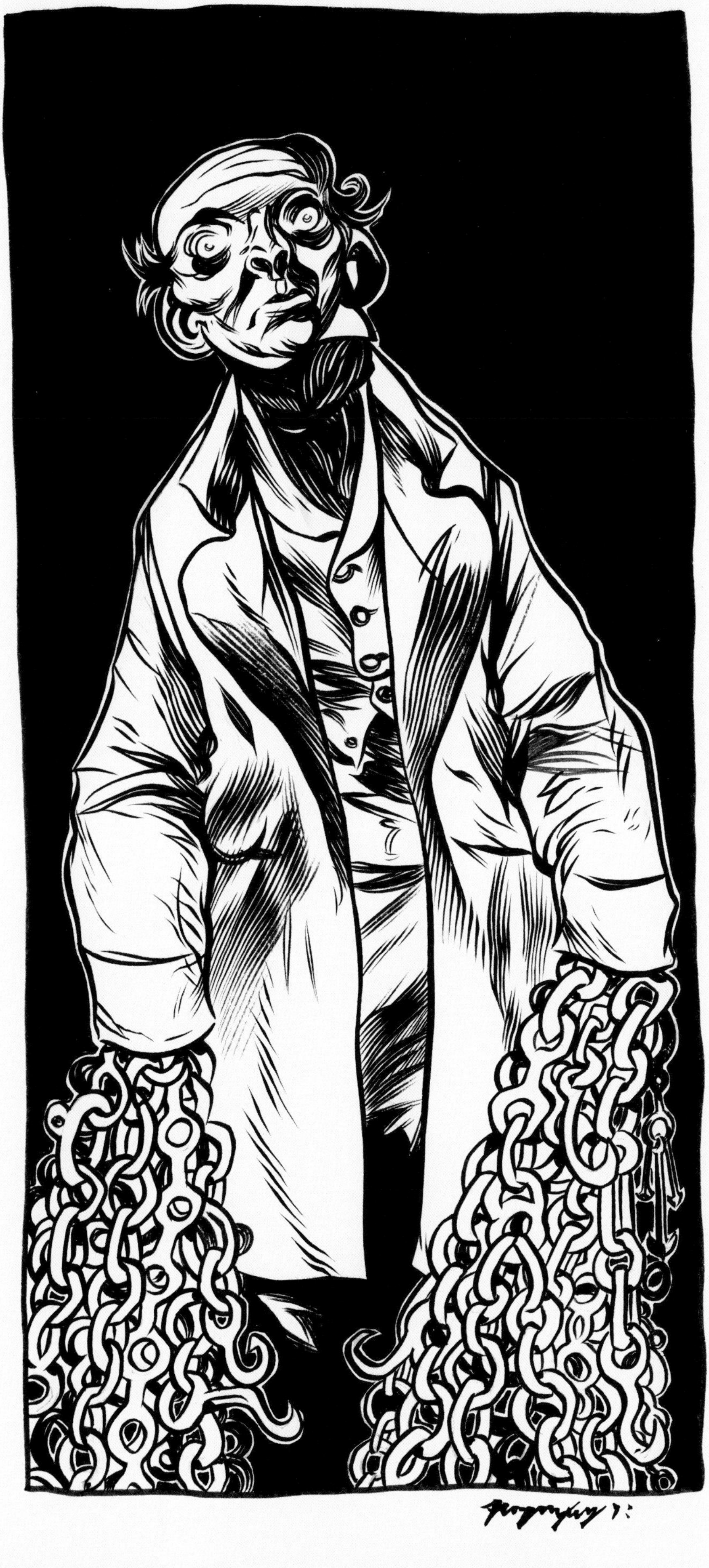

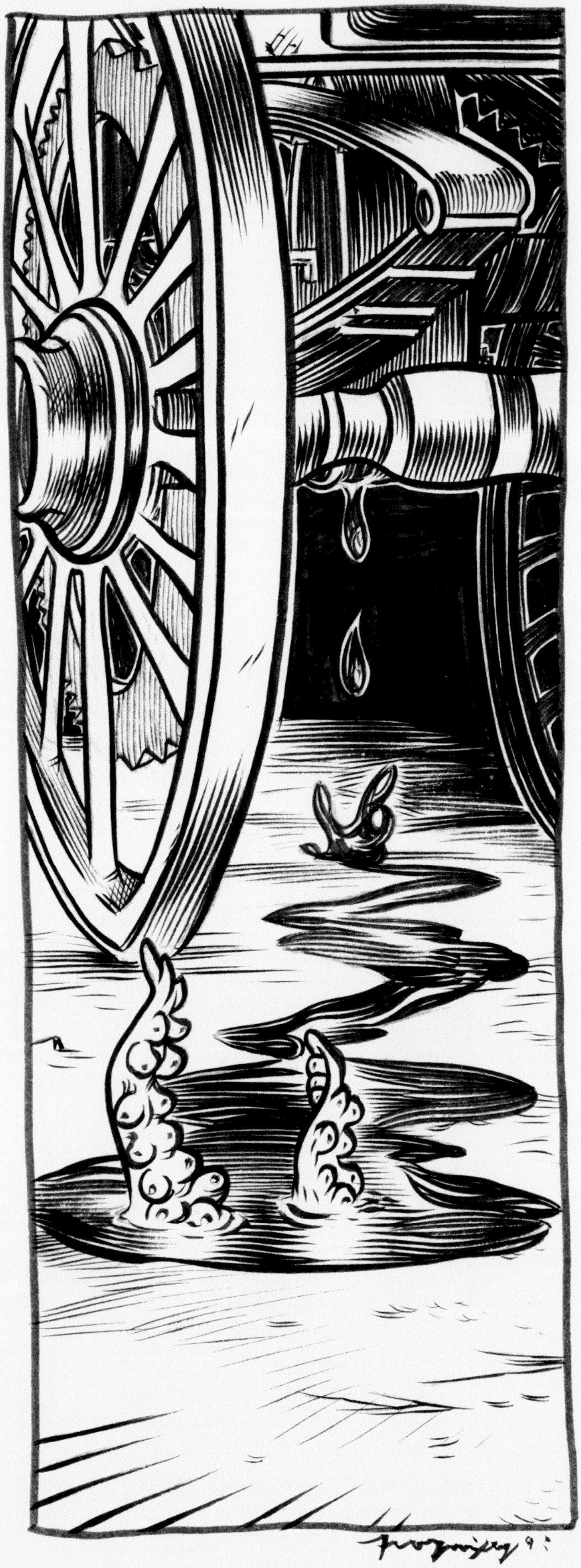

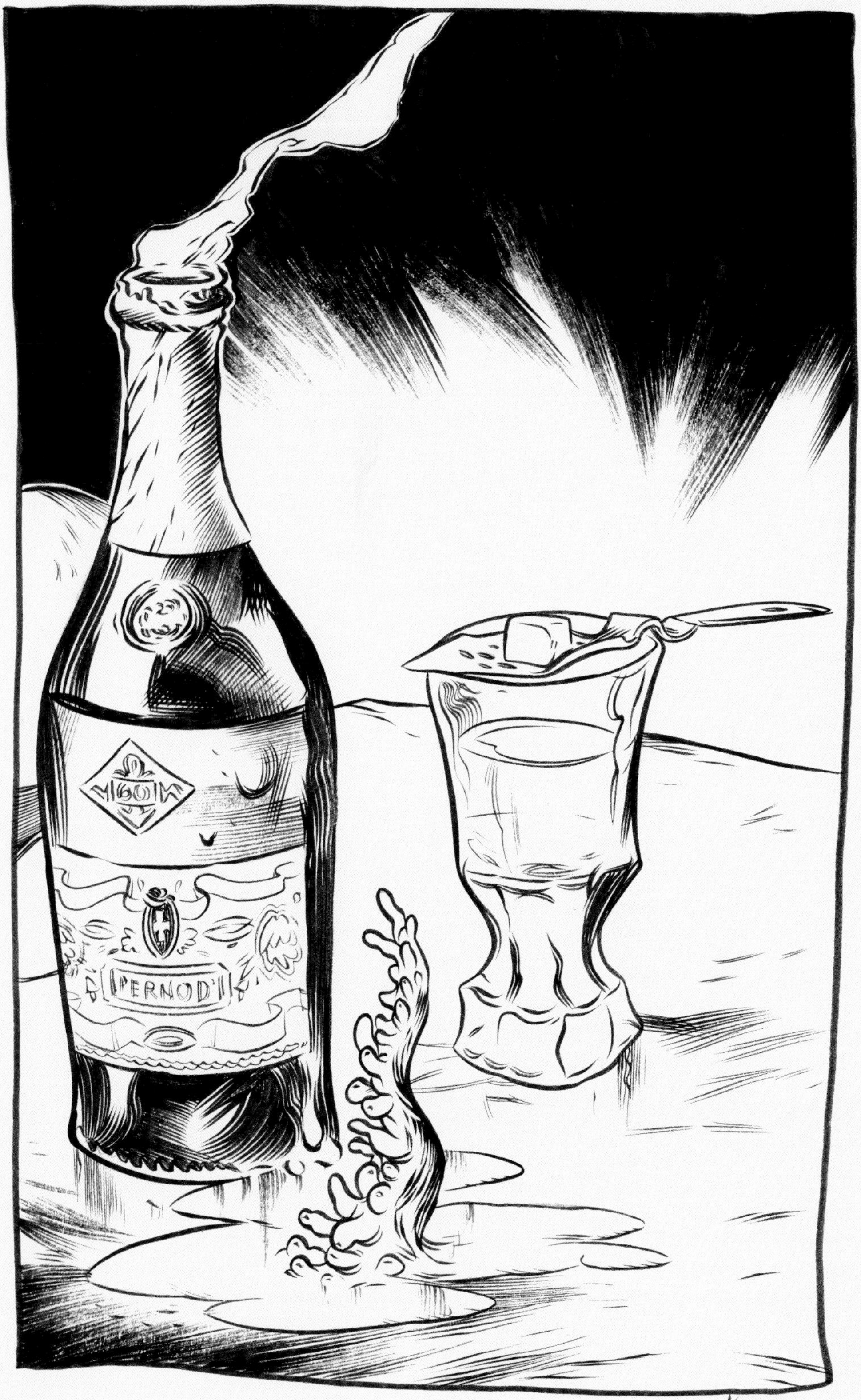
PERNOD

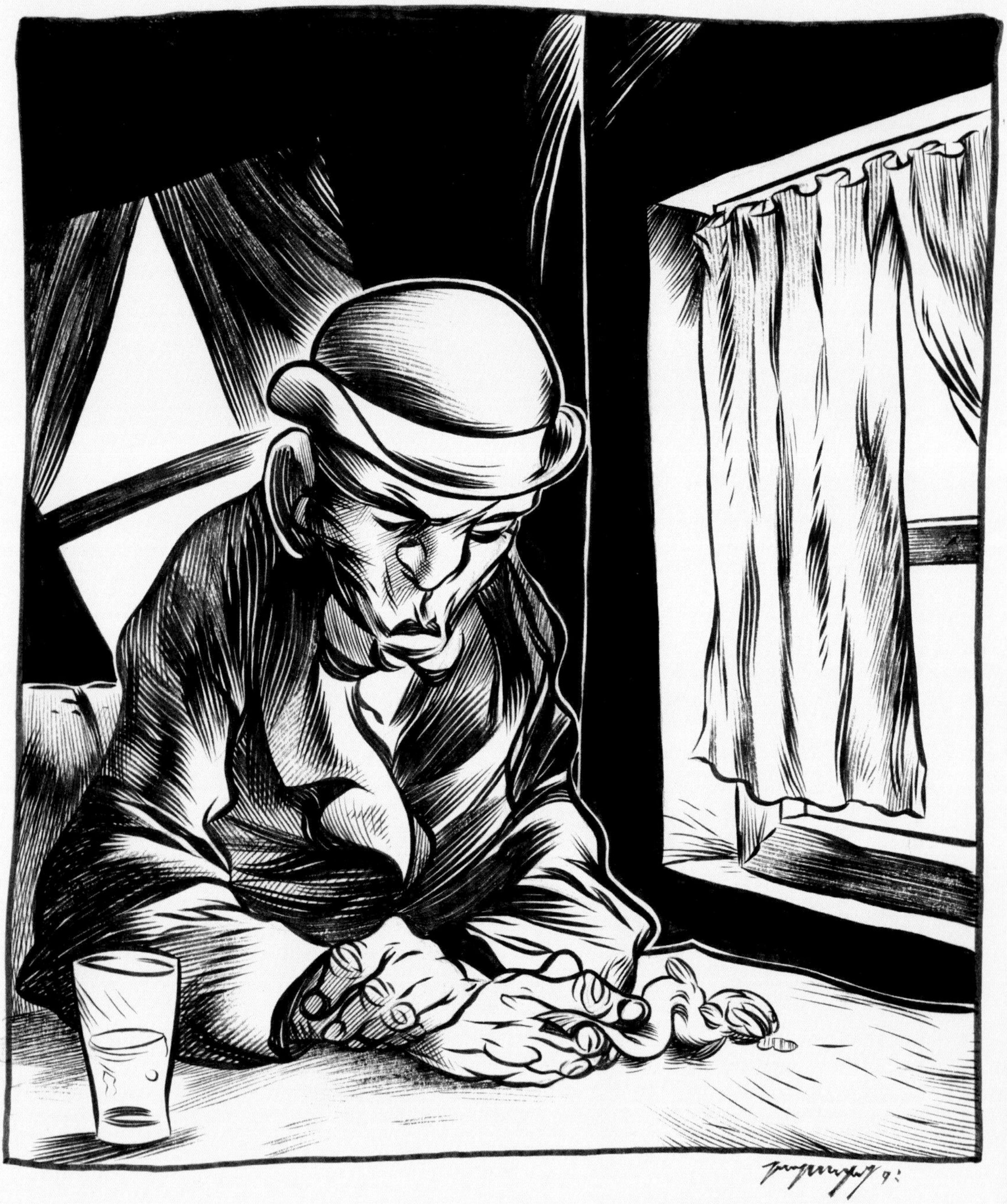

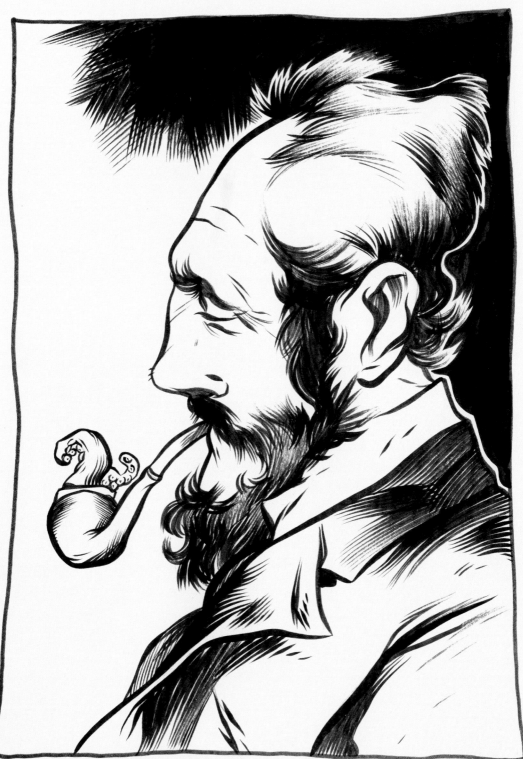

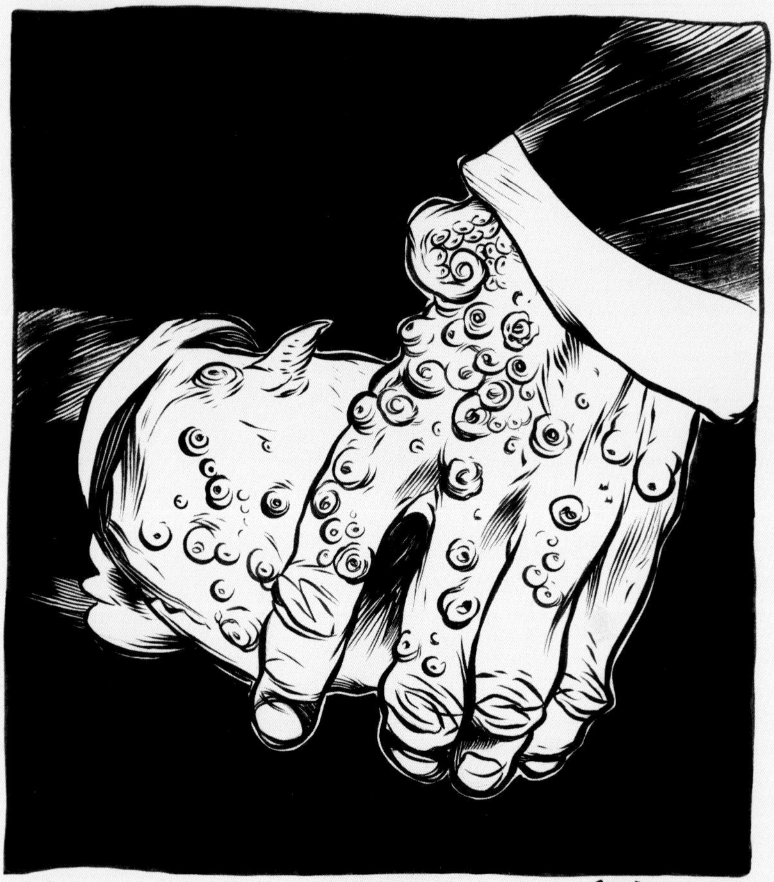

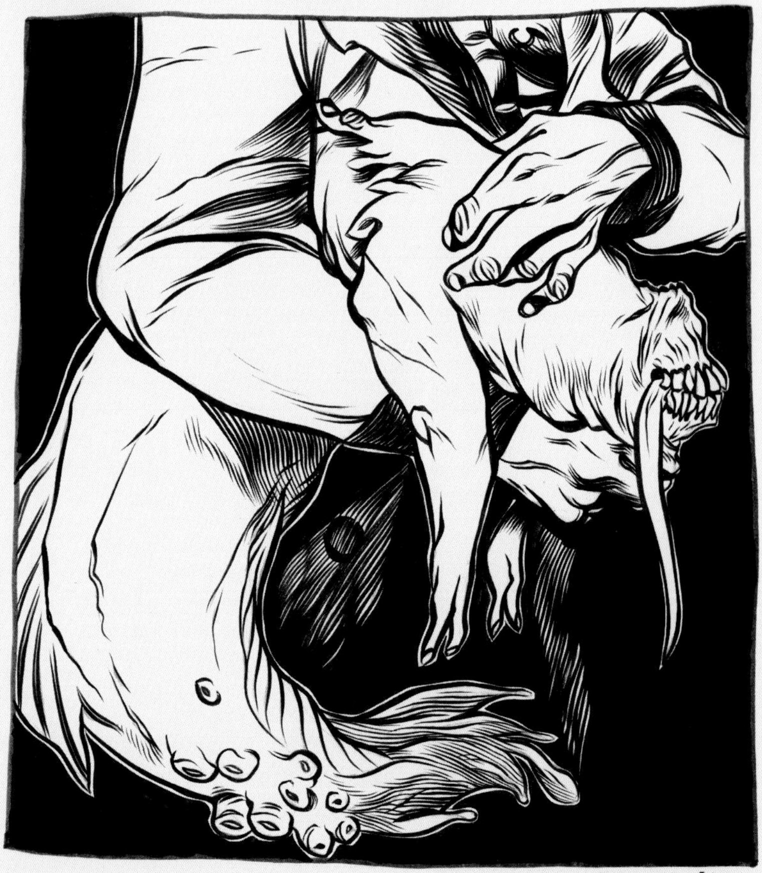

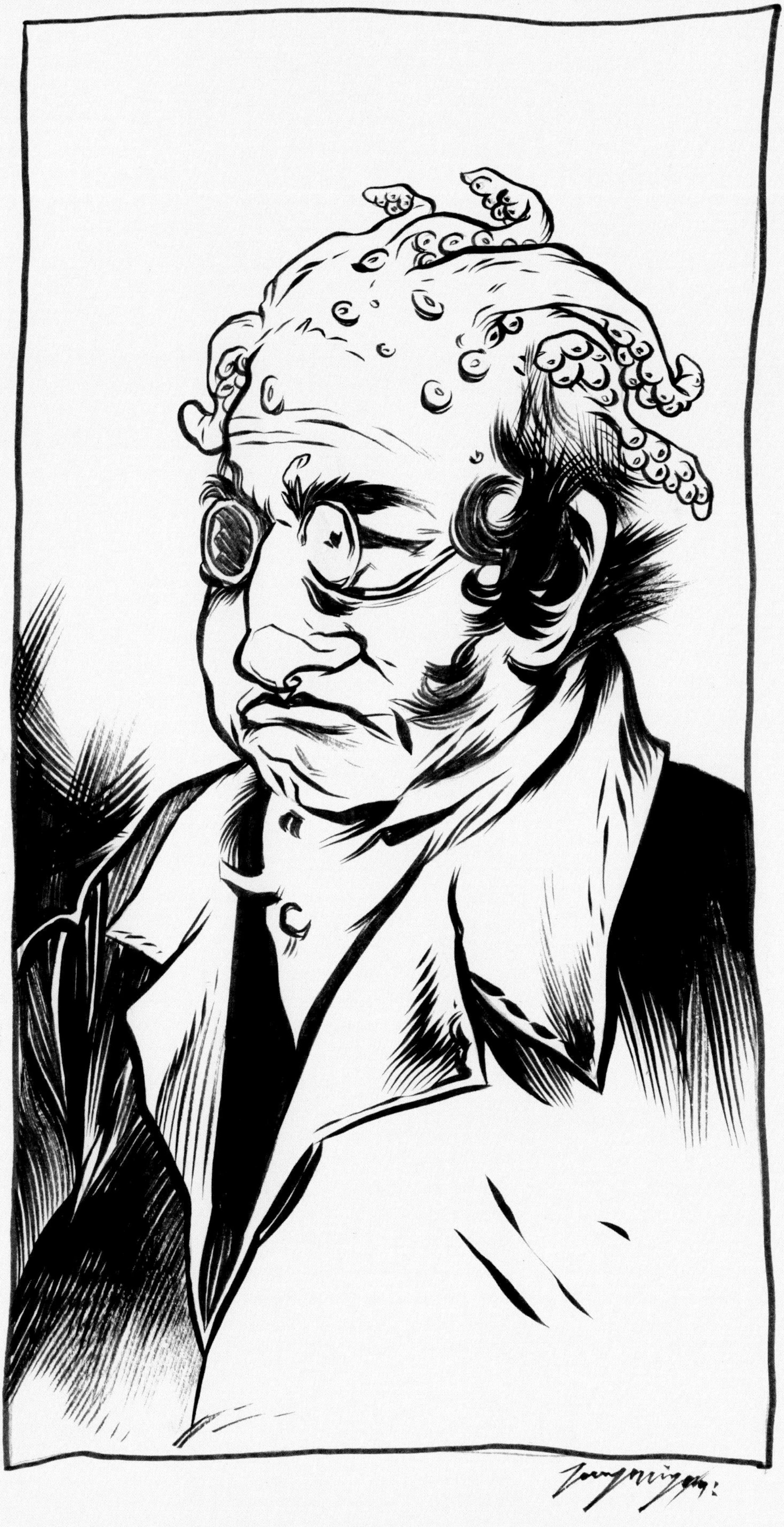

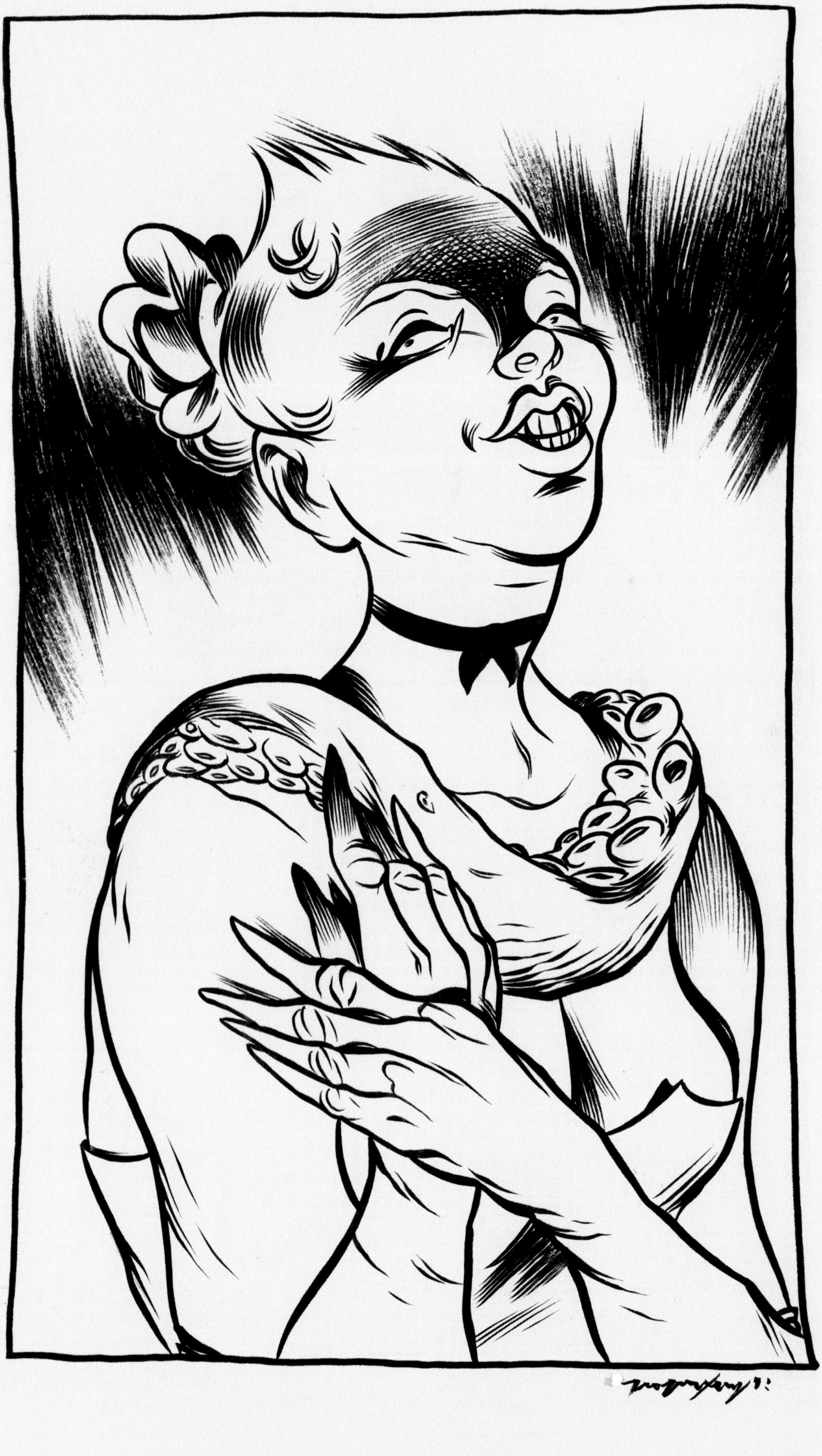

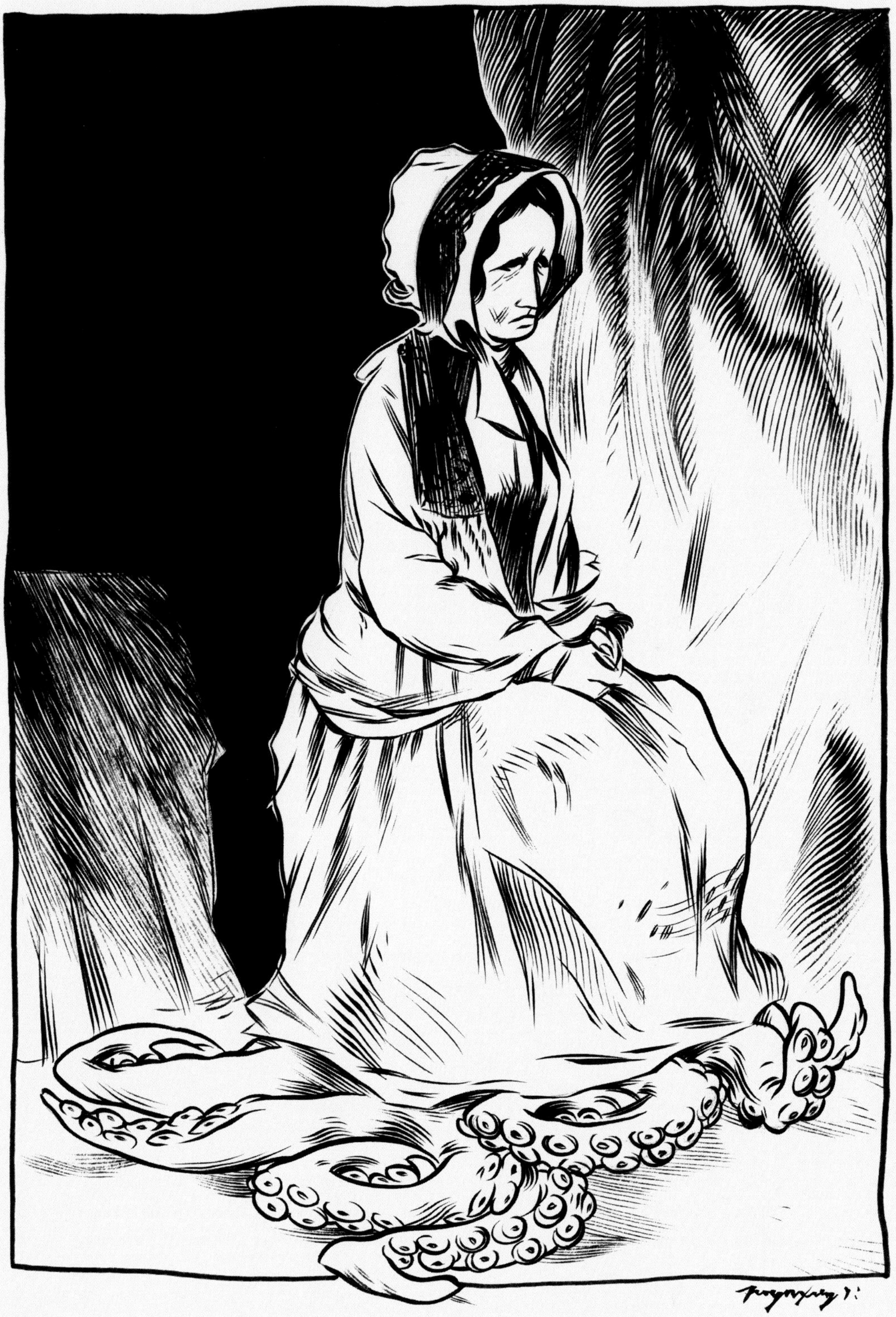

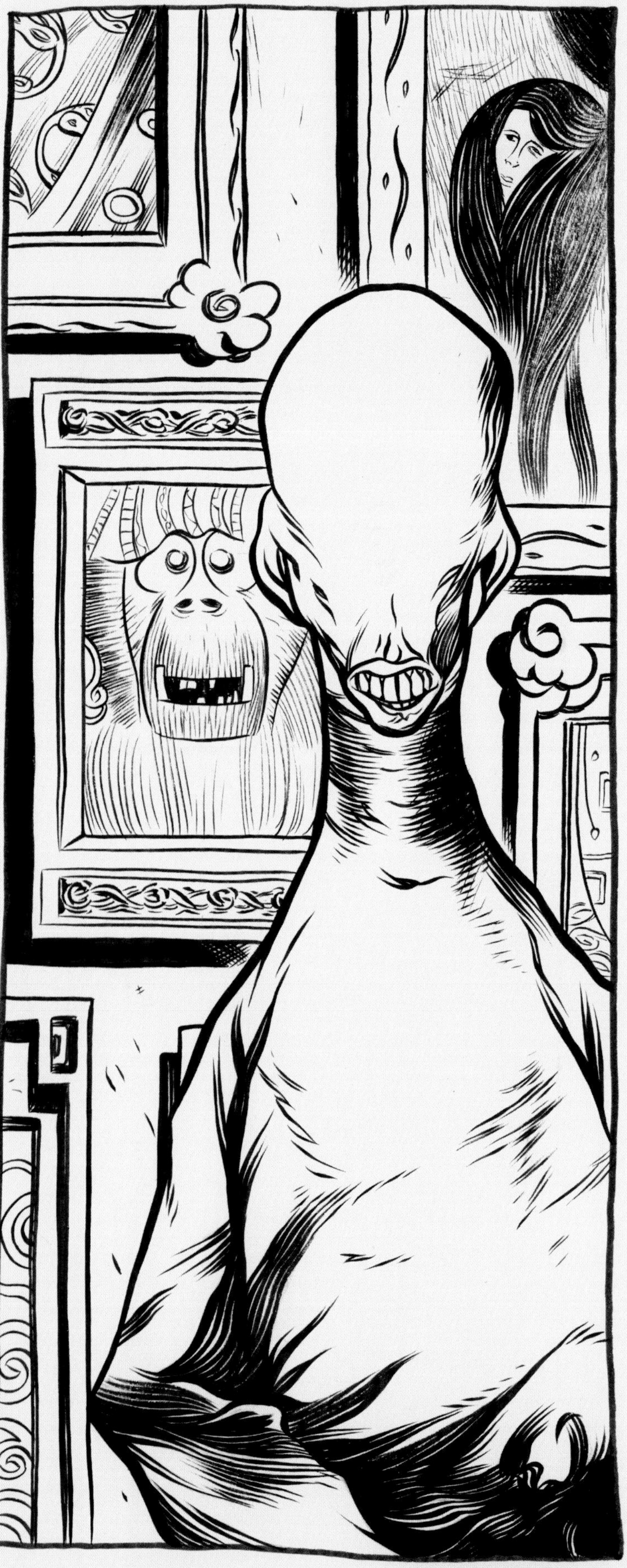

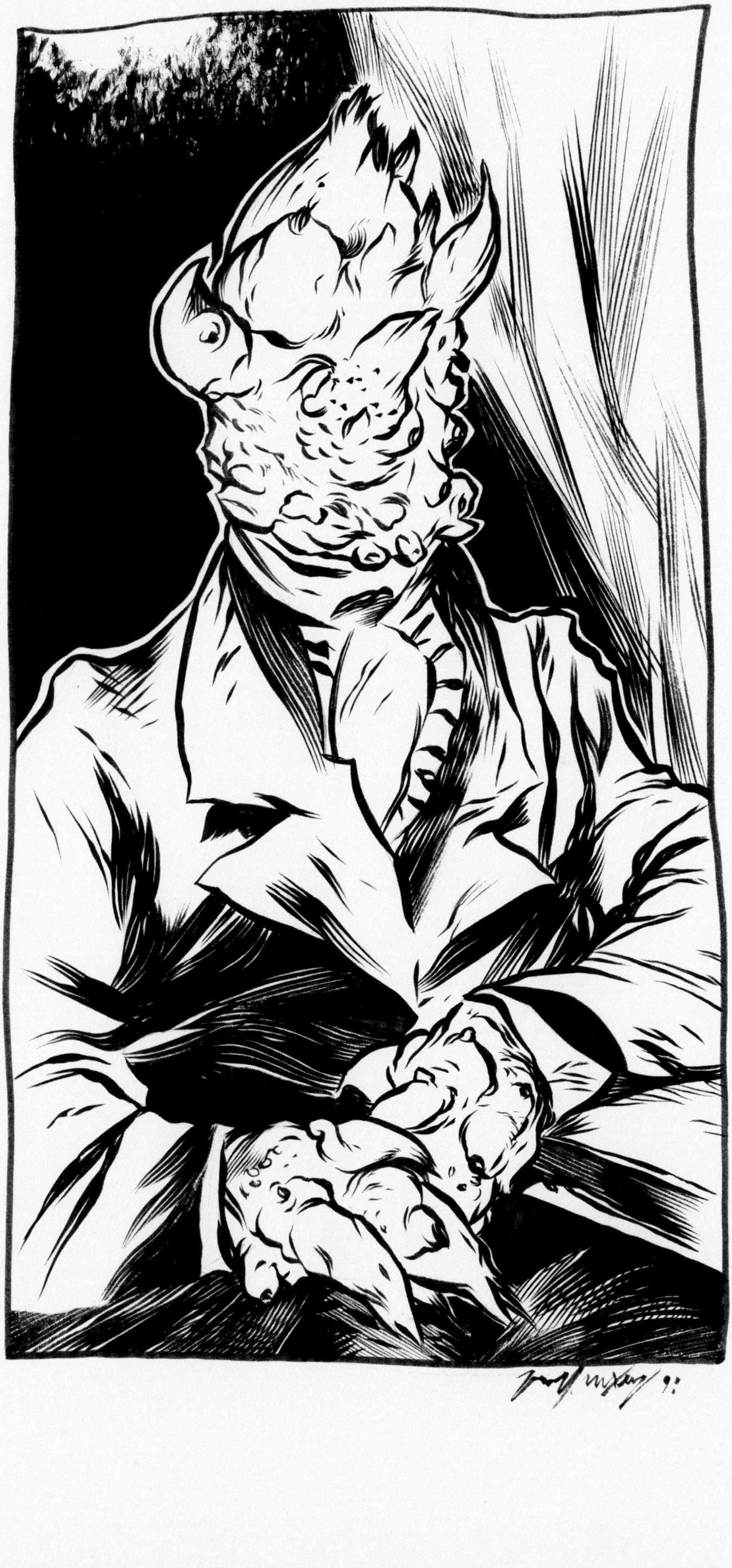

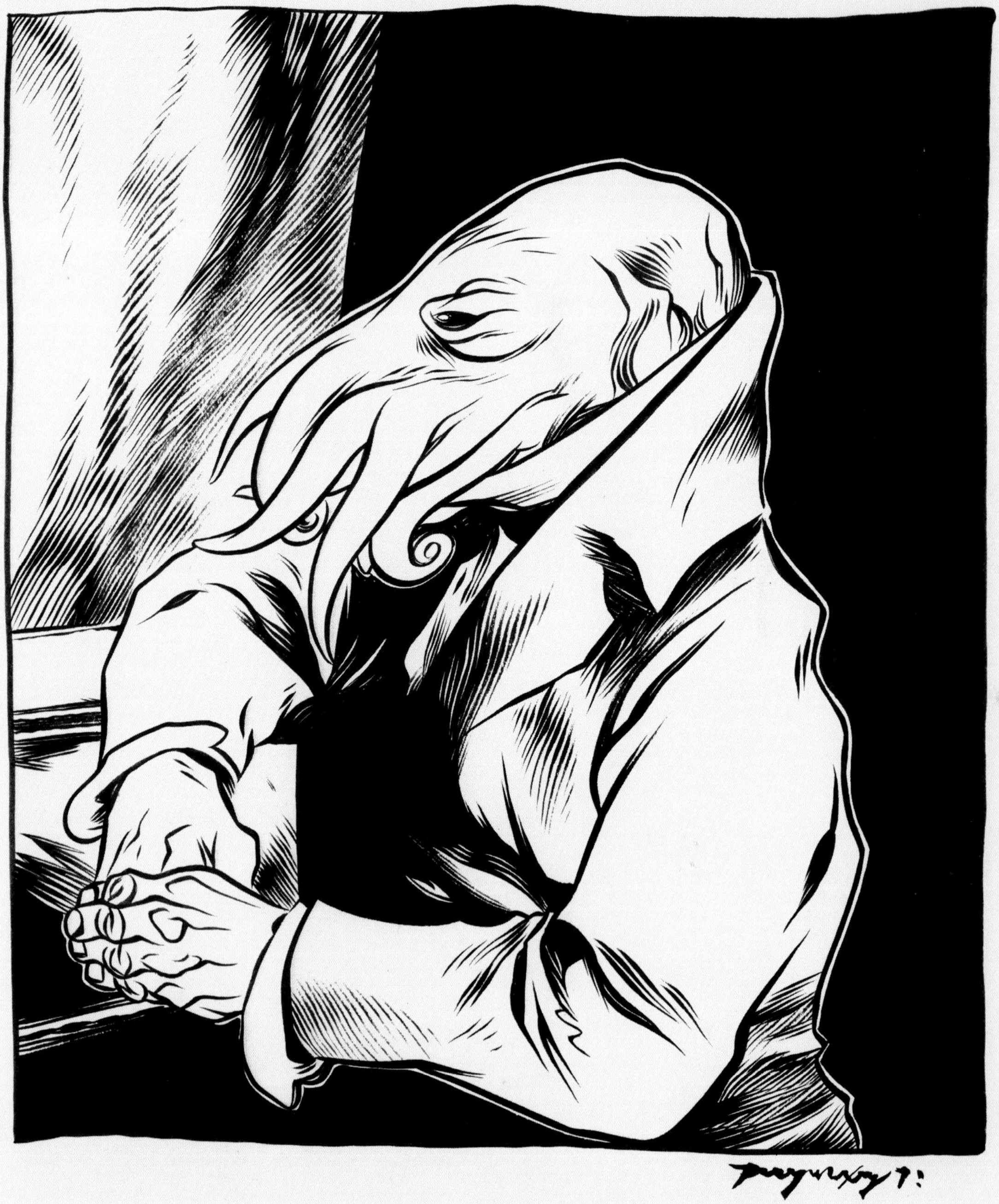

Following pages: Mike's covers for the single issues, re-colored by Dave for this edition.

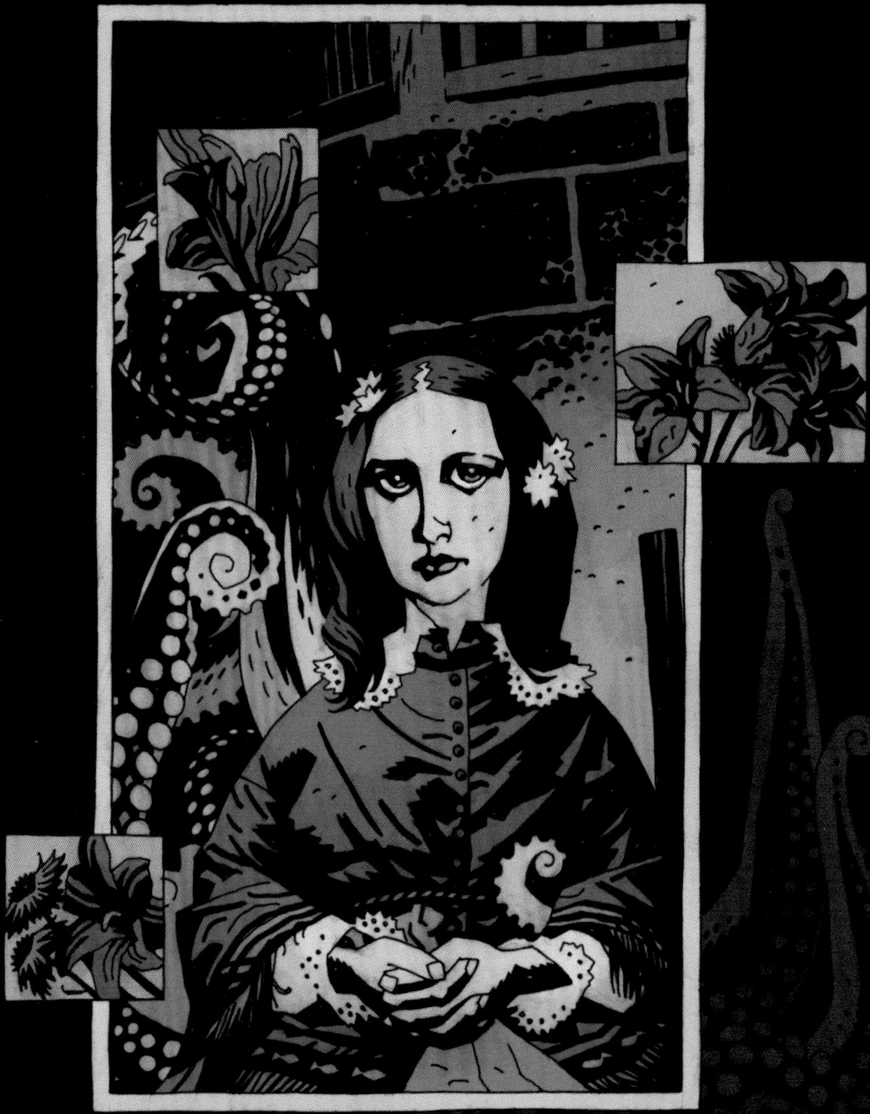

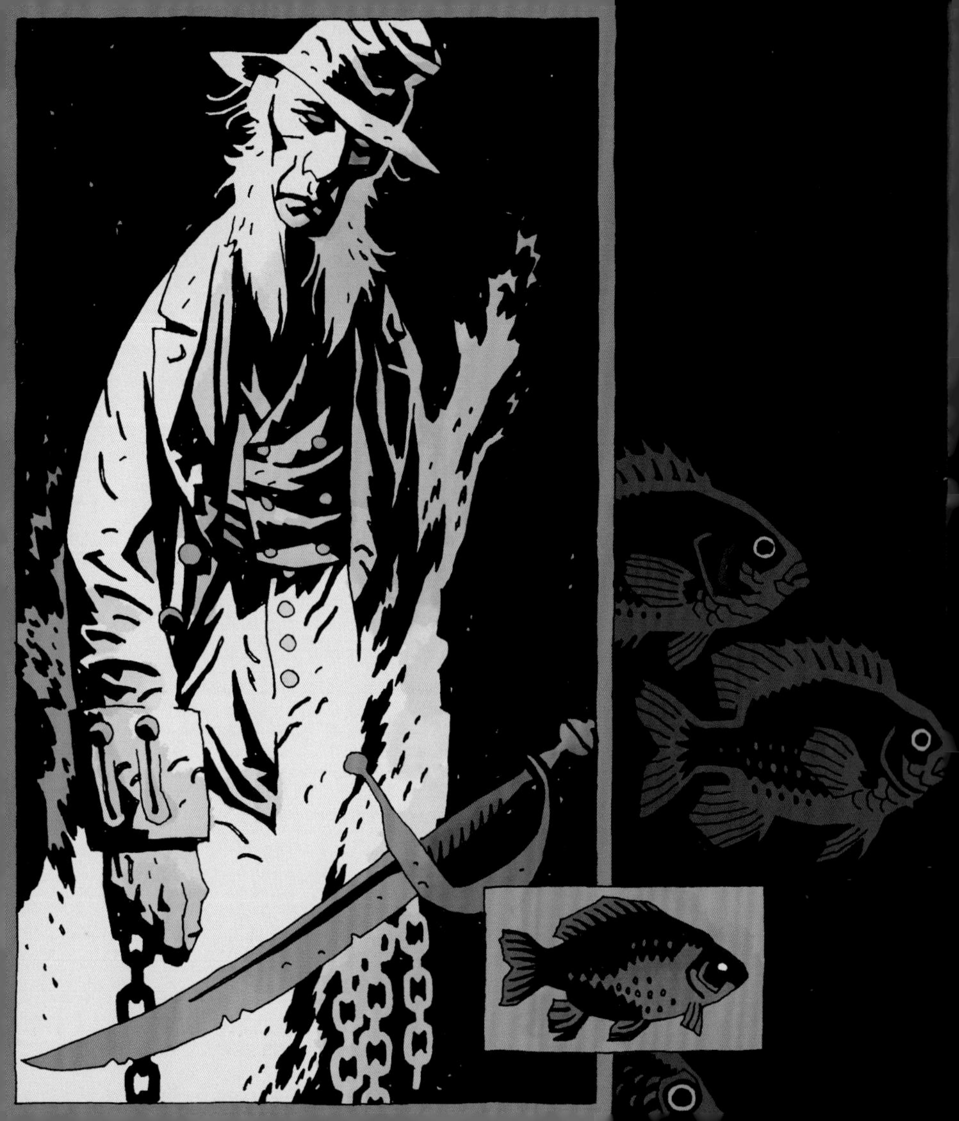

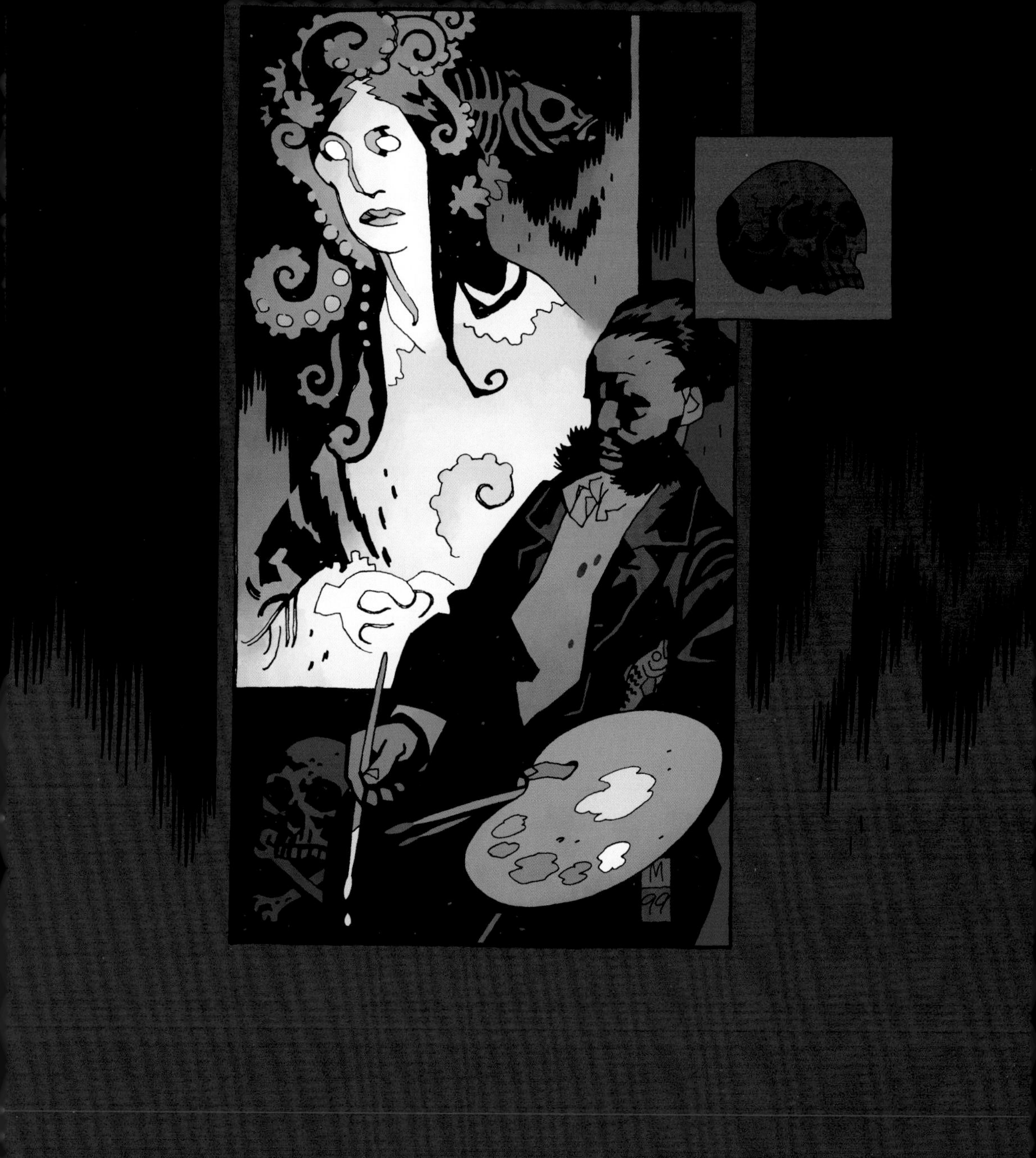
M
99

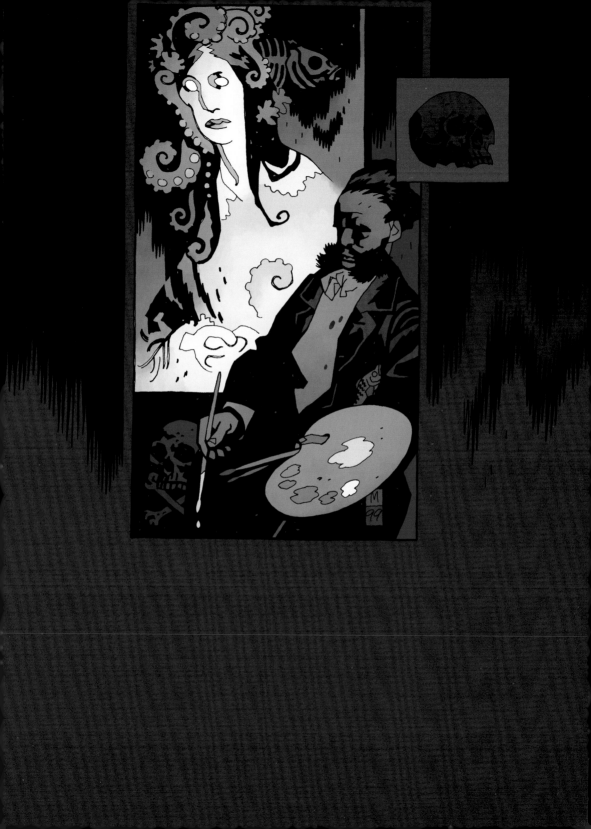

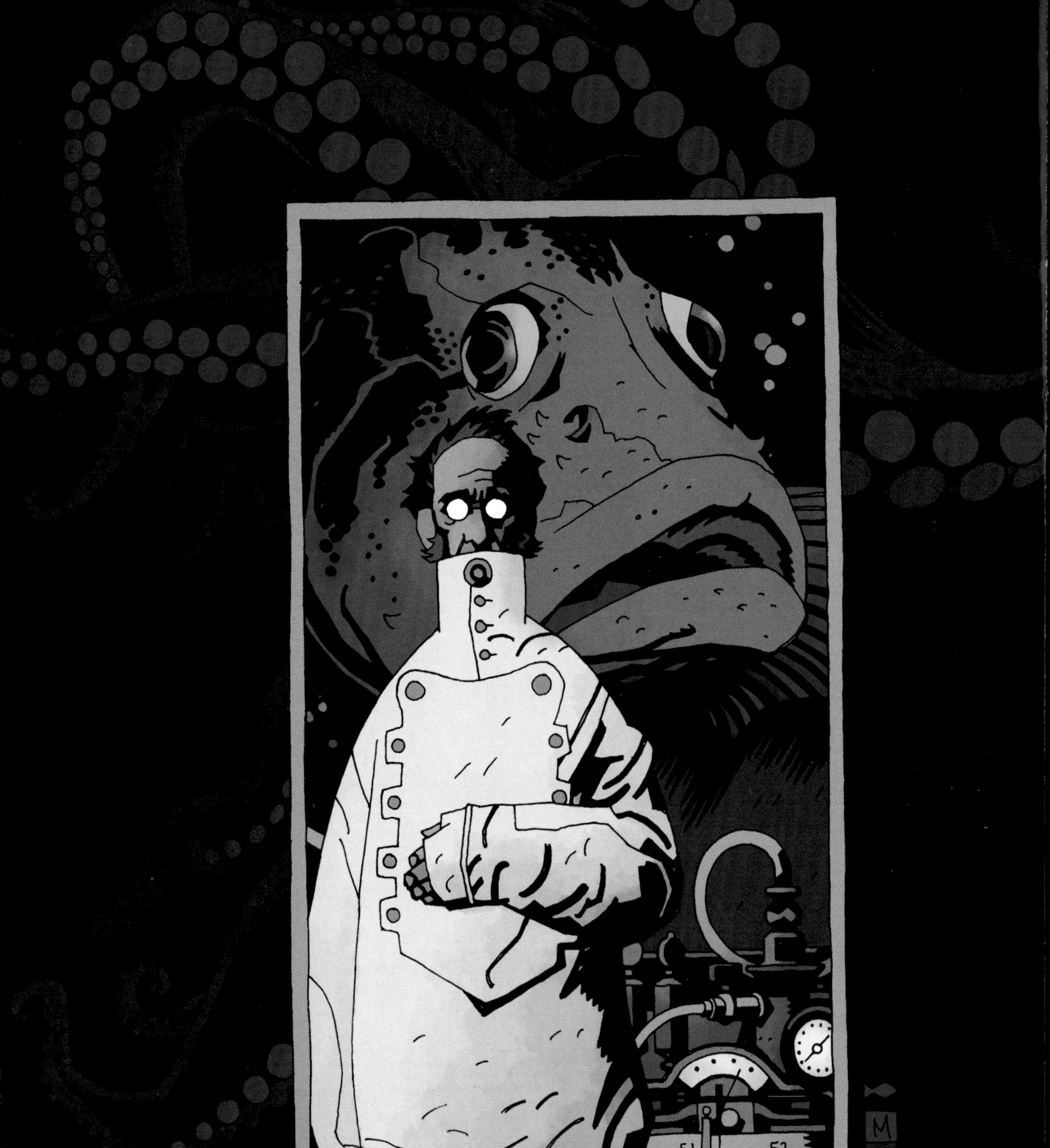
51
52

RECOMMENDED READING

MR. HIGGINS COMES HOME
Story by Mike Mignola
Art by Warwick Johnson-Cadwell
978-1-50670-466-1 · $14.99

THE BLACK SINISTER
Story by Kaare Andrews
Art by Troy Nixey
978-1-50670-337-4 · $9.99

ALEISTER & ADOLF
Story by Douglas Rushkoff
Art by Michael Avon Oeming
978-1-50670-104-2 · $19.99

**HARROW COUNTY VOLUME I:
COUNTLESS HAINTS**
Story by Cullen Bunn
Art by Tyler Crook
978-1-61655-780-5 · $14.99

DEATH HEAD
Story by Zack and Nick Keller
Art by Joanna Estep
978-1-61655-904-5 · $19.99

RAT GOD
Story and art by Richard Corben
978-1-61655-769-0 · $19.99

SHADOWS ON THE GRAVE
Story and art by Richard Corben
978-1-50670-391-6 · $19.99

CREEPY PRESENTS: RICHARD CORBEN
Story and art by Richard Corben and others
978-1-59582-919-1 · $29.99

**EDGAR ALLAN POE'S
SPIRITS OF THE DEAD**
Story and art by Richard Corben
978-1-61655-356-2 · $24.99

**ONLY THE END OF THE
WORLD AGAIN**
Story by Neil Gaiman and P. Craig Russell
Art by Troy Nixey
978-1-50670-612-2 · $19.99

**FORBIDDEN BRIDES OF THE FACELESS
SLAVES IN THE SECRET HOUSE OF THE
NIGHT OF DREAD DESIRE**
Story by Neil Gaiman
Art by Shane Oakley
978-1-50670-140-0 · $17.99

**CREATURES OF THE NIGHT
SECOND EDITION**
Story by Neil Gaiman
Art by Michael Zulli
978-1-56970-025-0 · $12.99

NEIL GAIMAN'S A STUDY IN EMERALD
*Story by Neil Gaiman, Rafael Albuquerque,
and Rafael Scavone*
Art by Rafael Albuquerue
978-1-50670-393-0 · $17.99

**GARY GIANNI'S MONSTERMEN
AND OTHER SCARY STORIES**
Story and art by Gary Gianni
978-1-50670-480-7 · $19.99

DEPT. H VOLUME I: PRESSURE
Story and art by Matt Kindt
978-1-61655-989-2 · $19.99

MIND MGMT VOLUME I: THE MANAGER
Story and art by Matt Kindt
978-1-59582-797-5 · $19.99

**LEGACY: AN OFF-COLOR
NOVELLA FOR YOU TO COLOR**
Story by Chuck Palahniuk
Art by Mike Norton and Steve Morris
978-1-50670-615-3 · $19.99

**BAIT: OFF-COLOR STORIES
FOR YOU TO COLOR**
Stories by Chuck Palahniuk
Art by Duncan Fegredo, Joëlle Jones, and others
978-1-50670-311-4 · $19.99

THE DARK HORSE BOOK OF HORROR
Stories by Mike Mignola, Evan Dorkin, and others
Art by Mike Mignola, Jill Thompson, and others
978-1-50670-372-5 · $19.99

AVAILABLE AT YOUR LOCAL COMICS SHOP OR BOOKSTORE

*To find a comics shop in your area, visit comicshoplocator.com. For more information or to order direct, visit DarkHorse.com
or call 1-800-862-0052. Mon.–Fri. 9 AM to 5 PM Pacific Time. Prices and availability subject to change without notice.*

Also by Mike Mignola

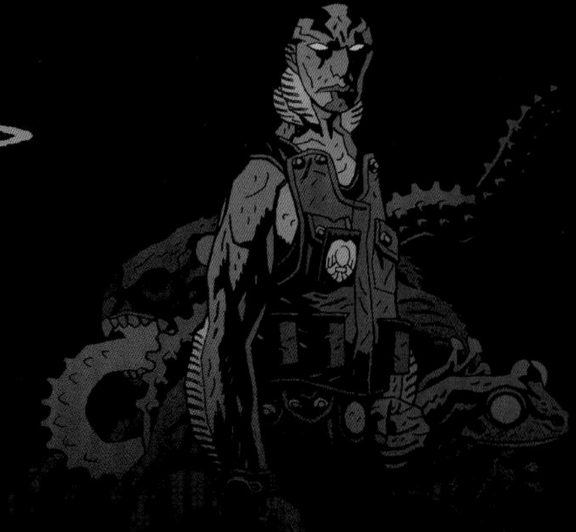

B.P.R.D. PLAGUE OF FROGS
VOLUME 1
with John Arcudi, Guy Davis, and others
TPB: ISBN 978-1-59582-675-6 | $19.99

VOLUME 2
ISBN 978-1-59582-676-3 | $24.99

VOLUME 3
ISBN 978-1-61655-622-8 | $24.99

VOLUME 4
ISBN 978-1-61655-641-9 | $24.99

1946–1948
with Joshua Dysart, Paul Azaceta, Fábio Moon, Gabriel Bá, Max Fiumara, and Arcudi
ISBN 978-1-61655-646-4 | $34.99

BEING HUMAN
with Scott Allie, Arcudi, Davis, and others
ISBN 978-1-59582-756-2 | $17.99

VAMPIRE
with Moon and Bá
ISBN 978-1-61655-196-4 | $19.99

B.P.R.D. HELL ON EARTH
VOLUME 1
with Allie, Arcudi, Davis, Tyler Crook, and others
ISBN 978-1-50670-360-2 | $34.99

VOLUME 2
ISBN 978-1-50670-388-6 | $34.99

A COLD DAY IN HELL
with Arcudi, Peter Snejbjerg, and Laurence Campbell
ISBN 978-1-61655-199-5 | $19.99

THE REIGN OF THE BLACK FLAME
with Arcudi and Harren
ISBN 978-1-61655-471-2 | $19.99

THE DEVIL'S WINGS
with Arcudi, Campbell, Joe Querio, and Crook
ISBN 978-1-61655-617-4 | $19.99

LAKE OF FIRE
with Arcudi and Crook
ISBN 978-1-61655-402-6 | $19.99

FLESH AND STONE
with Arcudi and Harren
ISBN 978-1-61655-762-1 | $19.99

METAMORPHOSIS
with Arcudi, Snejbjerg, and Julián Totino Tedesco
ISBN 978-1-61655-794-2 | $19.99

END OF DAYS
with Arcudi and Campbell
ISBN 978-1-61655-910-6 | $19.99

THE EXORCIST
with Cameron Stewart, Chris Roberson, and Mike Norton
ISBN 978-1-50670-011-3 | $19.99

COMETH THE HOUR
with Arcudi and Campbell
ISBN 978-1-50670-131-8 | $19.99

ABE SAPIEN
THE DROWNING
with Jason Shawn Alexander
ISBN 978-1-59582-185-0 | $17.99

THE DEVIL DOES NOT JEST AND OTHER STORIES
with Arcudi, Harren, and others
ISBN 978-1-59582-925-2 | $17.99

DARK AND TERRIBLE
VOLUME 1
with Allie, S. Fiumara, and M. Fiumara
ISBN 978-1-50670-538-5 | $34.99

VOLUME 2
ISBN 978-1-50670-385-5 | $34.99

LOST LIVES AND OTHER STORIES
with Allie, Arcudi, Michael Avon Oeming, and others
ISBN 978-1-50670-220-9 | $19.99

LOBSTER JOHNSON
THE IRON PROMETHEUS
with Arcudi, Tonci Zonjic, and others
ISBN 978-1-59307-975-8 | $17.99

THE BURNING HAND
ISBN 978-1-61655-031-8 | $17.99

SATAN SMELLS A RAT
ISBN 978-1-61655-203-9 | $18.99

GET THE LOBSTER
ISBN 978-1-61655-505-4 | $19.99

THE PIRATE'S GHOST AND METAL MONSTERS OF MIDTOWN
ISBN 978-1-50670-206-3 | $19.99

A CHAIN FORGED IN LIFE
ISBN 978-1-50670-178-3 | $19.99

WITCHFINDER
IN THE SERVICE OF ANGELS
with Ben Stenbeck
ISBN 978-1-59582-483-7 | $17.99

LOST AND GONE FOREVER
with Arcudi and John Severin
ISBN 978-1-59582-794-4 | $17.99

THE MYSTERIES OF UNLAND
with Kim Newman, Maura McHugh, and Crook
ISBN 978-1-61655-630-3 | $19.99

CITY OF THE DEAD
with Roberson and Stenbeck
ISBN 978-1-50670-166-0 | $19.99

RISE OF THE BLACK FLAME
with Roberson and Christopher Mitten
ISBN 978-1-50670-155-4 | $19.99

THE VISITOR: HOW AND WHY HE STAYED
with Roberson, Paul Grist, and Bill Crabtree
ISBN 978-1-50670-345-9 | $19.99

FRANKENSTEIN UNDERGROUND
with Stenbeck
ISBN 978-1-61655-782-9 | $19.99

JOE GOLEM: OCCULT DETECTIVE—
THE RAT CATCHER & THE SUNKEN DEAD
with Christopher Golden and Patric Reynolds
ISBN 978-1-61655-964-9 | $24.99

BALTIMORE
THE PLAGUE SHIPS
with Golden, Stenbeck, and Peter Bergting
ISBN 978-1-59582-677-0 | $24.99

THE CURSE BELLS
ISBN 978-1-59582-674-9 | $24.99

A PASSING STRANGER AND OTHER STORIES
ISBN 978-1-61655-182-7 | $24.99

CHAPEL OF BONES
ISBN 978-1-61655-328-9 | $24.99

THE APOSTLE AND THE WITCH OF HARJU
ISBN 978-1-61655-618-1 | $24.99

THE CULT OF THE RED KING
ISBN 978-1-61655-821-5 | $24.99

EMPTY GRAVES
ISBN 978-1-50670-042-7 | $24.99

THE RED KINGDOM
ISBN 978-1-50670-197-4 | $24.99

NOVELS
LOBSTER JOHNSON: THE SATAN FACTORY
with Thomas E. Sniegoski
ISBN 978-1-59582-203-1 | $12.95

JOE GOLEM AND THE DROWNING CITY
with Golden
ISBN 978-1-59582-971-9 | $99.99

BALTIMORE; OR, THE STEADFAST TIN SOLDIER & THE VAMPIRE
with Golden
ISBN 978-1-61655-803-1 | $12.99

DARK HORSE BOOKS
DarkHorse.com

AVAILABLE AT YOUR LOCAL COMICS SHOP OR BOOKSTORE! • To find a comics shop in your area, visit comicshoplocator.com.
For more information or to order direct visit DarkHorse.com or call 1-800-862-0052 Mon.–Fri. 9 AM to 5 PM Pacific Time.
Prices and availability subject to change without notice.

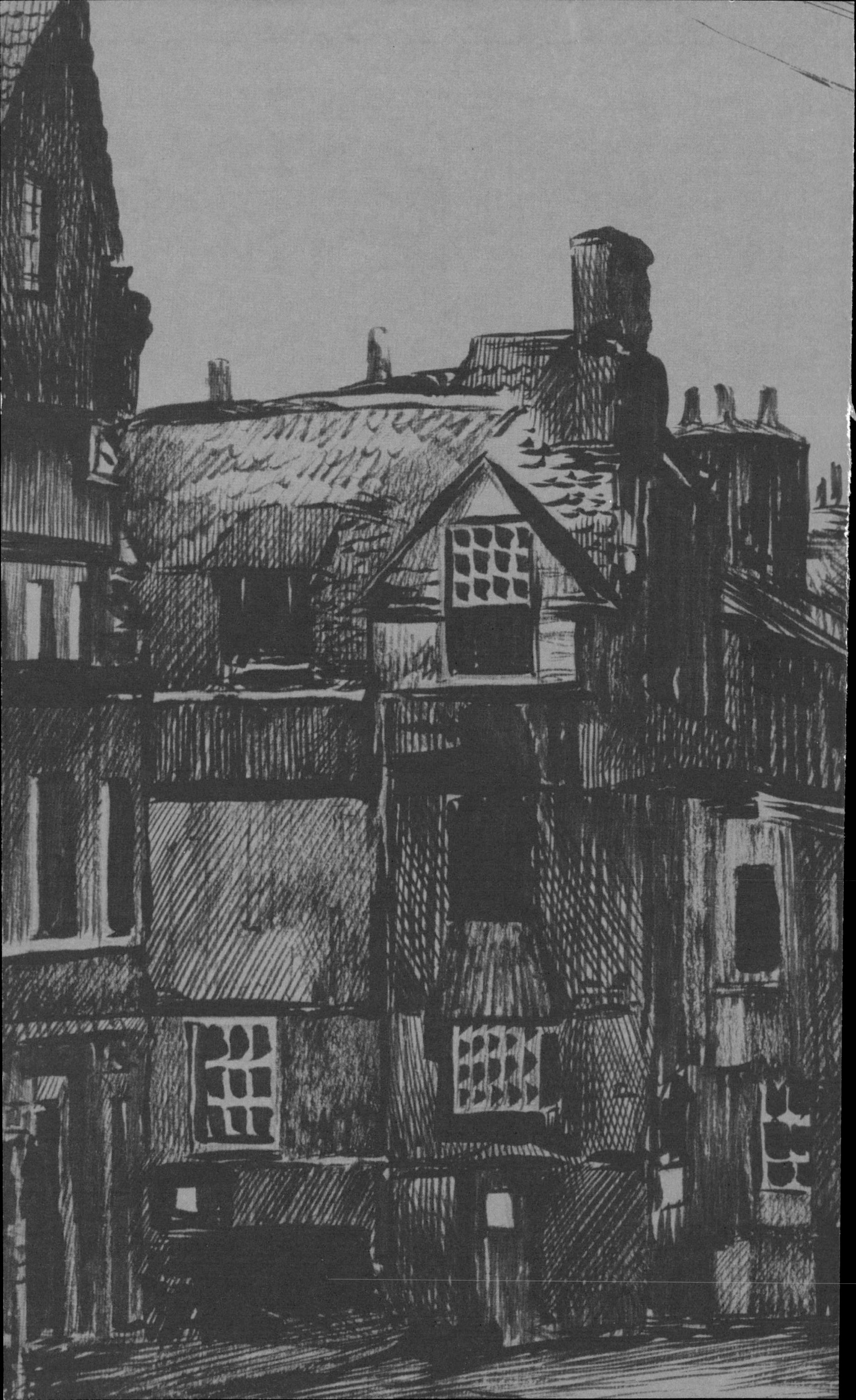